AFTER THE RAJ

AFTER THE RAJ

THE LAST STAYERS-ON AND
THE LEGACY OF BRITISH INDIA

Hugh Purcell

First published 2008
This edition published 2011

The History Press
The Mill, Brimscombe Port
Stroud, Gloucestershire, GL5 2QG
www.thehistorypress.co.uk

British Library Cataloguing in Publication Data.
A catalogue record for this book is available from the British Library.

ISBN 978 0 7509 4787 9

Typesetting and origination by The History Press
Printed in Great Britain
Manufacturing managed by Jellyfish Print Solutions Ltd

CONTENTS

PREFACE

When I was asked by my publisher to write about the last days of the Raj, I said no. So much has already been written, some of it exemplary popular history like James Morris's *Farewell the Trumpets* and Geoffrey Moorhouse's *India Britannica*. However, on my frequent visits to India over the last forty years I have often wondered what happened to the Raj – whatever that word means exactly. It did not just disappear. On my first visit in 1964 there was still a thriving British commercial community in Calcutta and British planters still dominated the tea gardens. Over the hill stations and formerly British clubs hung a mist of Raj nostalgia. All that has gone except among enclaves of Anglo-Indians who still yearn for a country they have never seen. But you do not need to look far to find a lively legacy of the Raj; the Indian heritage industry taps into it, the Indian armed forces keep alive its traditions, the Indian Christian churches sing its hymns, the wonderful Indo-British language still comes up with new anglicisms. Above all there are still a few remarkable survivors living in India connecting the present with the past.

Obviously I am grateful to the stayers-on who trusted me and my tape recorder. If they had suspicions of me as a member of the mass media that has tended to caricature the *koi hais* and *mems* of the Raj, they did not show it. They are among the very, very last remnants of the Raj who decided not to go Home, and I am proud to tell their stories. By now, anyway, they are no longer identified with British rule but are thought of as Britons (some with Indian passports) who have played an active part in the making of modern India. They have lived through nearly a century of change, and that change seems to be accelerating. Now, in fact, it is more common to speak of Indian Britain than British India. Over one million Indians live in the UK, another half million visit annually, 20,000 Indian students are study-ing here and India is the third largest foreign investor; it is a sort of raj in reverse.

Just after I handed in this manuscript to my editor, Jim Crawley of Sutton Publishing, I went to India for a fifth time in ten months. I was leading a British party round sites of the Indian Mutiny, 150 years after that sad and terrible event. Unwittingly we caused a second 'Indian mutiny', although thankfully it never got beyond riot, sloganising and the hurling of empty plastic bottles and dung. But it caused me to think more personally about any 'after the Raj' spe-cial relationship between India and Britain, and I conclude my book with these thoughts in a postscript.

When I decided to contact the last stayers-on of the Raj still living in India and connect each with a legacy of British rule, I knew I had two invaluable sources. The first was the British Association for Cemeteries in South Asia (BACSA). Over the last two years its Secretary and founder Theon Wilkinson MBE and the editor of its magazine *Chowkidar*, Dr Rosie Llewellyn-Jones, have given me addresses, emails, books, magazines, letters, the lot. The second was a now defunct magazine called the *Indo-British Review* edited by Antony Copley of the University of Kent. For over a quarter of a century the journal published essays about many aspects of recent Indo-British history, and I found particularly useful its themed edi-tions on the BBC in India, 1932–94, and on the Indian Armed Forces before and after Independence. My thanks to these three for permis-sion to quote from their articles.

I also want to thank Sir David Goodall, Sir Anthony and Jenifer Hayward, Robert and Laura Sykes and Lyon Rousel for allowing me to interview them in the UK. I am grateful to Derek Perry and Larry Brown for permission to use their articles on the 'Koi-hai' website (www.koi-hai.com) and to David Air for making this possi-ble. Graham and Thelma Anthony kindly allowed me to quote from

After the Raj

notes they made from the minutes of the Royal Bombay Yacht Club, and Tony and Jackie Lord supplied information and photographs of 'Papa' Wakefield. The Tollygunge Club in Kolkata sent me background material, as did Malcolm Brown about the Anglo-Indians of that town; my thanks to them. Denise Love allowed me to use her MA thesis 'Anglo-Indian Community and Identity during British Rule in South Asia, 1820–1947'. Neelima Mathur in Delhi provided all kinds of help. Mark Tully and Adam Clapham went out of their way to help an old BBC colleague, and in Mumbai Aiyub and Farida Hoosenally were very generous. Thanks to Carol Woodhead who transcribed the tapes and made the sandwiches while she was doing so. Finally a big thank-you to my dear partner, Margaret Percy, who corrected with her usual determination my many mistakes, I hope.

I really did interview the last of the stayers-on, for since handing this manuscript to the publishers two have passed away, Frank Courtney and Nigel Hankin; Theon Wilkinson has died too. Finally, in between the hardback and paperback editions, Col. 'Papa' Wakefield and Joseph Galstaun also died. I make this clear again in the appropriate chapters but I have not altered the text otherwise because their profiles would lose the immediacy they possessed when I first wrote them.

Hugh Purcell
Yorkshire

THE RAJ AND THE STAYERS-ON

'WHy do you call it "The Raj"?' asked Anne Wright, who has lived in India since 1930. 'We never used the term when I was growing up. It's like saying that all tigers are Bengal tigers, which they aren't'. What she meant was that *raj* simply means 'rule', and there are all kinds of rule in India. She went on: 'I think it was that novelist chap who made the word famous after Independence,' and here she was referring to Paul Scott, whose *Raj Quartet* (filmed for TV as *The Jewel in the Crown*) was the last fictional word on the end of British rule.

'No, we never said "The Raj",' answered Theon Wilkinson, who was born in Cawnpore in 1924. 'We talked disparagingly about the "wakil's [lawyer's] Raj", meaning that smart Indian lawyers were tying the government in knots when it tried to deal with Gandhi's passive resistance campaign, but I never heard the word "Raj" in isolation all the time I was in India.' He left in 1946 to study Indian history at Oxford University. 'Perhaps historians and journalists writing around the time of Independence picked it up from the old days of the "Kampani Raj" [East India Company] that ended with the Mutiny in 1858 and quite naturally looked for an appropriate slick term to cover the next ninety years.'

'It was a word we used with a laugh,' remembered John Riddy, who worked in India in the 1950s, 'somewhat uneasily because we weren't quite certain what it meant. Did it imply criticism or praise? Probably, we thought, it was a word some commentator had invented to put a retrospective glamour on things, a kind of solace because we had lost it.'

It was clearly time for me to consult the authority. This is *Hanklyn-Janklin*, a dictionary of Indo-British words written by Nigel Hankin, who has lived in Delhi since 1946. As usual he has the answer. 'Raj', he writes, is a Hindi and before that Aryan or Sanskrit word meaning 'rule'. He goes on:

> *The Raj, 'the days of the Raj'* post-Independence, references the period of British rule. Before 1947 Britons tended to term their occupation 'the Empire', or 'the Indian Empire'. But 'Kampani raj' was a Hindustani expression for the British government of India up to 1858. As used today the term is an Anglicism; in no Indian tongue can 'The Raj' refer to British rule.

'The Raj', as used in book titles, TV series and themed décor in pubs, is now part of the heritage industry. It has become an onomatopoeic word that conjures up visions of a *durbar* (a royal assembly), where maharajas on caparisoned elephants pay homage to the King Emperor while the band plays Elgar's *Pomp and Circumstance*; or of a *shikar* (hunt) where Britons wearing *topis* (short for the Hindi word *sola topi* or 'sun hat') stand proudly behind a tiger they have shot. Perhaps we should be grateful. These days the Raj is not a politically correct concept. No national museum, for instance, put on an exhibition to mark the 150th anniversary of the Indian Mutiny (1857–8), and the British Empire and Commonwealth Museum in Bristol did not receive a government grant, so it was forced to close. According to Dr Rosie Llewellyn-Jones, who edits a magazine about British India called *Chowkidar*, 'you wouldn't get far at SOAS [the School of Oriental and African Studies] if you wanted to write something sympathetic about the Raj'. Nevertheless, its reputation was even worse in the 1970s. The India-born author Charles Allen and a sympathetic producer Michael Mason tried to persuade BBC Radio to let them compile an oral history called *Plain Tales from the Raj*. It was an uphill task. BBC TV had recently broadcast *The British Empire* series, the bias of which, says Charles Allen, was very evident:

> The 1857 Mutiny was recreated on Bagshot Common: the scene consisted of one cannon, one Pandy [mutineer] lashed to same, a gunner, one memsahib mounted sidesaddle on a horse and lots of smoke. With much rattling of drums, the wretched Pandy was blown to pieces and the memsahib's dress drenched in blood. That was it: all the fault of the wicked memsahib.[1]

Charles Allen's persuasion was successful. Three programmes grew into a longer radio series and then a second one. Eventually his book sold half a million copies. This should have proved to the BBC and the government that the experience of 'the Raj' is deeply embedded in our national subconscious. Scratch the surface, or these days trawl the internet, and there in the history of many families is a soldier who served on the Khyber Pass, a Welsh missionary who spent his life in Assam, perhaps an Anglo-Indian who worked on the railways. Charles Allen claimed that the success of his series took the politics out of the British Raj and allowed it to become history. Perhaps it did, except in the minds of museum curators, TV producers and some academics; and what is the heritage industry if not a sentimental, nostalgic, form of history?

British India was not, strictly speaking, the Raj. It was certainly not a colony. Talk of those who 'stayed-on' after Independence as 'old colonials' is, says Theon Wilkinson, making the exception that proves the rule. 'You see it was not a settler society, like most of the Empire. The Brits went out to make their money or serve in the army and then they came Home, with a capital H! In my day, to prove the point, the India Office was separate from the Colonial Office.' That is why in the years before Independence there was no white settler mentality to resist the rising tide of Indian nationalism.

This point struck me as in need of more investigation, so I called in to ask my neighbour in Yorkshire, John Riddy – Riddy of the Raj to me – whose private collection of 7,500 books on British India is the largest in the country, presumably in the whole world. 'Where do

I start?' he asked himself, looking at me over the strawberries on his
kitchen table. 'Actually, I am the person to ask, as I did my Ph.D. on
landownership in India under the East India Company.' He lent back
from the kitchen table. 'Forgive me if I start with indigo …'

Ten minutes later he looked at me enquiringly to see if I had
followed his exposition. It went like this. Unlike elsewhere in the
burgeoning empire of 200 years ago, freehold land in India was very
difficult to acquire. When British merchants tried to grow indigo
shrubs to produce the highly profitable colour dye, they found that
the land of the rich alluvial plains by the Ganges and Brahmaputra
rivers was already owned in a complex network of leases. As they
could not buy land themselves, they had to employ poor whites
and *badmashees* (local thugs) to bribe and force the peasant farmers
to grow what they could not eat instead of what they could eat.
Many ugly skirmishes took place, says Riddy, that have still not been
properly written up. Indigo gave the East India Company a terrible reputation, so much so that in the 1840s it passed legislation
giving the peasant farmer the basic right to grow what he wanted to
grow on his own soil. During twenty-year reviews of the East India
Company in Parliament (1793, 1813, 1833) the question was always
asked 'Could we settle in India? Should we settle?' Riddy of the Raj
gathered himself for the answer:

> All the senior men gave evidence, Warren Hastings, 'Boy' Malcolm
> and so on. Their conclusion was that there were 200 million rela-
> tively civilised Indians who were quite capable of being ruled if
> you left their religion and land alone. The Indian was prepared to
> pay taxes to a remote, perhaps incomprehensible, even semi-divine
> authority; but not to a settler community. The roughhouse indigo
> experience loomed large. Don't risk it again! Don't encourage the
> lower classes to emigrate because they will upset the British reputa-
> tion. Practical discouragements were put in the way of Brits who
> might be tempted to try and buy land. For instance, Company pen-
> sions had to be claimed outside India unless you were prepared to
> lose a lot of money.

And so the die was cast. I was tempted to put words into John's mouth to conclude his peroration. Before I left I asked him about the 'stayers-on', the collective noun that applies throughout the former British Empire to those who remained behind after Independence to make what was left of their lives in the new nation. As he had worked for six years in India a decade after the 'midnight hour' on 15 August 1947 when Jawaharlal Nehru declared 'we are a sovereign people today and we have rid ourselves of the burden of the past', he must have known quite a few? The question put him in a melancholy mood:

> Most hill stations had a few Brits past the breeding stage and not at all well off – former teachers, clergy, civil servants, engineers, nice *Daily Telegraph*-type Brits who regarded the Labour government in Britain with horror. They said 'we can't possibly retire to Tunbridge Wells, it's been taken over by dreadful socialists'. So staying-on was staying put until death came in its sweet majesty in your early 60s. That was the age when people like Tusker had their heart attacks. In India the climate is hellish. You work for twenty-five years with an active life for another four or five years and then increasing decrepitude, with the servants taking over.

Colonel 'Tusker' Smalley is the central character of Paul Scott's novel *Staying On*, which won the Booker Prize in 1977. In the TV version he is played by Trevor Howard and his wife Lucy by Celia Johnson. As they starred together in the wartime romance *Brief Encounter*, you might expect that this time it is a film about requited love, but it is not. It is a film about growing old in a somewhat unhappy marriage. 'It's so bloody depressing,' said John. 'I really cannot pick it up again: unlike *Kim*' (by Rudyard Kipling, written in 1901). He brightened. 'Now there's a book I keep coming back to. I recommend it to anyone who wants to understand the mind of Empire; a fantastic source!'

It is 1972 and the Smalleys are in retirement at the hill station of Pankot, the last survivors of the Raj in the town. Lucy says they feel like relics that might be on a tourist itinerary with the Taj Mahal

and the Elephanta caves. Several of her points of view must have
marked that generation of stayers-on, who had spent their working lives in India before Independence. First there is the link to the
past: they and their Indian neighbours cannot escape the imperial
past and the freedom struggle. Lucy says: 'however friendly you were
with the Indians of your own generation, there was something in
that relationship of a distant but diminishing but not yet dead echo
of the sound of the tocsin.' Then there is the question of respect:
the British in India had retained their confidence because they were
held in respect, even if this was by the outward and visible symbols
of respect rather than by any inner, truer, feeling. After Independence
this respect seemed gradually to disappear, and the loss hits the
Smalleys hard. They are dependent for their living on the grasping
owner of Smith's hotel, Mrs Bhoolabhoy, whose only respect is for
the possession of money. Tusker's response is a fury that disguises his
humiliation. Mrs Bhoolabhoy's letter to the Smalleys giving them
notice to quit because of 'planning developments' brings on his fatal
heart attack. Lucy is bereft, the more so because she realises that she
does not fit in modern India. Not that she fitted in the India of the
Raj either. In fact, she realises, she has exchanged the small-minded,
status-conscious world of army wives for the emerging Indian
middle class. 'There was this new race of sahibs and memsahibs
who had taken the place of generals and Mrs Generals, and she and
Tusker had become for them almost as far down the social scale as
the Eurasians [Anglo-Indians] were in the days of the Raj.' Her cry
at the very end of *Staying On* – 'Oh, Tusker, Tusker, Tusker, how can
you make me stay here by myself while you yourself go home?' – is
a recognition that she will spend the rest of her days as an outsider
in India.

There were any number of real-life 'relics' of the Raj scattered
round the hill stations up until the 1980s. These were the stayers-on
the Indians called *koi hais* and *mems*. *Koi hai* means literally 'anyone
there?', and, says *Hanklyn-Janklin*, 'it is the call with which, in British
days, masters were alleged to summon their servants. Hence "an old
koi hai" means a long-term European resident of India.' It is used of
the caricature old Brit with a red face who shouts '*Koi hai*? Fetch me

my *chhota-peg!*' (a single whisky as opposed to a *burra peg*, a double whisky). The *mem(sahib)*, of course, is usually his wife, or widow; 'relict' one might say. By the 1980s the *mems* outnumbered the *koi hais*. To the old *koi hais* and *mems* and to some Anglo-Indians today, fellow stayers-on who preferred social not to say sexual relationships with Indians were accused of going *jungli* or 'native' – no longer an unforgivable crime but certainly deserving of social disapproval. My friend Adam Clapham made a TV documentary in which, at the hill station of Ootacamund known by everyone as Ooty, he encountered the spinster Elfrida Gaye, to me the caricature stayer-on *mem* except in one respect:

> She was pale, shy, softly spoken in a pedantically correct Home Counties accent, dressed like a 1930s aunt. And she was completely broke, living in a guesthouse paid for by surreptitious handouts from the other British who had stayed on. She painted really rather good watercolours of Kensington Gardens, of Norland nannies and high-backed prams – of boys in sailor suits and girls in wide-brimmed straw hats – scenes from half a century before. However, it soon became apparent that Elfrida had never been to England, never ventured abroad.[2]

In fact, although Elfrida had convinced herself that she was English, 'she was almost certainly Anglo-Indian and not at all proud of it'. The world of the Anglo-Indians, children of a mixed relationship who stayed on in India but still yearn for a country they have never seen, is one that I visit in Chapter Seven.

The sad hill station stayers-on met first by John Riddy, and then, twenty years later, by Adam Clapham, those who were at least middle-aged at the time of Independence, have all passed away. In fact they were not representative of the stayers-on during the quarter of a century after Independence. The figures supplied by the British High Commission in India in the early 1970s provide a clearer picture. In 1947, about 55,000 British civilians returned home so that, in 1951, there were 28,000 British residents in India, most of whom had been born in the United Kingdom. By 1961 the number had halved to around 14,000, and ten years later it had more than halved again to

6,500. Crucially, most of the men were still in work. The senior rank of the Indian Civil Service had 'Indianised' (the phrase used) long before Independence, so by August 1947 only 630 Britons remained out of a total cadre of 1,150, and one month later the number was down to thirty-three! The Indianisation of the armed forces had taken longer but was complete by 1960. Of those stayers-on who remained in work in 1966 nearly 1,000 were tea planters and their families, over 500 of them living in north-east India (see Chapter Two). That left those in industry and commerce, many in senior positions and most in Calcutta (see Chapter One). The same year, 1966, the total number of these *boxwallahs*, the phrase used in Raj days to mean the broad band of businessmen, was estimated at between 2,000 and 3,000, though this included those on short-term secondment as well as long-term residents. The year 1966 was significant, indeed catastrophic, for the stayers-on. The huge rupee devaluation that June meant that the cost of exchanging to pounds sterling went up by over one-third. The date is still remembered apocalyptically as 6/6/66, when many stayers-on decided to call it a day.

The 1960s were a watershed for the British remaining in India. The 1950s had been a halcyon period, an Indian summer; the 1970s became a stormy period, a hanging-on in a foreign country. The 1960s separated the two decades, politically by the end of a 'special relationship' and accelerated Indianisation; economically by devaluation and punitive taxation.

The stayers-on whom I interviewed are very different from their predecessors. Three were in their thirties in 1947, most were born in India in the 1920s or 1930s, and others arrived just before Independence. No one could call them outsiders or relic(t)s of the Raj. They have matured with the new nation itself, and, although most have kept their British citizenship, they have adapted to India without imperial hang-ups. I doubt if they would have lived so long had they not. All of them whom I asked intend to pass the remainder of their days in India. They intend to be buried there too, and I believe this is a key indicator of where we think we belong.

The latest figures about stayers-on from the British High Commission are not very helpful. Apparently in 2006 there were

11,205 British nationals living with residence visas in the four main towns of India – that is New Delhi, Mumbai (formerly Bombay), Chennai (Madras) and Kolkata (Calcutta). Interestingly, over 6,000 were in Mumbai and only 600 in Kolkata, and this reflects the new business reality. Most of these must be relatively short-stay business people, at least those not intending to stay on, who are working once again near the west coast where the East India Company began. The High Commission says 'most major British companies consider it now "business critical" to have partnerships in India', and most of these are in the 'Mumbai region'. Where does that leave our old stayers-on? They must be well over seventy to qualify, and I wager on the basis of circumstantial research that the total number, excluding Anglo-Indians, is probably no more than twenty out of an Indian population of 1.2 billion.

The figures supplied by the High Commission about the economic relationship between the UK and India tell an extraordinary story. In 2006 the UK was still the third biggest inward investor in India and the fourth largest trading partner. What is record-breaking, literally, is the investment of India in the UK: 'In 2005– 2006 for the first time ever the amount of money invested into the UK by Indian companies overtook the amount invested in India by British companies. This is an amazing leap for India on the UK investor's chart from No. 8 to No. 3, an increase over the previous year of 110%.'[3] In 2007 there are one million British Indians living in the UK, twenty Indian companies are listed on the Stock Exchange and 430 Indian firms are based in London alone – that is 30 per cent of all foreign investment in the capital. It is getting on for economic imperialism in reverse. Incidentally, a rumour went the rounds of British Mumbai when I was last there in 2006 that 17,000 British passport-owners had returned to live in Gujarat, 'no doubt all called Patel'. This makes it all the harder to separate out the stayers-on.

I have chosen my stayers-on not just because they have spent interesting lives but because their careers are illustrative of the legacy of British India. Ask anybody who knows the recent history of India, and they will agree that the 350 years of the Kampani Raj, the British Raj, the British Empire or occupation – whatever you want to call it and for better or worse – passed on the following: the English language, the Christian faith, a constitution and a civil service, the railways, the tea industry, the regimental traditions of the army, a heritage industry, the managing agency commercial system, tiger shooting and now tiger conservation (in partnership with the maharajas) and the mixed race of Anglo-Indians. It also passed on the judiciary, an elite form of private education and cricket – and no doubt other things too that are not in this book because I could not find any continuity of character, still alive today, through whom to introduce the subject. If you read on, then, you will find a mixture of biography and theme. The book is what it says it is: 'After the Raj: the last stayers-on and the legacy of British India.'

On one of my visits to India to research this book I read *Out of India* by Michael Foss, whose family returned to England when he was eleven in 1948. On the flight I underlined this passage:

> Even in the photos I can see that the imposition of the Raj, under the lens of time, was a moment out of history. A turning aside. It could not last, it was an anomaly. India lapped at it, and washed over it, and submerged it for ever, like a lost city obliterated by an inevitable rise of the waters. But it retains the mystery and eerie seductiveness of lost cities, a forlorn piece of the archaeology of the human spirit, grandly – triumphantly – *wrong* in the wrong place.
>
> Surely, among the criticisms and excuses for their conduct, we can smile at a people who made such an unforeseen, wholehearted and dedicated mistake.[4]

I thought I would discuss this evocative and provocative conclusion with the stayers-on I met. I was too late. The Raj has indeed been submerged by modern India and with it their own interest in arguing about it. One or two were wary when I asked them for their own opinions; perhaps they did not wish to cause offence to their host country, the government of which is still sensitive about such matters. One or two came out with the cliché about 'at least we gave India a language, cricket and the railways', but it was not a subject of much interest. For others it obviously had been a question that they had once agonised over, but the time for that had long passed. Only Mark Tully, as always generous to his interviewer, gave me a considered answer (see Chapter Six).

On one area of comparison only did my stayers-on speak out and that was corruption. While agreeing that the Raj had been self-serving, they were convinced it had also been incorruptible at the higher levels of the Indian Civil Service, and this example – this principle – had percolated down. The government 'servant' under the Raj, said more than one, had cared about the high standards of British rule: 'It was a matter of trust that was handed down.' Elderly Indians I met said much the same. Indeed, one talked about this 'trust' with wonder because, he said, honesty in government was simply not part of the Indian tradition. The stayers-on I met had encountered minor corruption in day-to-day matters such as obtaining planning permission, extending their residential visas and doing business with politicians. Their reaction depended on temperament. The late Bob Wright (see Chapter One) said 'always act first and argue afterwards'. Another said 'keep a sense of humour', citing the time when he had needed a vaccination with a certificate and the doctor had offered him two prices with the question 'do you need a certificate or the jab as well?' A third, actually the son of Joubert Van Ingen, the taxidermist stayer-on in Mysore (see Chapter Four), blamed himself for not being corrupt. 'It's a cultural habit and I can't learn it. I'm always losing out because I obey the rules.' None of them was so excoriating as the long-suffering Lucy Smalley in *Staying On*. She admitted to herself that she was 'filled with anger at the emerging Indian middle-class of wheelers and dealers who with their corrupt practices, their utter indifference to the state of the nation, their use of political power for personal gain, were ruining the country'.

Although *After the Raj* is what it says it is, it is not as it should be. British India covered the Indian subcontinent, and I have excluded Pakistan, Bangladesh, Sri Lanka and, apart from a visit to Karnataka, the very distinct world of south India. The other deficiency in my mind is that I do not really understand India. I am well aware of the saying 'it takes seven weeks to become an expert on India and seven years to achieve ignorance', and after frequent visits over the

last forty years I believe that ignorance is quite an achievement. I
have never lived in India, although, oddly but definitely, I sometimes
imagine I have lived in British India in a past life. Most of the British
who lived in India did not understand it either, and this, in my view,
is the greatest criticism of the Raj. Michael Foss writes in another
graphic paragraph:

> Like all the British of the Raj, adult or child, I was a part of two worlds.
> I and my kind lived *on* India but not *in* it. One world – the super-
> structure of our lives provided by the Raj – was manifest, too plain
> to be missed by even the greatest dunderhead. This other world, this
> shadowland, was a place for our averted eyes – if not a dirty secret, at
> least a slightly disreputable tale, hardly mentioned in decent company.
>
> The land, the climate, the day, the moments of existence belonged
> to all of us. But the two worlds moved, as it were, on parallel tracks,
> intimately close but separated by the indestructible veil of our histo-
> ries. Our rules for living were not their rules.

These two worlds exist today, at least for the 400,000 Britons who
visit India annually. Our superstructure now is the luxury hotel, the
first- or second-class air-conditioned coaches on the railways, the
international culture of the tourist industry. The shadowland is what
we perceive through the (usually dirty) plate-glass window – the
shrouded figures squatting round kerosene fires in the Kolkata back
streets as we travel in from the airport in the early morning; the
lines of bare figures, also squatting, as they attend to their ablutions
in fields next to the railway lines, also in the early morning. Often
we do not have the symbolic protection of plate glass as we push
our way through smelly, seething markets, or past groups of intense
worshippers in temples and mosques. This is not the India of the
'emerging middle class', with which we are united by language and
consumerism, but the India 'out there', nearly a billion strong and
unfathomable: a mystery if not a secret. More intellectually, books
like V.S. Naipaul's *India* (1998) or films like Satyajit Ray's *The Chess
Players* (1977) are the closest we will get to understanding the unique
phenomena of India that are the Hindu caste system and the variety

of religious practice. Indeed, we might not even know they exist. Yet we are tourists, passing through, while under the Raj the British lived in India, not for a lifetime but for many years.

The views of two anglophile Indians whom I encountered writing this book are relevant here. After several years living in England D.K. Palit joined the British Indian Army in 1938 in Baluchistan, and many years later he wrote enthusiastically about the relationship between British officers and the Baluchi private soldiers of his regiment. But he still felt a race apart from his brother officers:

> There was almost no social contact between British and Indian officers in the army. I don't know of a single case where a British and Indian were friendly. I was never asked by my commanding officer, my second in command or my company commander for a meal or a cup of tea in his house. There was just no contact even though we fought the same enemy. The British officers loved the life here and their nostalgia is based on that – not on any love of Indian society, because they had none … They lived their lives in cantonments. Little Englanders all over.[5]

So much for some kind of mystical relationship between the two races. The journalist and author Khushwant Singh, who admires British fair play and incorruptibility, believes the British in his lifetime were 'nabobs', arrogant and patronising:

> The British in India were never close to the Indians. If they ever made any friends it was in a benign attitude towards their servants, not at higher levels. British nostalgia for India is really a figment of their imagination. Most of them hated this country when they were here and hardly had any Indian friends to call their own.[6]

If we want evidence for this today, then we need look no further than the former British clubs, which were not Indianised until the 1960s. If we wander round the Royal Bombay Yacht Club or Tollygunge Club in Kolkata, it is easy to see them in former years as symbols of white supremacy. They existed to keep Indians out.

How else could they be bastions of Britain in a foreign land? 'What is the difference between the Yacht Club in Bombay and the Bengal Club in Calcutta?' the Maharaja of Baroda asked the writer Somerset Maugham: 'The first does not allow Indians or dogs; the second allows dogs'.

Probably there are survivors of the Raj at home in the UK who find this Indian criticism hard to take. After all, they experienced little personal animosity when they were in India, and westernised Indians of their era often share the same nostalgia for aspects of the Raj. Moreover, Indian ignorance of the Raj was as great as the other way round at that time. The socialist writer Inder Malhotra, who as a student was in the crowd with Khushwant Singh when Nehru proclaimed Independence at the 'midnight hour', describes how his little niece saw a statue of George V in 1961. He told her that it was a statue to the King Emperor: 'She laughed at me and said "No, uncle, you are trying to pull my leg! It can't be. How could anyone come here and rule us? We are so many millions of people."'

Given that the British retreated to their clubs and cantonments, shielded by their *topis*, protected by their hierarchical 'orders of precedence' and distracted by sport and *shikars*, is it any wonder that the realities of Indian society eluded them? But thoughtful men like Michael Foss's father, a soldier of the Raj who confessed towards the end of his life to 'an infatuation with India', nevertheless admitted: 'The relationship went sour. We lacked sympathy and understanding. We wanted too much and gave too little, not in terms of administration of politics or economics, where, I think, we did quite well, but in our paucity of imagination, our stuffy emotions and lack of heart. Another case, I'm afraid, of British constipation.' This is a subtle way of saying that the British did not try and understand India and I believe this was the case.

No doubt the early generation of stayers-on who retreated to the hill stations – enclaves of Britishness, just as McCluskiegunge was intended as a homeland for Anglo-Indians (see Chapter Five) – protected themselves from the real India down below. The next generation, the very last, the people I met, are very different. They have grown old in the State of India and for sixty years in most cases

have lived *in* it, not *on* it. For Nigel Hankin it was a conscious decision way back in 1948. Watching the funeral of Mahatma Gandhi,
he was aware for the first time of 'something of his stature in India'
and, at the same time, of the insularity of the British. He determined
to find the real India, and now he sits enjoying his beer with Indian
friends discussing the subject he has made his own, the Indo-British
language (see Chapter Three). Fr Ian Weathrall OBE is the last non-
Indian Brother of the Delhi Brotherhood, and he has spent over half
a century as a missionary, helping to unite the Christian Church in
north India and working in the slums beyond the Yamuna River (see
Chapter Three). Sir Mark Tully has become a sort of Indian national
treasure for interpreting India back to Indians through the BBC
World Service. 'What you British don't understand', said an Indian
newspaper editor, 'is that we Indians also regard Mark as one of us'
(see Chapter Six). Colonel 'Papa' Wakefield, the tiger-hunter turned
wildlife conservationist, may behave like a *koi hai* of the Indian Army,
but he was married to an Indian *rani* (the widow of a maharaja),
works for Indians and says defiantly that he is Indian (see Chapter
Four). Bob Powell Jones, the tea planter in Assam, has a Khasi wife,
Dorothy, and a Khasi employer, Nayantra Lakyrsiew Mon Sawain,
who intends to make boutique tea for Harrods (see Chapter Two).
Lieutenant-Colonel Graham Tullet OBE and Major Frank Courtney
OBE, MC are past Presidents of the Royal Bombay Yacht Club, virtually the last British survivors of a club that now has 1,200 Indian
members (see Chapter Seven). Anne Wright MBE is a paradox. For
years she and her late husband, Bob Wright OBE, known as Raja
Wright, were the leaders of the staying-on community in Kolkata
and enjoyed their status at Tollygunge Club as flamboyant colonial
figures toughing it out in India. Yet Anne is an Indian citizen and has
always had many Indian friends, for the maharajas and Indian members of the ICS were always accepted in British society (see Chapter
One). The Anglo-Indian Kitty Texiera of McCluskiegunge is to my
mind a brave example for her mixed race of the need to assimilate in
order to survive. Although proud of her roots, she has three Indian
children by a tribal Indian and has no doubts that her future is in
Indian society (see Chapter Five). That leaves just one relic of the

Raj, the very old Joubert Van Ingen. As he spent his career as a taxidermist, perhaps that is appropriate (see Chapter Four).

RIDDY OF THE RAJ

The idea to write this book came after a visit I made to John
Riddy in 2004. He entertained me with an intellectual enthusiasm
about the British in India that must be unique, as evidenced by his
extraordinary library. Moreover, he had worked in the Indian cotton
industry in the early years after the Raj, and this was a deeply felt
experience that still seemed to haunt him. I wrote an account of my
visit at the time.

John met me in the garden of his Yorkshire village home, a large,
genial figure who could be a retired farmer in these parts, except
that he wore a red peaked cap with the yellow and black insignia of
Ferrari cars, and a Mozart opera drifted towards us out of the kitchen
window. Even outside he was hemmed in by books. The garage was
full of packing cases; the specially built summer house had book-
shelves lining all the walls, leaving room only for a large double bed
in the middle. He muttered about being 'banished' and then took me
into the house. Once again every wall apart from the kitchen was
lined with books: stacks of them on the floor reaching halfway up
the walls; boxes of monographs, calendars of state papers (*The Court
Minutes of the East India Company, 1500–1680*), shelves of memoirs
(*Rugby and India* by Sir Alexander Arbuthnot), lines of official gazetteers (*The District Gazetteers of India, 1904–1913*, over 200 volumes). I
noticed that many had page markers.

John stood over the tea he had prepared in the kitchen; half bottles
of three different dry sherries and *patum peperium* sandwiches made
according to the Gentleman's Relish recipe of 1826. It reminded him
of another tea he had taken in Ackroyd's bungalow outside Sholapur
in 1958. John had joined the Bombay Company on impulse, having
been turned down by the Foreign Office, and so he found himself
aged twenty-five as Assistant Manager of the Parbhat and Vedanta
cotton mills, a gigantic plant of 3,000 looms and 30,000 Indians

stretching over miles of dusty plain between Poona (now Pune) and
Hyderabad. There were three other Britons, all over sixty. 'None
of them enjoyed India any more. Their ambition was to retire to a
paradise like Malvern.' Ralph Ackroyd was one of them. He was the
engineer with a genius for making the 'clanking, derelict, Victorian
machinery work past its die-by date', John said. They had hardly
exchanged a word for many weeks when Ackroyd invited Riddy
for tea. They sat under the fan on the veranda, the older man with
a 'carapace of shyness' and the younger tongue-tied with loneliness.
To John's amazement there were cream buns on the table. 'Young
men like cream buns,' said Ackroyd. 'I had them flown in from Aden.'
Equally amazing was Ackroyd's 'O'-gauge train set. During tea the
toy trains sped through tunnels in the walls and reappeared on mini-
ature viaducts in the garden. John felt a wave of homesickness as he
saw the LNER insignia.

Poor Ackroyd had a sad secret. No one knew what had happened
to his first wife, but his second, a young woman with 'the vestiges of
beauty', had been overcome by 'the total loneliness of the place and
the surreptitious apartheid of our Indian neighbours'. She had done
a bunk. A passing American had stopped for the night, and early the
next morning she had hidden in the boot of his car. An hour away
from Sholapur, she had banged on the boot and thrown herself on
his mercy. They had married, and Ackroyd was left with his 'O' gauge.

John began collecting books four years after he returned home to
become a research student at Oxford University. At the Turl bookshop in Oxford he bought the six volumes of John Mill's *History of
British India*, the third edition of 1826, for three shillings. 'Pernicious!
This was the first history of the Raj. Mills painted the hues in bold,
his tones were stark, evil was evil. Only mission Christianity could
save the Indian soul!' Many of John's collected works are cast-offs
from university libraries that should have known better. *The Moral
and Material Progress of India* came from a skip outside Cardiff
University. This was an annual report from the India Office to show
how the British had fulfilled their stewardship since the Mutiny, a
volume a year between 1859 and 1942. John has the sequence 1918–
38. 'Note how the volumes become thicker as the voice becomes

shriller in defence of the Raj.' Alas, *Progress* ended just before the Empire itself. 'Eternal marble revealed as melting ice,' said John, relishing the phrase. In this connection I noticed twelve thick volumes on a lower shelf: *India: The Transition of Power.* 'Wilson's idea, the liar! He thought that if the Government printed all the documents then partition could be justified. It couldn't. It was not worthy of us. Playing the communal card has left a terrible legacy that could even involve the world in nuclear conflict.'

Whether the Parbhat and Vedanta mills contributed to the moral and material progress of India John doubts. After a few sherries he experiences shock and awe at the very memory of the place. 'A Blakian vision! A Stygian hell! In the loom sheds the smashing sound as shuttles slammed at enormous speed into the cast iron frames … The clacking of leather drive belts that turned great ghouts of water issuing from the ceiling into clouds of mist to keep the machines moist … The smell of sweat, stale urine and worse.' John had to make a tour of inspection every day, dripping with discomfort. The Indian men were naked apart from 'the most exiguous *dhoti* and the women's gauze-thin *saris* slipped from their bodies. Many were shapely! I sometimes lingered.' John took refuge in the cool of evening by searching the top crevices of the deep artesian wells for pigmy owls and dangerous snakes. Sometimes, wretchedly homesick, he would gaze at the silent machinery, taking comfort from the metal plate 'Made in Bolton, Lancs'.

John's own morals exemplified the self-discipline of the Raj. When he disembarked at Bombay, a company director had greeted him with: 'Riddy? I knew your father. Taught me at school. Word of advice first – don't s★★t on your own doorstep.' Baffled, John decided to inspect the doorstep. He toyed with the advice offered by Rafferty, who was another of the Sholapur stayers-on: 'Get one of the *cheechee* (Anglo-Indian) engineers to send up his sister; she'll show you her *sitar* (musical instrument), or something.' John hated Rafferty because Rafferty hated Indians. His favourite talk after a *chhota-peg* was of the 1930s, when he had beaten up Congress Party rioters with a *lathi* (stick with steel rim used by police) when serving with the British special police in Calcutta.

Later, John travelled through an India heavy with the imprint of
the Raj and stayed at clubs still British in membership but Indianising
fast. After his return to Britain he wrote to each, offering to provide an English home for history books from the libraries. Packing
cases arrived full of tomes riddled with white ants and pale from light
fatigue. Over 1,000 books were sent by the Bengal Club of Calcutta;
other collections arrived from Darjeeling and Nainital. What were his
A1 collector's items? He looked flustered, as if this was an improper
question, but then he spread out on the bed in his summer house a
maritime survey of the Hoogly estuary printed in 1780 that showed
the dry docks where the East India Company repaired its ships. Only
twenty-four copies had been made, one for each director. Even rarer
is Major James Rennell's second edition *Charts of India*, a carto-
graphical survey compiled about the same time and kept in one folio
binding. All the first edition has been destroyed, and only a dozen of
the second remain: 'I have the twelfth and it's in the bank.'

By this time we had tasted the sherries and moved on to champagne. John had shown me his garage, apologising for the 'lighter
books' stuffed into packing cases. These included tourist vade
mecums going back to the nineteenth century and 'my collection
of gardening books'. A generously illustrated copy of *The Perfumed
Garden* gave him particular pleasure.

Riddy has contributed to the scholarship of the Raj. In particular
he has recently published *Courtesy in Conflict: The Strange Character
of the Briton in Indian and Pakistani English Fiction.* 'Almost always the
Briton has been shown as brutal, barbaric, very intelligent and essen-
tial for the resolution of India's destiny. As this statement has not been
challenged I assume it has found acceptance.' John's special study is
of the College of Fort William set up by the East India Company in
1801 to 'teach its ignorant adolescents about India'. At this time there
were no texts available to study the vernacular languages. Popular
culture depended on the oral tradition:

> By the combination of the amateur scholarship of the Company's
> European servants and savants recruited in India, the orthography and
> grammar of India's languages were settled, fonts were cast and texts

began to be printed. The College became part of Calcutta University in the 1850s. Who has even heard of it now? Who knows about its extraordinary achievement?

We sat in John's kitchen looking at his overgrown garden and, with the champagne inducing its *vin triste*, contemplated the fall of empires. I told him that on a recent visit to Delhi a taxi driver had offered to show me a ruin of the Raj. He had taken me instead to a Mughal ruin, Humayun's Tomb, but it was all the same to him. *Sic transit Gloria mundi!* I asked John, all in all, what he thought of the influence of the Raj? A long silence and then an *obita dicta*: 'For all the blemishes and misunderstandings, nonetheless it is my belief that our presence was better for the peoples of India than our non-presence and the exposure of Indians to the internal chaos caused by the collapse of the Mughal hegemony.'

When I last visited Riddy of the Raj his vast library had just been collected by York University. He had a team of helpers to stack it up in crates that resembled a Mount Ararat of books, because floodwater had lapped at the very base and then receded. He was bereft.

HER MAJESTY'S GOVERNMENT: AN OVERVIEW

'We are a free and sovereign people today and we have rid ourselves of the burden of the past. We look at the world with clear and friendly eyes and at the future with faith and confidence.' So said the new Prime Minister, Jawaharlal Nehru, on 15 August 1947. The Raj was the burden, but its legacy, of course, could not be laid down. In the intervening sixty years its influence has faded, its edifices crumbled, its institutions Indianised, its survivors reduced to a handful; but in many ways it is still part of modern India, as this book shows. What is the legacy at the highest, official, level? How has it affected relations between Her Majesty's Government and the Republic of India? I asked two High Commissioners (the equivalent of ambassadors) twenty years apart, the Rt Hon. John Freeman, who arrived

in India in 1965 and stayed for three years, the period twenty years
after Independence; and Sir David Goodall, who occupied the post
between 1987 and 1991, the period twenty years before the present.
Through conversation and once confidential papers now in the
National Archives I report their views.

I do the same with the British Council, which was integrated into
the High Commission in 1971. Lyon Roussel held senior positions in
India between 1960 and 1967, and Robert Sykes did likewise twenty
years later between 1987 and 1993. The two bodies represent diplomacy and culture, between which, says Lyon Roussel, 'there is a very
British and invisible demarcation line. We were not concerned with
the politics of the day but thought more in the longer term. You
could say that the Diplomatic Service looks after the weather while
the British Council concerns itself with the climate.' In both these
periods the weather was stormy, the climate changing.

John Freeman arrived on a gust of goodwill. His previous job in an
extraordinarily diverse career had been editor of the *New Statesman*,
which had campaigned for Indian independence since before the
war. He made it known quickly that he had been no friend of the
Raj. He and his wife, Catherine, a former TV producer, invited to the
High Commission a new generation of writers such as Khushwant
Singh and Prem Shankar Jha, who revelled in the decline of the *maa–
baap sarkar*, the paternalistic 'mother–father state' of the Congress
Party, which had run India politically and socially since 1947. The
atmosphere at the Freeman parties, remembers Jha, was 'like a room
full of fresh air'. Storm clouds, however, were banking up on the
horizon. Prime Minister Harold Wilson's tactless and wrong remark
that India was to blame for the second war with Pakistan (1965)
'hung round my [Freeman's] neck like an albatross'. Then came the
controversial Commonwealth Immigration Act of 1968, which prevented Kenyan Indians with UK passports from entering the UK.
Freeman was officially castigated on behalf of his government for
'bad faith that will destroy what little enthusiasm is still left [in India]
for the Commonwealth'. Above all was the personality of the new
Prime Minister, Indira Gandhi, who seemed to have none of her
father's affection for Britain. Freeman took a somewhat sexist view

of this. Writing about her 'quite remarkable waywardness and unreal-
ism in dealing with public business', he added a sentence or two that
he could have written for the *New Statesman* diary:

> Her femininity does, of course, play a considerable role in all this. But
> simple sex is not all. Before one can really get through to her, one has
> not only, as it were, to squeeze her hand, but also to dress up in her
> political clothes. Since her most deep-seated and darkling neuroses
> concern Britain, this is not always a course that can be commended to
> HM Commissioner.[7]

In his Final Despatch of July 1968 Freeman wrote that British–Indian
relations were in a state of 'post-colonial tension'. On the one side
was 'nostalgia' and on the other side 'neurosis', which showed itself in
hypersensitivity and suspicion. He had no time for the nostalgia: 'We
must pursue our direct interests, eschewing nostalgic recollections of
a special relation that over most fields no longer exists.' He had been
outraged when Lord Mountbatten had come over and offered to take
British guests at the Commission round 'my old house', by which he
meant the former Viceregal Lodge and now the *Rasthrapati Bhavan*
(the President's House). This patronising insensitivity accounted in
part for the 'neurosis'.

It took a very forgiving Indian not to be offended by some visible reminders of the Raj in New Delhi. I remember my first visit
in 1964 when an Indian student, who told me that Churchill considered Indians 'a beastly people with a beastly religion', took me
deliberately to the Government Secretariat built in the 1920s for
Raj rule and pointed out the ludicrous, condescending quotation
engraved in very large letters: 'Liberty will not descend to a people:
a people must raise themselves to liberty. It is a blessing which must
be earned before it can be enjoyed.' Indira Gandhi's neurosis, wrote
Freeman, took the form of suspicion about Britain's role in India's
conflict with Pakistan. He wrote in *Despatch* No. 9 in May 1967:

> She believes that we are constantly trying to manipulate Pakistan
> against India and intervene in a situation that did not call for out-

side interference ... She feels that it was consistent British policy to build up Pakistan as a threat and counterbalance to developing India. I replied that it was nothing of the sort:'It is a most earnest desire to see the two countries settle their disputes.'[8]

Under the surface Freeman detected a paradoxical attitude in official India towards Britain. On the one hand, politicians were constantly on the watch for any slighting comment about India in the British press, to which they replied 'in immoderate and occasionally abusive language'. On the other hand, when the British government 'cooled off its intercourse ... and behaved with detached friendliness' towards the Indian government, Indian politicians became anxious that they were no longer in any kind of special relationship. A bit like former lovers, it seems.

I put Freeman's points of view to Sir David Goodall, who had been appointed High Commissioner by Maggie Thatcher in 1987 with the order:'Don't forget we gave India democracy and our language'; to which Dennis Thatcher had added 'and the railways'. Then, showing her very human side, the Prime Minister had asked to be remembered to the Head Bearer at the High Commission, who on her previous visit had given her a potion to cure her stomach upset. 'If the servants' quarters need refurbishing,' she told Sir David, 'tell me. I'll squeeze money out of the Foreign Office.' He arrived soon after the assassination of Prime Minister Indira Gandhi by a Sikh. This was in retaliation for her orders to the army two years before to attack the Sikh Golden Temple at Amritsar, where extremists were holding out demanding a separate state. In 1987 India's official attitude to the Sikhs was still very touchy, as it had been to Pakistan in Freeman's time.

Sir David agreed succinctly with Freeman's description of a paradoxical attitude towards Britain by official India:

Twenty years later we were further down the road and there was an awareness of the extent to which Britain and India were growing apart. But the post-colonial feelings were still there. Some of this was bound up with *Schadenfreude*, at seeing the former imperial power diminished and its influence contracted. Yet there was a genuine sense of dismay that Britain was losing interest in India, as evidenced by the increase in overseas students' fees and reduced levels of bilateral aid.

I asked him if there was still suspicion, even paranoia, about the UK's foreign policy towards India. He agreed that there was, though the UK's supposed unholy alliance in his day was with Sikh separatists rather than Pakistanis: 'The British were perceived as helping the Sikh extremists. It was very, very difficult to persuade the Indian government that Britain was not interfering at all.' Underneath this paranoia, said Sir David, was the 'wound of partition':

> By the time I got to India there had been three wars with Pakistan and there was still the very neuralgic dispute of Kashmir, so the fragility, the troubled character of Indian society, arose in part from the wound of partition. Indians in my day obstinately believed that partition was engineered by the British to 'divide and rule'. As the Thai Ambassador, a wise old India-hand, said to me: 'Don't be deceived; the Indians love and admire the British in almost all respects. But the one thing they can't forgive you for is partition.'

Sir David said he had thought a lot about why this persistent wound refused to heal:

> I think it's intimately bound up with this sense of inner security. The explanation seems to be that not only was Pakistan carved out of what Indians see as the territory of the Indian nation, but that it was created and is maintained in being on a principle that strikes at the very heart of India's cohesion and survival: the principle that confessional iden- tity [religion] is a sufficient basis on which to build a separate nation. Moreover, as today there are 130 million Muslims in India – almost as many as there are in Pakistan – this created and still creates a suspicion of a huge potential Pakistani fifth column.

He added a shocking postscript to this discussion about suspicion. In his day there was still a small number of 'genuine stayers-on like retired missionaries and old ladies, classic stayers-on' who had trouble renewing their resident permits. He complained about this to one Indian minister, whom he would not name 'because he is still active in politics'. He replied: "'I don't care about them, they're all spies!" I said "Minister, you can't be serious?"' – visions of Lucy Smalley as a member of MI6 – 'talk about paranoia. That was the attitude of a Harvard educated Indian. He was talking about people who ran schools and hospitals and had been in India all their lives.'

Nevertheless, both High Commissioners agreed that there was a legacy of the Raj that united the two countries in a unique way. Freeman described it prosaically as 'a shared backgound of language, culture, professional and administrative practices'. He evaluated it in the terms of national self-interest that he wanted HMG to adopt: 'It should continue to give us an advantage for a good few years yet.' Sir David described the legacy more romantically:

> When I presented my Letters of Commission to the President of India, I felt the ghosts of empire thick about me. I took the salute in the forecourt of Viceregal Lodge flanked by officers of the Viceroy's – now President's – Bodyguard ('only the name has changed' the Commandant said afterwards) while the band played 'God Save the Queen' and imperial New Delhi lay spread out in front of me. The Britishness of the pageantry only echoes the Britishness of more important things: of the language, of the parliamentary institutions, of the judicial framework, of the style and discipline of the armed forces.
>
> People dismiss language and say 'You know, it's only the language', but language is a very, very culturally pervasive thing. Look at someone like the writer Vikram Seth. Is he Indian or British? He couldn't possibly think as he does if he had not come out of an Indo-British culture. We are still one of the largest investors in India [in 2006 the third largest behind the USA and, believe it or not, Mauritius]. People said to me: 'If you are looking for a foreign partner, then most Indian companies would prefer a British partner.' This is partly a matter of language.

Writing again in terms of national self-interest, Freeman singled out Aid as 'the most important single weapon we at present deploy …

It is our principal contribution to develop India on a stable, non-Communist line.' Sir David endorsed the importance of Aid: 'It was rather like the nuclear bomb. It gave you a seat at the high table.' However, interestingly, he denied that giving Aid was solely for the national interest: 'Although a lot of us felt dealing with the Indian government was a pain, we also recognised that we had an obligation to the country of India as a result of our history.'

Soon after Sir David left, a new Indian government guided by the World Bank gradually dismantled the bureaucratic nightmare of a socialist economy known disparagingly as the Licence Raj and introduced liberal, free-trade, measures. The boom began. Relations with Britain began to improve: 'The Indian Foreign Minister announced: "Relations with Britain are now normal, which is most unusual." That was about right. They were never like relations with other countries. They just couldn't be, because of the past.'

Knowing how much Sir David Goodall had tried to get outside '2 KG' (2 King George's Avenue, the official residence of the High Commissioner) and explore the real country, I bought his book *Remembering India*. I thought I would learn something more than from most diplomats' memoirs. And so I did, for it is a collection of his paintings. He is an accomplished watercolourist in the tradition of artists like Thomas and William Daniell who, he says, 'first gave people in Europe a vision of what India looked like'.

Whereas themes of continuity run through the Foreign Office's relations with India, in the case of the British Council there seem to be more themes of discontinuity. When Lyon and Elizabeth Roussel arrived in Bombay in 1960 to work for the British Council, their briefing came from a now defunct book called *The Main Tasks*. These were: 'the propagation of English; the dissemination of the written word; the promotion of British Arts; the exchange of people'. India, Lyon reminded me in 2006, an indulgent smile on his face after a good lunch in his Woodstock garden, was the 'jewel in the crown' of the British Council:

The Indians so loved English culture! Shakespeare was our best ambassador! My library in Bombay was the busiest Council library in the world. We had 12,000 members, a waiting list of 8,000, a stock of 55,000 books and 200 papers and periodicals. The secret of our success was that we employed local people to run things and we had fifty in Bombay alone [one was Foy Nissen; see Chapter Seven]. Their service reflected a devotion to Britain whether we deserved it or not.[9]

Cut now to a restaurant near Andover in Hampshire in 2007 and the company of Robert and Laura Sykes. He took over the British Council office in Calcutta in 1987 and eventually became the Number 2 in India, 'rejoicing in the title of Councillor for Cultural Affairs, British High Commission, British Council Division':

Libraries? The whole concept is going out of the window now. I don't know how many survive. Most of the information we provide is on-line. Anyway, the mission of encouraging Indians to read books as literature is no longer top of the list. The identity of the British Council as a book library has more or less had its day. These days our aim is to get young Indian postgraduates to enrol in distant learning or come to the UK to study for an MBA and so on. It's a question of targeting.

Back to Woodstock and the enthusiastic memories of Lyon Roussel of his time in Bombay in the 1960s:

If I had to name the three most successful arts events in British Council terms (mentioning only *en passant* one-night stands by British orchestras – you should have heard Malcolm Sargent conducting the LSO playing an arrangement of the Indian National anthem!), I would plump for: a Young Vic tour directed by Dennis Carey that included Hamlet with 18-year-old Sarah Badel as a superb Ophelia. The Indians simply love Shakespeare, don't they? A gentleman behind us quoted the whole play from memory and just a little ahead of the actors' delivery to show he really knew it. Then a tour by Julian Bream, a sure success in a country where the stringed instrument is so appreciated. And then Emlyn Williams with readings from Dickens. No one who has not seen and heard Emlyn give these readings can imagine their power. The Indians were spellbound.

Robert Sykes in Andover was more reflective, even self-critical:

> The British Council is involved with big manifestations a lot less now.
> That's the buzz word, 'manifestations'. My Henry Moore was one of
> the last. Thinking about it afterwards, was it wise to invest £100,000
> for an exhibition of sculpture that travelled round India? Is that going
> to be an enduring way of opening the eyes of key young Indians to
> the West? I rather doubt it. What we were after in my day, still are, are
> the new young technocrats of India and examining what we have to
> offer them.

The British Council seems a lot less fun than it used to be – like the
BBC, for whom I worked for thirty years. It is all up on computers now, mission statements emailed to staff, the target raj, endless
budgeting 'adjustments'. Out are 'The Main Tasks' ('a bit pompous'
said Robert Sykes) and in is the mantra 'the British Council has rapidly become one of the main delivery agents for educational and
human resource development aid' (Robert Sykes again). Probably
one reason for this is that it is now fully integrated into HMG –
and, of course, HMG sets the standards for presentational spin. It
was a structural change with a strange origin. In 1971, so Robert
Sykes told me, a Russian cultural centre in south India collapsed
causing Indian fatalities. 'This gave the Indian government the pre-
text of taking control. They did not want too many Brits with their
propaganda around in their libraries.' From then on the Indian government insisted that foreign libraries, arts centres and so on could
operate only in towns where the country concerned had a diplomatic presence, otherwise they were to be run in partnership with
the Indian Council for Cultural Relations (ICCR). The response of
HMG was 'a piece of fancy footwork'. The High Commissioner of
the time, Sir Maurice James, who was Laura Sykes's father, decided
to incorporate the British Council offices in the four main towns
of New Delhi, Calcutta, Madras and Bombay into a division of the
High Commission – 'fancy diplomatic titles', CD plates, the lot.
Robert said it made life a lot easier and more comfortable. More
centralised and bureaucratic too?

The main aim of the British Council has always been the teaching of English. But whereas in nearly every other country of the world the Council runs institutes where the public may enrol, pay a fee and learn English, that is not allowed in India. The reason is that English is an official Indian language, so designated in the constitution (see Chapter Three), and therefore it cannot be taught by a foreign agency. The British Council instead specialises in the teaching of teachers, with a cadre of consultants and online materials. Since the 1970s, however, it has branched into other forms of aid. Now it is the Department for International Development (DFID) UK that provides the commissions, so that the British Council has become one of the main delivery agents for education, training and human-resource development aid. That was another reason why Robert Sykes approved of his status with HMG: 'It was much easier to bid for these contracts if I could present my visiting card from the High Commission as it gave me a *locus standi.*'

I read him Freeman's view that 'Aid is the most important single weapon we at present deploy in India', much more so than the cultivation of any supposed special relationship. Not surprisingly he agreed:

> He was absolutely right, of course, and my father in law would have said so too. We can't rely on sentiment, on the old special relationship. If we provide a huge project in family health care in Bihar, or safer drinking water in the Deccan, or a big project about primary education in Hyderabad, that's much more important.

Of course it is, but I could not get out of my mind Lyon and Elizabeth Roussel sitting in a hushed Bombay theatre and watching Sarah Badel play Ophelia, while an Indian sitting next to them recited her lines.

Chapter One

THE WRIGHTS OF TOLLYGUNGE

The last time I met Bob Wright OBE was in 2004 over breakfast at the famous Tollygunge Club in Kolkata, where he lived. I waited for him in the *shamiana* (an Urdu word meaning a sort of luxury canopy for outdoor functions) and watched golfers on the eighteenth green. Round me were the new nabobs of Kolkata, wealthy Bengali and Marwari businessmen and their wives. As Bob entered with his Labrador dog, Becky, still every inch a *burra sahib* (Urdu for 'great master', as used by servants), conversation fell silent. Men rose to their feet. 'Good morning, Bob!' He took it in his stride. 'Do sit down,' he said, inspecting the room. I half expected a salute. There was something imperious about Bob, and he revelled in it. He boasted that the only public figure who did not come to visit him – and new Deputy High Commissioners would always call to pay their respects – was his dentist, because he could not carry his equipment. Bob Wright was regarded by the British community in Kolkata as the leader of the stayers-on and by his many Indian friends as the last of the *koi hais*. The *Hindustani Times* once said he was the 'most influential figure in Calcutta after Mother Teresa'. Now he is dead. In March 2005 his faithful Becky died, and he passed away a few weeks later. Fifteen hundred mourners followed the funeral cortège from Tollygunge to the crematorium, aware that with the death of 'Raja Wright' the era of post-Independence British Calcutta had finally ended.

From 1971 to 1997 Bob Wright was the so-called 'managing member', in effect the managing director, of the famous Tollygunge Club. He and his wife Anne lived in the old clubhouse that had been built by an indigo planter in the early nineteenth century and soon after housed the widow and sons of the deceased Tipu Sultan. It is a white colonnaded palace, more typical of Calcutta in the eighteenth century, with an 80-foot-long sitting room that made Anne weep, so she told me, at the prospect of furnishing it. Now the area around it is one of the most beautiful golf courses in India, but originally it was known as the *Sahibanbagicha* or 'garden of the white men'. Anne wrote: 'Golfers may lose their balls in the lake where the bronze winged jacana teaches her chicks to walk on the lotus leaves, but it is a small sacrifice to make to preserve this Eden.' Bob saved Tolly (as it should be called, without the definite article) from collapse and made it one of the most desired clubs in India.

In the 1970s the journalist Simon Winchester described Tolly as 'an island of imperial memories hidden within the kind of neat and self-satisfied Calcutta suburbs that John Betjeman might easily recognise'.[1] Thirty years later the memories remain, but the suburbs have been replaced by the usual city chaos of India that followed expansion southwards in the wake of the metro. Bob ended his days in a small apartment behind the new club buildings; no longer the Raja but more the Tusker of the Paul Scott novel *Staying On*, bemoaning the new management and beset by the indignities of old age. Anne lives in Delhi when she is at home. Seemingly as youthful and tomboyish as ever, she divides her time between her horse stud at Tikli Bottom (in fact a place name rather than a *cri de cœur* of the British in India) and her wildlife sanctuary in Khanha National Park called Kipling Camp.

Bob was born in India in 1924 and Anne Layard went out to India from Hampshire aged one in 1930. They met in Calcutta soon after the war and married in 1950. For the next half-century their life was at the centre of the expat community of Calcutta, which numbered around 4,000 at the beginning and a few dozen or so of the last stayers-on at the very end. Latterly much of Bob's time was spent in the somewhat depressing business of repairing cemeteries, managing

Anglo–Indian retirement homes and running the remains of the UK Citizens' Association. Formerly, for twenty-five years in fact, he was a *boxwallah* working his way up the prestigious managing agency of Andrew Yule, the largest in India. This chapter should also be called '*Boxwallah* Bob', because it tells the story of the decline and death of the managing agencies that were the main institutional form of Raj commerce for well over half a century.

James Morris wrote in *Places*:

> In the 1950s and 60s the British business society still thrived in Calcutta. It was a direct and living relic of the City of Palaces [as the hugely rich Calcutta was dubbed in the eighteenth century] – itself a community of *boxwallahs* in the days when the Honourable Company humbly received concessions from the Nawab of Bengal. The British businessman made Calcutta. It sprang from the loins of five-per-cent. There was nothing here before the Company came, but out of the dividendal urge arose the first and most terrifying of all monuments to the westernisation of the East. Go-downs, factories, counting houses were the core of the city and around them the Bengalis swarmed in fascination.[2]

In the twentieth century managing agencies succeeded the counting houses. Bob Wright and his long-time friend Anthony Hayward, who worked his way from the family firm of Haywards Gin and up the agency of Shaw Wallace during the same period, witnessed the initial post-war flowering and then the final withering-away of the British commercial community of Calcutta. In the words of James Morris again: 'Now [he wrote in 1972] like a tissue finally rejecting a graft, Calcutta has finally rejected the *boxwallahs*: the chemistry of nationalisation, taxation, trade unionism has forced them out at last, and the transplant of three centuries has just this minute ended.'

Sir Anthony Hayward, known in the Oriental Club as 'the last of the *boxwallahs*', because in 1977–8 he was the last British President of the Associated Chambers of Commerce and Industry of India, now lives in Sandwich in Kent. He and his wife Jenifer arrived in Calcutta at the same time as the Wrights and have been close friends since. This is their story too.

It was the *boxwallah* Job Charnock who founded Calcutta in 1696 and it was the *boxwallah* Bob Wright who supervised the demise of the British in Calcutta 300 years later. It is a young city, younger than New York, and for most of its history it was the capital city of the British Raj. Yet the British found it a most unpleasant city to live in. In 1863 Sir Charles Trevelyan asked rhetorically: 'Find, if you can, a more uninviting spot than Calcutta. It unites every condition of a perfectly unhealthy situation. Human efforts could do little to make it worse; but that little has been done faithfully and assiduously.' For half the year the heat is to blame. 'It is enough', said Mark Twain, 'to make a brass doorknob mushy'; sufficient, it is said, to expand the colossal steel mesh of the Howrah Bridge four feet during the day. It was the heat that exacerbated the plague of cholera that filled the oldest British cemetery in Park Street. It was the heat that exacerbated the other plagues too; the sectarian violence, the industrial riots, the poverty and homelessness. It reduces everyone to irritability and listlessness between the months of April and August. 'For certain months', rhymed Kipling in 'A Tale of Two Cities', 'we boil and stew', which is why the British with money fled the city:

> Fled, with each returning spring-tide from its ills,
> To the Hills.
> From the clammy fogs of morning, from the blaze
> Of old days,
> From the sickness of the noontide, from the heat,
> Beat retreat.

Yet nowhere do the ghosts of the British collective past return more evocatively than to Calcutta. The most evocative view is from the Hooghly River. Take a boat from Fairlie Ghat near BBD Bagh, formerly Dalhousie Square, where the British built their first fort in 1696. Chug upstream under the Howrah Bridge, which carries a million people daily between Howrah on the west bank and Calcutta proper on the east. On both sides you pass semi-ruins of the old go-downs, factories and counting houses. Jute, tea, rice and cotton from all points east were stored here before being shipped on to Europe. Then downstream towards the sea are the long lines of wharves at Garden Reach, from where the massed masts and then funnels of Victorian merchant steamers once propelled these cargoes back to the mother country. The old imperial energy is still there, crumbling but visible. Walk along Strand Road South and search on the walls for the faded announcements of trade – First Class Tailors, Hamilton the Jewellers, Spence's Hotel.

To imagine the city that the early traders built you need a different perspective. In the eighteenth century Calcutta was known as the City of Palaces or the St Petersburg of the East. It may have been self-regarding, greedy and sinful, but the ostentatious Georgian tombs in Park Street cemetery are monuments to the richest, most elegant colonial city of all. If you sit on the grass of the Maidan (an Urdu word meaning open ground in a city) and look north, with the paintings of Calcutta by Thomas and William Daniell in your mind, then a mirage appears; shimmering under the blue sky are stately rows of white plastered, neo-classical buildings in the Grecian style, elegant vistas of terraces as Nash might have built them, arched gateways through which further colonnaded palaces appear. Behind are the spires of St Andrews and St Johns. Only the storks perched on ornamental urns or imperial lions give any hint that this is a world away from London or St Petersburg in 1800.

The polished brass plaques in the metropolitan cathedral of St Paul's – where the memorial service to Bob Wright was held – tell a different story again. Here is the grandiosity of empire, of the superiority of 'the Heaven-born', as senior members of the Indian Civil Service were called. Notice a monument to a judge, also a champion pig-sticker, who deserves the encomium 'well done, thy good and faithful servant'. Imagine the congregation of sixty years ago, the Wrights and Haywards among them, surrounded by marble statuary and cooled by ranks of electric fans, singing the hymn of imperial retreat: 'So be it Lord, thy throne shall never like earth's proud empires pass away.'

Separated on the south side of the Maidan by Cathedral Road is the vast Victoria Memorial, arguably the most impressive monument to the Raj. Lord Curzon proposed it as 'a great imperial duty' to commemorate his beloved Queen, who had just died. Little did he know that it would also become a memorial to imperial Calcutta, for the capital of the Raj passed to Delhi in 1911 while it was being built. Curzon saw it as his Taj Mahal, though built in the Italian renaissance style, and like his inspiration it is made of dazzling Rajasthan marble, reflected in ornamental pools. He wanted 'a monumental and grand building where all classes will learn the lessons of history and see revived before their eyes the marvels of the past'. So the inside is stuffed with imperial trophies, from a lock of Lady Canning's hair to the swords of defeated princes. You may wonder what today's Indian schoolchildren think as they wander open-mouthed through the Durbar Room to Queen Mary's Room and across to the Royal Gallery.

A miracle of Calcutta is that, although the past is another country, the descendant of the Raj may still visit it today. It is another country to the Wrights and Haywards too, but as they lived in it for half a century, it is to them far more than the sound of imperial echoes.

Although Anne Wright is one of the very few remaining stayers-on with an Indian passport, she is a true daughter of the Raj. On her father's side, the Layard family, service in the colonies went back for two centuries. Her grandfather was Lord Chief Justice of Ceylon; her great-great-uncle, Sir Henry, discovered Ninevah – 'though he never did get to India,' said Anne – and her father, Austen, became a very senior member of the Indian Civil Service. When he arrived at the Gateway of India in Bombay after the First World War, there waiting for him – and wearing his battledress with two rows of medals – was his new bearer, Khali Khan, who stayed with him until his resignation from the ICS in 1948. 'He used to wear his medals when he served at table,' Anne said. 'They would dangle in the soup when he lent over to serve guests.' In one of Anne's photo albums there is a citation presented to her father by his Indian staff when he was Commissioner of the Central Provinces between 1943 and 1945: 'Let us pray to God that this benign Governor will rule over India. Let us sing songs of praise to British justice and to A. H. Layard.' Next to it is a letter: 'I'm very glad to see that you have added lustre to the name of the Central Provinces by being given the CIE [Companion of the Indian Empire]. Please accept my heartiest congratulations. Haydon – Governor CP.' One of Anne's first memories is of standing with her young sister and governess at the side of the King's Way (now Rajpath) in New Delhi, all wearing large white *topis*, and watching her father as Deputy Commissioner process past with the Viceroy Lord Willingdon in 1934. She remembers her nursery rhymes too and recites her *ayah's* version with delight:

> *Chhota Jack Horner*
> *Kona par beta*
> *Khatata Christmas mithai*
> *Angli gussaya*
> *Kishmish nikhala*
> *Bola 'kya good boy ham hai'.*

In 1938 Anne's father became Deputy Commissioner of Central Provinces (now Madhya Pradesh), and she longed for summer in the Gawilgarh Hills. Leaving her father festering in the heat of Nagpore, the family escaped by car to the remote hill station of Chikhaldhara, the domestic animals following on behind as best they could for the 120-mile journey. Here Anne, a fearless little girl, spent all day on her pony, sometimes riding bareback on her own baby elephant and once surprising a leopard in the kitchen. It was a *Swallows and Amazon* childhood that she described to me looking at her scrapbook:

> Here's a map I drew. That's Gavilgarh Fort that Wellington captured [1803] and I've written 'Julian shot two tigers in the fort'. We used to hunt for cannon balls and play in the old British cemetery. Here the map says 'Tiger killed cow here' and, what's this? [Childish handwriting] 'Here we saw a monkey murdered by dogs.' Here's Sunrise Cottage and Mont Capri, where we lived when Daddy was Commissioner – it's still there – and here's Elephant House, where the elephants played. And here are the rules of our Jackal Gang: 'Before anybody can enter the gang they have to go through trials of valour e.g. jumping, climbing, strength, daring and bravery. If there are quar-

rels between gang members they must come to Judy for justice. Tell tale tits to grown ups is forbidden.' Childish stuff, of course.

Boarding school back Home in England (with a capital H of course) was bound to be an anticlimax: 'Ugh! How I hated it. Suddenly I was being ticked off for not cleaning the bath, something I had never done in my whole life.' Finishing school in Switzerland was more to her taste, and then she returned to India aged eighteen, sporty and pretty. In 1948 she went with Lord Mountbatten's party to Gandhi's cremation 'but it was too frightening for words, such a huge crowd surrounding the body we had to leave'. Soon she was in Calcutta, where her father, now an Advisor to the second British High Commissioner, General Nye, was on a mission to decide who should obtain British passports. It was here that she met Bob Wright.

Robert Hamilton Wright was born in 1924 in Calcutta, where his father was Commissioner of Police. At the age of five he, too, returned Home for his education and eventually became Head of School at Cheltenham, the public school that turned out more senior Indian Civil Servants than any other. His 'cum summa laude' education continued with a rugby blue and Presidency of the Hawk's Club at Cambridge University, as well as a degree in Engineering; then it was war service 'in tanks', as he put it, and a bad injury on D-Day. After a spell with the Sudan Rifles, he returned to Calcutta in August 1947, looking like a raffish David Niven in his self-appointed role as eligible bachelor. His diary relates:

Arrived in Bombay on the good ship *Strathmore*, then trouping, and was still quite uncomfortable, but I made friends with Lord Kenneth Inchcape, who was consorting with a very attractive young wife. By the Bombay–Nagpore mail across to Calcutta (then in the middle of riots), met at Howrah station and installed in the Andrew Yule chummery [bachelor digs] with four other young bachelors. Two of them insisted on having B-class parties with the local ladies, when the other three of us were told to make ourselves scarce.

The riots Bob Wright dismisses within parentheses may have seemed marginal to a newcomer sheltering in the oases of the Tollygunge or Ballygunge, where the affluent British played and lived, but from 1943 onwards for three decades Calcutta was afflicted with death in the streets, destruction and despair on an extreme scale. This was additional to the everyday awfulness of the city that caused Kipling to describe it as 'the city of dreadful night', where 'above the packed and pestilential town / death looked down'.

In 1943 the rice crop failed, and the capture of Burma by the Japanese followed by British procrastination meant that it was not replaced. For several months over that summer 11,000 people died of starvation every week in Calcutta. The *Manchester Guardian* described everyday scenes: 'Thousands of emaciated destitutes roamed the streets in a ceaseless quest for food, scouring dustbins and devouring rotten remains of castaway fruit and food. Rickety children clutching imploringly the tattered garments barely covering the bones of their mothers are seen in all quarters of the city.'

Three years later, starting in August 1946, mobs of Muslims and Hindus set upon each other in an orgy of pre-Partition madness. Once again the streets were littered with corpses bloating and rotting in the heat. Because of the scruples of the Indian caste system it was often the British who carted the corpses away, issued with waterproof anti-gas clothing and 'stench masks'. The fear and evil of the Goddess Kali, after whom some say Calcutta was named, hung over the city. A year later came Partition. The scene in Calcutta was dramatic, as the late *boxwallah* Owain Jenkins described it:

It was August 15 1947. The Punjab was a scene of dreadful slaughter. For months Calcutta had been on the boil with every chance of a return to the large-scale communal massacres of the previous year. Mahatma Gandhi had installed himself in the middle of north Calcutta calling for peace and 'fasting unto death' on an open stage exposed to the public view. At any moment he could have been torn to pieces. Then the mood changed and suddenly the town was full of open lorries packed with Hindus and Muslims embracing one another and chanting *ek ho!* – 'be one!' By the afternoon the mobs

were confident enough to run happily hand in hand into the grounds
of Government House, thronging the marble halls and removing
everything that could be carried away. The Governor, Sir Frederick
Burrows, left for England and retirement by a side door.[3]

It was too good to last. When Bob Wright arrived a few days later,
the destructive tide of partition, a man-made *tsunami*, washed up
on the streets of Calcutta. East Bengal became East Pakistan, and
4 million Hindus fled into India over the border only 65 kilometres away. They squatted in the streets of Calcutta, so that the city
took on the appearance of an enormous relief centre, crowded with
homeless, hungry and desperate newcomers. From this time date the
encampments on Howrah station, so that some families of squat-
ters must now be in their third generation. The influx of Hindus
inflamed sectarian tensions. The British naturally enough assumed
they were immune to them, but in 1951 the Managing Director of
Andrew Yule, Sir Leslie Cameron, was killed by a mob of Hindus
while trying to protect a Muslim who was sharing his car at the time.
This must have shocked the Wrights if nothing else did.

Bob Wright was also caught up in the industrial violence that
now broke out and continued for several years. The managing
agencies were targeted, and the commercial centre of Clive Street,
renamed Netaji Subhas Chandra Bose Road in honour of the 'freedom fighter' and founder of the Indian National Army (see Chapter
Two), was at the centre of it. Owain Jenkins remembered that on
one occasion the street was 'packed wall to wall with a sea of shouting clerks' and in his own Works Office 'typewriters and calculators
were hammered flat, chairs, tables, drawing boards and instruments
broken to small pieces'. In part this was revenge, the looters getting
their own back for being looted all the years of the Raj, but it was
also heavily political. The communist trade unions and the Congress
trade unions (socialist in outlook) were competing for power, and
when the Congress Party in Delhi brought in a tranche of pro-
labour legislation – at any cost to productivity – the labour unrest
quietened down, until the late 1960s. Then it was the turn of the
Naxalites, a communist splinter group believing in violent revolution

(see Chapter Two), and this time the Wrights were affected in a very personal way. In 1971 a terrorist shot dead the chief accountant of Tollygunge Club in his office. That was when Bob took over.

At Andrew Yule's, Bob Wright's first task was to learn Hindi, for which he was provided with a *munshi babu* (language teacher) to give him six classes a week. He learnt more than one lesson:

> I had no chance of passing the exam. The *munshi* appreciated this and said he had a son, a very good boy, B.Com (failed), who was desperate for a job. It so happened that I was, even then, responsible for engaging clerks. I got him the job. The results of the exam came out and to the astonishment of all my colleagues I was placed as number one – my first and early experience of corruption in Calcutta!

Yule's was the biggest managing agency in Calcutta, employing sixty or so British 'covenanted' (contracted) assistants in its main office. When Bob Wright joined, it managed ten jute mills, a paper mill, forty tea gardens, two power stations and the largest group of coalmines in India. These were all British owned and known as 'sterling companies'. It was also one of the most prestigious agencies, being classed as 'old Scots' together with McCleod & Co., Jardine Henderson and McNeil & Barry. Apparently in the old days they rarely employed Englishmen never mind Indians. The top managing agencies controlled the business life of Calcutta. The Managing Director of Andrew Yule, for example, was President of the Chamber of Commerce every third year, for which he obtained a knighthood.

The managing agencies dated from the 1880s and their function was straightforward. The *boxwallahs* who founded the mills and the tea gardens rarely wanted to stay in India, so they returned Home, set up a head office in London and employed an agent to manage their company for them in India. Particularly if the mills and tea gardens were remote in location and small in size, it made sense to share with other similar companies the infrastructure of accountants, solicitors and secretaries and base the paperwork in Calcutta, where, in any event, the commodity was bound. Hence the agencies became commercial umbrellas with agreements to manage companies they might

not necessarily own or even control. The next stage was for the
agency to float the company and take 20 per cent or so of the equity,
while the original owner back Home sold his shares and retired with
a profit. In the first years after Independence foreign-exchange controls did not exist so after floatation masses of money was taken out
by partners and remitted Home. Anthony Hayward's agency, Shaw
Wallace, became a public company in 1947 and 40 per cent of the
equity was held at its London headquarters. Called R.G. Shaw &
Co. Ltd, it was based in Leadenhall Street, for years the home of the
East India Company. Anthony Hayward said: 'It was traditionally run
by retired partners from Calcutta; financially a good deal and they
did little work.' The trouble was that many of the companies back
in Calcutta were consequently starved of capital. It was not unusual
for the agencies to have less than a 10 per cent holding in companies
they managed. The writing was on the wall, but few in the 1950s
worried about it.

Bob Wright worked his way round Andrew Yule, 'moving through
the various departments of finance, tea and a paper mill. The work
was not hard in those days and we were encouraged to play as much
sport as possible. We had at least one afternoon off for golf.' Bob
did not need encouragement to play sport. He captained the Boffins
Rugby Club, which played all over India, and in due course he
became President of the Calcutta Polo Club and a Steward of the
Turf Club. *Burra sahib* indeed! Managing a paper mill gave him the
opportunity to visit the jungles of Bihar and Orissa to secure long-
term bamboo leases, for the supply of bamboo from East Bengal
had ceased with Partition. And this gave him the excuse for a *shikar*.
The best time was the *Durga puja* in October, a five-day festival in
Bengal in honour of the goddess Durga followed by a public holiday.
Colonel Wakefield was employed as *shikari* (huntsman, see Chapter
Four), a block of forest was reserved in Palamau (Bihar) and the
Haywards came along for a 'fairly drunken week of fun'. Anthony
Hayward commemorated the event with 'Jungle Jaunts and Jollities':

While other people stay at home
And booze away the *pujas* (prayers),

Our friends the Wrights make copious plans
To drive away in huge cars
And slaughter beasts in jungles deep
With hearty Hallelujahs!

It must have seemed a marriage made in heaven when Bob and Anne fell in love, but, according to Anne, her family did not approve: 'Bob was a *boxwallah* you see and we were used to mixing in different social circles. Calcutta with the *boxwallahs* was not really the place to be.' It was one of the greatest ironies of the Raj that its most prosperous city, based on commerce, looked down on businessmen. Although Andrew Yule was considered one of the poshest of managing agencies, joined by ex-public school boys from the poshest of schools as a substitute for the ICS, it was still 'commerce' and dangerously close to 'trade'. After all, the term *boxwallah* comes from traders who in the early days carried their merchandise from bungalow to bungalow in boxes. Consequently, only the partners in a managing agency were eligible for membership of the very snooty Bengal Club.

The British in India had their own caste system. Such was the rigid social hierarchy that up until the 1920s a hostess needed to research a government publication *The Warrant of Precedence* before planning the seating at a dinner party. Among civilians, businessmen ranked way down the table below government officers. 'Mind you,' said Anne, 'the ICS had its hierarchy too, and down at the bottom were the PWD chaps, men employed by the Public Works Department.' Within commerce the commodity mattered. Working in tea was far superior to working in jute, because the former was popular among gentlemen amateurs and the latter required skilled technicians. As for trade, Sir Owain Jenkins, the author of the autobiography *Merchant Prince* (1987), pointed out the silliness of snobbery when he wrote that it was socially permissible to sit at a desk and sell nails by the barrel but not to stand at a counter and sell them by the pound; such was the prejudice against retailers. 'Shopkeepers!' said Anne. But Bob worked his charm, and the couple married on Anne's twenty-first birthday in June 1950.

For over twenty years the Wrights lived at 14 Ballygunge Road, that affluent and well-ordered British suburb 'south of Park Street', as the area was called. Here lived the *burra sahibs* in Regency-style houses complete, in the Wrights' case, with *porte cochère*, marble entrance hall and grand staircase. The gardens were more like small parks, too, with species of deer and crane in abundance next to the lawns and flowerbeds carefully tended by the *malis* (gardeners). Society consisted, said Owain Jenkins, 'of a body of similar people divided vertically according to its spare-time interests – racing people, riding people, cricket, tennis and bridge addicts'. Anne said: 'We were all mad keen gardeners and it was frightening the amount of time you spent feeding people at incredible dinner parties – continental food, of course.'

This society must have been too tame for Anne for she added her own animal *menagerie*:

> The first pet we had was a lion, but he never did anything naughty. Then we had a tiger that was a bit naughty. It escaped once and went to sleep in one of the guest's beds. We used to take it to dinner parties, and one time it ate a maharaja's chair from the bottom up. Then we had a leopard that was always naughty. Of course we gave them to zoos when they were no longer cubs. We released the leopard into the wild. One of our main pets, though, was a mongoose that we had for eighteen years and the children absolutely adored it. We called it Pepe and it went with Rupert [her son] to England when he started school. There was no quarantine in those days. When it escaped we pretended it was a cat. You see I had spent my life with wild animals when I was a girl.

When Anne showed me her photo album it opened at an *Alice in Wonderland*-like page. There was a horse standing at the table during a dinner party:

> Yes, that's right, that's Ballygunge. It was a very sweet polo pony called Figura. She's just standing there. It was a kind of party thing to do. [Anne turned the page.] And this is polo in Calcutta. I used to play for

the Police Team, on equal terms with the men of course. [Turns page.]
And here's the leopard hanging onto some washing at Ballygunge. It
absolutely loved the cat, who thought she was its mummy, however
big the leopard grew.

British expat society was youthful and war free. Independence
appeared to make little difference, and money was there for the
taking. 'We had a fabulous time,' said Anne: 'You used to go into a
room and all the men were six foot tall and Old Etonians.' There
were formal dances like the Go Lightly, which was organised by
The Unceremonials, a *burra sahib* club started in the 1890s as an
antidote to stuffy Government House parties. The club was limited
to twenty-one members, and, said Anthony Hayward, 'nobody paid
anything until the end of the year, when the total cost was divided
between the members whether you had used the club or not.
All the members were partners in their firms and money did not
matter.' In due course Bob Wright became a member. At the other
end was the 'Vingt et Un', an annual dance organised by twelve
bachelors as a payback to the *burra sahibs* for all the hospitality they
had received. 'It was a real slap-up show,' remembered Anne, 'Italian
chefs, champagne, cabaret, very good bands. You danced all night.'
She paused as if listening to other imperial echoes: of the thud and
thwack of polo matches, of the rifle crack when tiger shooting,
of the splash of young men falling into swimming pools wearing
evening dress.

I asked Anthony Hayward if Indians entered this social world:

Sir Anthony: Maharajas certainly came into it. Really it was just Indian
           royalty.
Me: Looking back now, how do you react to that?
Sir Anthony: The managing agency houses only employed their first
           Indians in the mid-1950s, so you did not actually have
           an opportunity to meet Indians of good family until
           then. Looking back it was very odd, very odd. Before
           Independence one wondered what would happen –
           whether the Indians would turf everybody out, whether

> there would be a blood bath. In fact everybody heaved
> an almighty sigh of relief when everything went on just
> as before apart from changing a few names.

If Indianisation had begun, few seemed aware of it then. Anthony Hayward says that it was at best a half-hearted acceptance: 'There was certainly a bar. When Indians first became "covenanted non-overseas assistants", they were expected not only to come from good families but to have gone to university in England.' A university education was certainly not required for their British colleagues. An Indian view comes from a Bengali accountant, R.N. Sen, who worked for Price Waterhouse. 'In the British companies the ranking used to be as follows: British, other white people, Anglo-Indians and, lastly, Indians.'[4] Apparently up until the early 1940s apartheid existed in Clive Street with separate toilet and eating facilities. However, wrote Sen: 'The British had one great quality. They knew they were ignorant and therefore would allow themselves to be led by a few capable people.' Presumably that is why he was invited to be a partner in the accountants Price Waterhouse in 1952. The invitation came at a lunch in the Bengal Club, where 'we ate separately in an ante-room'.

As may be imagined, in a society far from Home that preferred the company of its own kind, there were many British clubs in Calcutta. The snootiest residential club then and now was the Bengal Club founded in 1827. During the Raj years it did not serve Indian food, nor were Indians mentioned in the club rules. Anthony Hayward attended the heated debate in 1959 when members narrowly voted Indians to join. His own argument in favour was simple: 'If you are called the Bengal Club, you can hardly prevent Bengalis from joining.' Yet such was the hostility that several *burra sahibs* resigned, and Indians did not want to join for several years. One of the first was R.N. Sen, who was proposed in 1963 and felt uncomfortable at its continuing snobbery: 'The British Empire had to be liquidated through a long-drawn-out process. I hope our snobbery also will pass away in due course.' He was over optimistic. Very recently a friend of mine was signed in at the Bengal Club and was asked where he was from. 'Delhi,' he replied, so the receptionist wrote in the ledger under

'Town of Residence' *mofussil*, a British Indian term meaning 'the back of beyond' or 'out in the sticks': such is the Bengal Club's snobbery about the town that replaced Calcutta as the nation's capital.

Most of Calcutta's clubs ignored the existence of women as well as Indians. At the Tolly country club, which then, as now, had at least a five-year waiting list to join, a wife was afforded the official status of 'Permanent Guest'. This was obviously a time when matrimony was a more durable institution than today. Bob Wright told me that in those days Indians were allowed to join but not to vote – 'but who wants to vote?' he asked disarmingly. He added that Americans were not welcome either and certainly not the Japanese.

The club always associated with these halcyon times was the 300 Club, described by Owain Jenkins as 'an oasis of civilisation in a world of damp clothes, leaking thatch, Mepacrine [for the treatment of dysentery] and mosquitoes'; he might have added 'in a world of stuffiness and snobbery too'. It was formed in 1937 by a charming, irreverent but determined young businessman named Allan Lockhart. He was indignant at the selection procedure of the Saturday Club, then the centre for regular sports and dancing among the British community. It did admit women, but that was as far as it went as a gesture towards the modern age. An officious committee grilled all aspiring members and rejected those of inadequate social standing, members of the retail trade, citizens of countries that had opposed Britain in the First World War and, it went without saying, Indians or those of mixed descent. The story went that Allan Lockhart invited to the club without permission a chorus line of young English girls who were part of a touring company. The girls monopolised the men, whether married or bachelor, old or young. Lockhart was summoned before the selection committee, where a senior lady accused him of bringing in actresses, probably 'tarts'. Owain Jenkins takes up the story:

> Not so, said Lockhart. These were young ladies of impeccable, not to say impregnable, virtue who had shown themselves proof against all his arts. 'Which', he added, 'is more than I can say for many members of this club.' Whether he really added 'present company not excepted',

legend does not say. There was in any case a shocked silence, during
which Lockhart raked his interrogators with cold grey eyes. He then
rose and, with a smile of infinite charm, withdrew. It was typical of the
committee that it should have reported Lockhart's behaviour to his
employers, demanding disciplinary action.

So Lockhart founded a new club, limited to 300 members, that was
open to anybody who shared his tastes and could afford it; Indians
were particularly welcome. He bought an ostentatious house on
three floors called Phillips Folly. Here he was joined by an ex-cadet
of the Imperial Russian Navy, Boris Lissanevich and his sexy wife
Kyra, who became the resident cabaret dancers. They brought
with them from central Europe a pianist, a steward and a chef who
introduced Bœuf Stroganoff and Chicken Kiev. There was a regular
three-piece band of piano, violin or sax and drums that were bashed
with much noise by 'Fuzz', the Filipino drummer who slept under
the stairs. Small tables with shaded lights in alcoves and ante-rooms
and a dark red décor emanated an intimate, louche, ambience. In
winter guests danced on a marble floor; in summer on a teakwood
floor placed in the garden under a Gulmohr tree and a canopy of
flowers. The opening night was a riot. Soon it became the place to
be seen, particularly late at night after renegades from the Saturday
Club crept in, intent, as all members were, on the simple pursuit of
pleasure. It was open twenty-four hours a day and managed the bar
bills by the simple expedient of varying their colour depending on
the hour of the night; a whisky at dawn cost several times more than
a whisky at sundown.

In the 1950s Colonel John Wakefield (see Chapter Four) was a
regular member of the 300 Club. Today he has several stories to tell:

I knew a Dr Mukerjee, and one night in February 1951 he was
joined at the bar by a Nepalese general. The general was in civilian
clothes and so were the three Nepalese with him. The general was
in a hell of a hurry because he'd just seen his girlfriend dancing with
somebody else. So he said to Mukerjee: 'Doc, meet my friend the
King. King – Doc.' And then he walked away. Mukerjee tried to be

polite. He said: 'We haven't been introduced properly. Is your name King?' The Nepali shook his head, so Mukerjee said without thinking: 'In that case I'm not Doc, I'm Jesus Christ, how do you do?' The two little Nepali chaps nearly fainted with shock. 'King' explained: 'I am King Tribhuvan of Nepal, but I'm incognito tonight as I should be in Delhi.' He was due there to plan the overthrow of the Rani regime. [The exiled King Tribhuvan of Nepal was plotting with the Indian government to return to Kathmandu and overthrow the reactionary Rana family that had supplanted him with his grandson Gyanendra, a puppet ruler. The putsch was successful.] And that's how Boris got the Yak and Yeti hotel in Kathmandu. It was the first foreign hotel in Nepal.

That this last dance of the Raj, taking to the floor well after the 'stroke of the midnight hour', could exist side by side with a city overwhelmed by poverty and destitution and a municipality increasingly revolutionary in politics is further proof that, in Simon Winchester's words, 'Calcutta is a city in a state of permanent surprise, where amazement is around every crumbling corner'.

For the British in Calcutta the 1950s must have seemed one long, unexpected, Indian summer. The reality was that they had stayed on in a third world country with socialist politics and an increasingly independent mindset. The special relationship with the Raj was getting to be a thing of the past. The 1960s were a rude awakening.

First came the end of so-called post-war credits. During the Second World War the Indian government had built up a substantial sterling balance in London for the services it had provided for the allied armies, and after Independence the new Indian government claimed this back in generous convertibility terms for British manufactured goods. During the first two Five-Year Plans, 1951–61, British exports to India achieved record levels, and Britain was still regarded as the principal supplier of industrial goods. To the British in India this must have been an unexpected windfall. Cars, white goods, beer, everything British crossed the world as, in effect, aid to India. Then all this ended; the sterling balances were run right down. Whereas in 1960 the British share of total Indian imports was 18 per cent, by 1970 it was down to 6 per cent. With the end of post-war credits came also the end of large-scale remittances of capital back to London.

The second shock was devaluation on 6 June 1966, when the value of the rupee against the pound fell by over one-third. It was so dramatic that Anthony Hayward refers to the date in apocalyptic terms as '6/6/66'. Thirdly, increasing throughout the decade came heavy taxation. Salaries of highly paid foreigners had to be approved by the Indian government, and, as a British survey reported in 1967: 'It is virtually impossible to obtain Government approval for a salary worth more than £2,750 per annum after tax'.[5] (That sounds minuscule in today's terms, but it is still huge compared to the average Indian income at that time of less than £25 per year.) Anthony Hayward went further: 'The government introduced a dividend tax, then an expenditure tax and a wealth tax, so that meant that when these taxes were added to a very high income tax of 50 per cent it was certainly possible for total tax to be over 100 per cent.'

Finally, creepingly, came the nationalisation of industry. It followed a Soviet socialist model, and this meant a jungle of laws, regulations and controls that made a happy hunting ground for corrupt politicians and bureaucrats. One Indian industrialist said there were thirteen industrial inspectors who could close his factory down and none of them was interested in what he was supposed to inspect but only in the payoff he was due to receive. This was the Licence Raj (see Chapter Six). Anthony Hayward remembers it with distaste:

> In Shaw Wallace we had to employ a senior man in Delhi whose sole function was to open doors, smooth the path, to government departments. You had to play the system. In order to get a file to move from desk to desk, the peon who did the actual moving had to be paid a back-hander. It was entirely frustrating. When I was Chairman, I spent half my time talking to trade unions and the other half talking to the government about licences and things.

A symbol of this era still evident on Indian roads is the Hindustani Ambassador car, which is, in effect, the 1957 Morris Oxford put together in Calcutta. Looking not unlike a bowler hat on wheels, it has a sturdy frame and high road clearance that make it a suitable vehicle for India, and it is spacious enough to cram in six or so passengers. Nevertheless, its precious licence for production in India allowed it to reign supreme over Indian roads long after it should have been overtaken by later models. For years it was a symbol of India's industrial inefficiency, but now it has become a collector's item.

Devaluation, heavy taxation, the end of post-war credit and creeping socialism, all these new economic realities discouraged the *burra sahibs* and the *chhota sahibs* (smaller masters) from staying on. In 1968 only 2,000 British citizens were left on the books of the High Commission in Calcutta, and by 1970 this number had shrunk to 1,350. 'The British are thus reduced', wrote Geoffrey Moorhouse, 'to roughly the same number of people as were in Calcutta a few years before the Black Hole happened.'[6] Bob Wright wrote: 'At this stage I was very keen to retire to Britain and buy a small house and start a new career.' His time at Andrew Yule, where he now managed the largest group of coalmines in India and served as Chairman of the Indian Mining Association (later he called himself 'Old King Coal'), was coming to an end.

It was commonly accepted that the managing agencies were nearing the end of their days and this fatalism accelerated their decline. An attitude prevailed: let's get as much out as we can and then go Home. Indians like R.N. Sen thought the British were a lazy bunch: 'The *burra sahibs* did not realise that the days of *chhota hazri* [small breakfast], *burra hazri* [big breakfast], lunch and then the Club had now gone.' Bob Wright admitted: 'The writing had been on the wall for some time. There were rackets going on, such as the agencies charging a 10 per cent fee but then paying themselves commissions whether they made a profit or not, plus huge dividends.' And Anthony Hayward added: 'There is no doubt that by the 1960s the agencies had outlived their usefulness. The managed companies were starved of capital because the agencies were unwilling to put in their own funds or go to the Stock Market and dilute their shareholding.' This made the companies vulnerable to takeover and many were sold willingly or unwillingly to the Marwari business clan led in Calcutta by the Birla family. (The Marwaris were from Rajasthan and had originally made their money by acting as agents for the East India Company trading in India. Now the boot was on the other foot. The Marwaris had diversified into property, taken over rich areas of Calcutta and become unpopular among the Bengalis.) Further, the agencies had not moved with the times. New industries of electronics, chemicals and hi-tech had replaced the old primary industries of the nineteenth century, and they needed large inputs of capital and new patterns of management.

All these deficiencies played into the hands of the Indian government. They saw the managing agencies as undesirable and inefficient British bastions. In 1969 the Indian Companies (Amendment) Act abolished the system of managing companies by agencies, thus bringing to an end the main and most typical form of British economic involvement with India during the Raj (for more on this see Chapter Two). At the end the great Andrew Yule and Co. still managed nine companies, and a sign of its importance was that the Indian government bought it out. The next year coal was nationalised. Bob Wright was out of a job.

One important *boxwallah* stayed on. Shaw Wallace and Co. Ltd became an Indian company, but Anthony Hayward remained as the British Chairman. Perhaps he wished he had not, because the 1970s were a miserable time of industrial action in Calcutta, when far more days of work were lost through strikes and lockouts than elsewhere in India. The government in Delhi had given in over welfare legislation irrespective of productivity, and now the Marxist government of West Bengal gave in further, so that wages were too high and per capita production too low. The result was inflation and unemployment. R.N. Sen wrote at the time: 'Management is always concerned with labour problems and left with no time to work for the future of the company. Managers are exposed to personal insults and occasional violence so that the percentage of heart and blood pressure patients is high among this class.' The *gherao* or intimidating 'surround' of the manager's office became a Calcutta speciality (see Chapter Three). Sen added, surprisingly, that the departure of the British had left a void of management skills that Indians found hard to fill. Anthony Hayward experienced his share of endless negotiation and disruption, so that the encomium written for him when he left in 1978 to move on to Singapore has an ironic ring:

> Sir – Affectionate and forbearing, you were the father of our corporate family. Dignity came naturally to you and we were allowed a mind of our own and to speak it out. You nobly put behind you the moments of ruction we would sometimes in the process have. Never for you to abdicate decency or take leave of fair play or let spite encrust the soul.

In 1977 Anthony Hayward became President of the Bengali Chamber of Commerce and therefore of the Associated Chambers of India (ASSOCHAM), a precedent begun in the days of the Raj, when Calcutta was the headquarters of British business in India. In those days the organisation was described as an 'extension of government' and until 1940 the Viceroy himself would deliver the annual Finance Statement in the Chamber every January; rather like the Queen's Address to Parliament. In the 1950s, when Owain Jenkins was on the committee, the President was elected from the 270 managing directors of mostly British firms in Calcutta and on its premises were housed the offices of no fewer than twenty-seven Industrial Associations of which the most important were Tea, Coal, Jute and Engineering. The President would receive a knighthood after his year in office. With the end of the managing agencies and the decline of the primary industries like jute and coal, so the Chamber declined in importance. In Sir Anthony's day, however, it was still an important forum of chief executives, nearly all of them Indian. By this time the Marwari clan had set up a rival Federation of Indian Chambers of Commerce and Industry (FICCI). Sir Anthony was, as he put it with Kipling in mind, 'the last of the dreadful knights'.

Geoffrey Moorhouse watched what his fellow writer James Morris called 'the final rejection of the *boxwallahs*'. He wrote about it in *Calcutta*, reviewed by no less than Paul Scott as 'the best book on modern India I have read'. He had no time for the *burra sahibs* of the managing agencies, considering that they showed a 'blank incomprehension or indifference' to Indian life. This could not be levelled at Bob Wright or Anthony Hayward, but the stereotype is familiar:

> They joined their old established family firm after Oxbridge and National Service at the end of the War. Their homes are still palatial in scale and comfort, the residue of a century's healthy profits. Both husband and wife are in their early forties, they ride for exercise and are particularly keen on shikar. Their children are at school in England but come over to Calcutta for the holidays. The boys are called 'darling' by their father and mix gin and tonic for the grown ups. They see quite a bit of their parents for Mummy and Daddy always manage to spend a couple of months every year at Home.
>
> But now they have suffered the end of empire and their own supremacy in the city. They have endured the devaluation of their money and although they are still fabulously rich in the context of Calcutta it is not enough for them. In this city they have to stand by and watch not only the power vanish, but the old symbols of that power wither and shrink.

Moorhouse is referring to one particularly humiliating event, a shabby symbol of the British withdrawal:

> So many of these latter-day Moguls had taken themselves and their small fortunes back to Britain by the end of the 1960s that the Bengal Club sold off its impressive exterior and library. There never was a gloomier moment in Calcutta's long, long history of the Raj and its reach-me-downs. On the terrace, with its commanding view across the Maidan, there were thirteen bathtubs drawn up in line ahead, and they were all very grubby. Beside them were thirteen lavatory bowls and heaven knows what degraded future lay ahead of them. The corridors were piled with wicker rocking chairs, mahogany tables and springy bedsteads. When they actually auctioned this decrepit residue, practically everything in sight was knocked down to once subservient Indians. Who never, in Calcutta's history, would have been allowed past those wrought-iron gates for any other reason at all.[7]

Here the story of the Wrights might have ended; another middle-aged couple of *burra sahibs* retired with their wealth to Hampshire for hunting and a part-time job in the City. In fact the era of Raja Wright of Tollygunge was about to begin. Tolly had been founded in 1895 by Sir William Cruickshank as a club devoted to golf and equestrian sports. Mark Tully remembers being taken there by his nanny before the war to play on the swings and watch boys on the golf course waving flags on bamboo poles to stop the kites swooping down for balls or sandwiches. It was, however, in a bad way. Anne described it to me in typical terms when we were looking through her photo album:

> And here's the Tollygunge when Bob took it over in 1971. It was an
> absolute shambles. There was no money in the bank [in fact there was
> not much, 200,000 rupees] and the staff was all on strike. The chap
> who ran it before Bob – [turns another page] here's the Maharaja of
> Jaipur, we knew him very well – the chap before Bob, Colonel Lal,
> was shot dead by his caddy. He was a bandit.

Calcutta was beset by industrial unrest approaching anarchy. For whatever reason – a volatile and left-wing intelligentsia, powerful trade unions and awful poverty – West Bengal has a revolutionary tradition. It was shortly to elect its first and enduring Marxist city government (from 1977). Although the Marxists are interested more in bureaucracy than in direct action, they spawned a splinter group, the Naxalites (see Chapter Two), who were and still are violent revolutionaries. They terrorised Calcutta until the Indian Army at Mrs Gandhi's orders put them down forcibly. It was a Naxalite who shot Colonel Lal, in his office.

Bob was then on the committee of Tolly, and he accepted the challenge to become 'managing member'. The following year the Wrights moved into the second floor of the Club House, with its drawing room the length of three tennis courts, and Bob imposed the smack of firm order. Despite bombs on the veranda, threats on the phone and arson in the stables, 'I soon got rid of the bad hats and the good men rallied'. The opportunity came when one of the club ground staff, a Naxalite, assaulted an elderly official in broad daylight. Bob dismissed him peremptorily and then reported the action personally to Jyoti Basu, the Communist Deputy Minister of West Bengal. 'He confirmed,' said Bob, 'that he did not approve of premeditated daily assault.' Thus Raja Wright earned the deserved reputation of taking the law into his own hands and arguing the case later, in person at the highest level; effective in India if you can do it. He went on: 'We got the club fully working and very shortly on a profitable basis by securing additional members. These were mostly our suitable Indian friends on an absolutely equal basis.' 'Suitable' to Bob, that meant, of course. He always had the last word on who joined Tolly, which made him unpopular sometimes but led to his powerful reputation at the Oriental Club in London; a word from Bob and a visitor from India would be given temporary membership.

Over the next twenty years Bob defended Tolly against politicians and land speculators. He modernised it too, so that it is now one of the elite country and sporting clubs of India. In 1973 he prevented the West Bengal government from taking over the southern area of the 100 acres of parkland to build a football stadium by obtaining a photo of its Wembley equivalent and proving that the area demanded was unsuitable. He lost 25 acres to Metro Rail, but used the Land Acquisition money to construct new housing for club staff, new sports facilities like billiard and bridge rooms, squash courts and an outdoor swimming pool. In 1982 he closed down the racing track and converted the stand into air-conditioned bedrooms. By the time of the 1995 Centenary of Tolly Club the membership included Bengali Marxist politicians, Marwari business families, Sikh Indian Army top brass and anybody whom Bob did not disapprove of. Raja Wright of Tollygunge ruled.

Anne Wright played little part in this. When I asked her, tactlessly, how she felt 'living above the shop' (on the second floor of the Club house), she put me down in a cool *burra memsahib* way: 'No, I didn't do that. I had little to do with running the Tollygunge. A few social duties, I suppose.' She and her daughter Belinda had found a new vocation in wildlife preservation. In fact, wrote Bob, it was their newfound dedication to wildlife that 'forestalled' the Wright move

back Home in 1971. Just as well, he added, because 'neither was able
to boil an egg or make a cup of tea because all the cooking and
catering was done by our servants'.

The visitor to Tolly in the Wrights' day, as now, would turn off a
teeming, dirty street into a high-walled world of order and good
manners. Groomed lawns opened up the vista of the eighteenth-
century Club House. Green fairways separated woodland where the
flowering trees heralded the spring with brilliant colours of reds, yel-
lows and mauves. In the early morning blue jays and golden orioles
circled overhead and in the evening jackals howled, hanging around
the bushes waiting to be fed by one of Bob's 'chaps': 'We've got to do
all we can for the creatures,' he joked. Imperial echoes were a meta-
phor, but one sound was almost authentic North-West Frontier. This
was the fierce yell of Naib Khaju Khan (grandson of Austen Layard's
bearer) and the thumping hooves of Starlight, his chestnut stallion, as
they gave a demonstration of tent-pegging – now a sport but originally the skill of unhooking tent pegs with a lance at full gallop to
bring down the tent on top of those inside. The familiar sounds were
those of a country club – the pat of ball on tennis racket, the ping of
a golf driver on the tee and the clatter as a jump came down in the
gymkhana.

For years the Wrights were the people to know in Calcutta. They
were authentic stayers-on, living heritage monuments as valid as the
bricks and mortar of the Raj. They were flamboyant colonial figures
who had stayed to tough it out in modern India. Everyone beat a
path to their door, from Mother Teresa, for whose orphaned children
Bob organised a 'Tolly jolly' every year, to visiting journalists and
British tourists in search of Raj nostalgia. Mark Tully said he felt
sorry for the Wrights, because they were objects of curiosity and the
butt of snide comparisons between the lingering anachronism of the
Raj and the poverty of modern Calcutta. Bob was most probably too
grand to mind. In fact he loved acting the part of raffish Raja, particularly after his daily six pink gins, with stories of tent pegs, chhota
pegs, maharajas and tiger cubs at parties. 'Cad!' he declared: 'If I wrote
my biography I'd call it *The Cad of Calcutta*.' He was a part-time
film actor whose battered David Niven looks may be seen in several

Indian films like *Mrigaya*, for which he won a national award, and a British film *Bengal Nights*, in which he starred with John Hurt and Hugh Grant. 'John and I used to sit and drink while Hugh cavorted,' he said.

Visitors who left Tolly with photos of Bob and Anne Wright drinking pink gins in the *shamiana* would be mistaken if they dismissed them as caricatures of the Raj. They were, in the hinterland of their lives, distinguished and determined public servants who were awarded the OBE and MBE respectively.

Anne had been alerted to the plight of the tiger during the mid-1960s, when she witnessed a severe drought in Bihar. Wildlife would collect round the diminishing watering holes, making it easy for poachers to pick off the tigers. Anne, nothing if not determined, brought tankers to the edge of the forests and filled lorry tyres, split in half, with water. She had them carried by jeep into the forests. Soon after she campaigned for tiger sanctuaries, formed a close relationship in the cause with Mrs Gandhi and was in at the beginning of Project Tiger in 1973 (see Chapter Four). In fact she helped to identify the nine sanctuaries that were chosen. One of her photographs shows her father, Austen Layard, at a tiger shoot he organised for the Viceroy Lord Reading in 1924, but times had changed. 'I suppose I just got disgusted with the slaughter,' she said. She became a high-profile campaigner, a founder trustee of the World Wide Fund for Nature and for twenty years a member of the Indian Board for Wildlife. Then she set up the Rhino Foundation in Assam. 'Somewhere towards the end of the 1980s things began to slide,' she wrote in 1992, referring to government supervision, 'and a new generation of greedy people have edged their way into poaching. Things have reached a new high in their operations.' This was when her daughter Belinda took over. Formerly a distinguished wildlife photographer and filmmaker, she now became an investigative reporter, 'going underground' at great risk to herself to expose the illegal trade in poaching for the Chinese market, where tiger skins and body parts fetch high prices for their supposed medicinal properties.

Anne and Bob set up their own wildlife resort on the edge of Kanha National Park in the very centre of India. They called it

After the Raj

Kipling Camp, and here may be spotted the characters of *The Jungle Book*: Rikki Tikki Tavi the mongoose, Baloo the friendly bear and the majestic tiger Shere Khan. Whether Rudyard Kipling ever visited Kanha is unclear, though Bob did tell me that Kipling had an affair with the British forester's wife and would stay with her when her husband was away. No doubt that was one of his tall stories. One of the present, genuine, animal characters is Tara the elephant. The writer Mark Shand donated her to the Wrights after his *Travels on my Elephant*, and she 'has been living the life of a maharani for the past fifteen years, spoilt rotten'. These are the words of a young travel writer, Lucy Cleland, who visited Kipling Camp three years ago. I asked her to describe safari, Wright style:

> When I was there, it was presided over by two girls in their mid-twenties, one of them belonging to a famous aristocratic English family. They were, in turn, aided by a couple of GAP year students (again, the well-bred type), wanting their year away before university to get a 'real' taste of life, although, apart from location, there wasn't much change in their lives I imagine. They seemed to have a lovely time lolling about in the sun, playing cards and whipping up a cocktail come six o'clock, when the day's contingent had returned from the game drive. One afternoon, I took the opportunity (like thousands of women before me) to ride Tara on the two kilometre trip to the Banjar River for her daily bath. It was a story to tell back home. Tara loved to slip beneath the surface, then reappear, trunk first, to douse herself with cooling water. I scrubbed her all over with a stiff-bristled brush while she lay on her side, like a docile pup who wanted her belly scratched and she thanked me kindly for my attention by bowing down on her knees and trumpeting.
>
> In the evening, the girls organised a candlelit picnic by the river – this always happens once during anyone's stay. The notable part of it was that candles were stuck in elephant dung which guests were later invited to put into the river to watch them float down. You couldn't imagine anyone apart from the English getting such fun out of a candle in shit.

It is said that all Bengalis are Anglophile at heart, much more so than in Delhi or Bombay. To them Bob Wright was a popular figurehead of the expats and a minor celebrity. To the stayers-on themselves he was a tireless champion. In effect he was the UK's ex-officio perma-nent representative in east India and a more powerful personage than the Deputy High Commissioner.

For years he ran the United Kingdom Citizens Association (UKCA), which represented the stayers-on with the declaration 'the British community in India must speak with one voice'. In its heyday of the 1950s and 1960s the Calcutta Branch would meet in the Bengal Club, where its President would report, for example, on the progress of lobbying at Westminster to obtain government subsidy for the private school fees of expats. Then it declined in signifi-cance. When Anthony Hayward took over in the 1970s, the Deputy Commissioner asked him to travel to the *mofussil* and gather together stayers-on listed as British citizens. He said it was a sad occasion; elderly single women drinking tea but with nothing to say to each other. Then it was Bob Wright's turn. He supervised the transfer of mostly Anglo-Indian members into retirement homes where he was a governor and gave them little presents at Christmas (for the Anglo-Indians in Kolkata, see Chapter Five). When necessary he arranged a funeral. He told me that he had found an undertaker who could preserve the corpse long enough, even in the Calcutta heat, for any remaining family to fly out from the UK for the funeral; but perhaps that was another of his semi-jokes. Now the UKCA is defunct.

Probably a more enjoyable task was serving as Chairman of the Board of Trustees of the Dr Graham's Homes. The Homes actu-ally make up a school of about 800 boarders at Kalimpong, east of Darjeeling in the Himalayan foothills. They were founded in 1900 by a Church of Scotland missionary, the Revd John Anderson Graham, and called then the St Andrew's Colonial Homes. Their purpose was to provide homes and schooling for the illegitimate, often orphaned children, known as 'by-blows', of tea planters and local women. Later 'the children of the tea gardens' were augmented by similar mixed-parent offspring of the Army, Railways and Civil Service. Today the children are no longer solely or even mainly Anglo-Indian, but over half are still supported by charities. This was where Bob Wright came in. He took over the fund raising and in 1997 made a successful Christmas appeal in the *Daily Telegraph*. As is usually the way with charity schools that originally offered an austere Christian education (as, for example, many British public schools), the Dr Graham's Homes is now a prestigious school much sought after by parents.

Finally, Bob Wright was Chairman of the Historical Cemeteries Association and helped supervise the renovation of the famous Park Street Cemetery, but that is for Chapter Eight.

Among Bob's papers that Anne showed me were his enquiries about becoming an Indian citizen. At first sight, incredible but true; on reflection, understandable that, half a century after the end of the Raj, even very British stayers-on should become movers-on. 'Was Bob Indian or was he English?' asked one of his Bengali friends, writing his obituary for the *Calcutta Telegraph*: 'There was something quintessentially English about Bob Wright but he belonged to a more gracious epoch of social life in Calcutta. It was in India that he had most of his friends. But in a very real sense, Bob's identity was his own. With his death nobody will ever say *koi hai* in quite the same way.'

I asked Anne if life was better in the time of the Raj, but she was reluctant to be drawn. After a pause she said: 'I'll tell you in a nutshell. India was a better place because there were fewer people.' I for one would not argue with that.

Chapter Two

PLANTER BOB

I've failed for the navy and army, the
Church and the law, so you see
The only profession left me
– my last hope – an assistant in tea.
You may not believe me, but I'm chockfull of brains,
The one thing I can't do, is think hard.
But I'm sure I'll love tennis and polo and golf,
I can work hard and play hard and drink hard.
And this, it appears, at least, so one hears,
Is what's wanted. It sounds just like jam,
So I'll pack up my box and make tracks for the docks
And that heavenly place called Assam.

Bob Powell-Jones sits in his bungalow in Shillong, formerly the
capital of Assam but now the capital of the state of Meghalaya, and
recites the tea planters' song 'Distant Lands Enchantment'. He does
not look like the caricature retired tea planter with whipcord trousers, old tweed jacket, red face and gin in hand. He speaks softly and
earnestly, wears a tracksuit top over flannel trousers and a baseball
cap to cover his bald head. He is small and agile, in his mid-sixties,
and has something of the Welsh terrier about him. He is not retired.
In fact, Bob Powell-Jones is the last British tea planter from the old
days left in Assam who is still working. He was first employed in
1963 by the Makum (Assam) and Namdang Tea Company that was

British owned by the Kilburn family and by the Assam Railways and Trading Company. Now, forty-four years later, he is managing the Tara Tea Estate outside Shillong for his Khasi employer, Mrs Nayantara Lakyrsiew Mon Sawain. Their aim is to grow boutique tea for Harrods of London. No one can say that Bob has not used his brain to move with the times.

I contacted Bob through the 'Koi-hai' website, which serves as a club for the once tight-knit community that worked in north-east India, mostly as expat tea planters in Assam, and is now dispersed through the English-speaking world. Photos, memories, a notice board – all ways of remembering what was an unforgettable experience between, mostly, 1945 and 1970, climaxing in an annual dinner, which I attended in an Eastbourne hotel. They could have been retired farmers and their families anywhere, ruddy cheeked and beer drinking, except here and there the darker Anglo-Indian complexion; some with the rugged look of the frontier with tales of remote tea estates up near the Chinese border, others more sophisticated, former careerists for agencies like Andrew Yule who had been sent to manage the big estates nearer civilisation. Via 'Koi-hai' I also contacted Derek Perry and Larry Brown, both retired to Australia. Derek was born in Assam in 1935 and returned there from England to work in tea in the mid1950s. Larry and then Bob, still friends, arrived soon afterwards. Through their three experiences I may tell the story of the gradual Indianisation of Assam tea – 60 per cent of the tea produced in India – over the last sixty years.

The first eyewitness story, however, is of a journey to the tea gardens in 1929. It comes from Sir Owain Jenkins, who visited Assam six years before Derek Perry was born and ended his career as a London director of the Indian-owned managing agents Balmer Lawrie. For them he inspected the tea gardens in the 1960s and 1970s, when Bob Powell-Jones got to know him.

The Assam valley nestles between the foothills of the Himalayas in Arunachal Pradesh and the Naga Hills on the Myanmar (formerly Burma) border. The great Brahmaputra River cuts in between, flowing through the valley and sweeping down to the Bay of Bengal. In Owain Jenkins's day there were two ways of getting to Upper Assam, either by paddle steamer up the Brahmaputra, calling at the tea districts along the bank, or by the Assam Mail, which required three changes of steam train and took three days from Calcutta to reach the head of the valley at Dibrugarh.

Owain Jenkins and his *khidmatgar* (butler) Abdul boarded the Assam Mail at Sealdah Station in Calcutta, and the following morning he breakfasted on a ferry crossing the Brahmaputra River at Amingaon. Waiting on the far side was train number two, on a one-metre gauge and without corridors. It puffed up the flat floor of the valley, and Owain watched brown men in loincloths harvesting the rice alongside the track. At a brief stop Abdul appeared with mid-morning tea, for 'somewhere among the luggage was a square open topped kerosene tin for heating water; also a yellow spray-gun for the recently invented insecticide known as "Flit"'. Then the train halted for lunch and the passengers wandered along to the station refreshment room:

'May I start train, Sir, please?'

'Out of the question, Station Master. We haven't finished our fish yet.'

A heavy fellow in grey shirt and shorts with a red face and a shock of iron-grey hair was spokesman for the first-class passengers. He was typical of a certain kind of Assam planter. The life often produced massive men with huge arms and legs, fleshy rather than fat, and exposure to the sun in shorts, shirt and sola topi burnt them red or brown according to their complexion. Planting was a lovely calling in which solidity was the prime requirement. Cleverness was secondary. You needed a chap who could stick it out and deliver the goods.[1]

The next morning Owain Jenkins woke up aware that the train had stopped. Day was breaking. He pushed up the shutter of his window:

Outside was a road, and on it were an elephant and a man. The elephant, hung about with ropes and chains, was on her way to work, padding along in the dust on silent feet, with her trunk curled up and her cheeks sucked in like an old lady in carpet slippers who has left her teeth in the bathroom. I loved the elephant. The man was a surprise. Broad faced and flat of nose, he wore a loincloth striped in black and red made on a narrow loom from some coarse fibre. He carried a bow and on his back a quiver full of arrows; a broad knife was at his belt. His glossy hair was cut just above the shoulder and in his ears were ornaments of scarlet seeds. It was my first contact with the raw material of our estate labour – a young buck newly recruited and still in the carefree arrogance of tribal life on the plateaux of central India. I have never forgotten that supremely confident noble savage.

The Garden Labour Forces are still recruited most often from the poor states of Bihar and Orissa.

Eventually Owain Jenkins arrived at the terminus of Tinsukia:

As seen from my window there seemed an amiable confusion between road and rail. Surrounded by bullock carts and pedestrians, locomotives stood about in the open, exposing parts of themselves usually discreetly concealed by station platforms. They were splendid creatures with high smokestacks, headlight and cowcatcher, straight from a western film. This was the marshalling yard of the Dibru–Sadiya Railway – built in 1881 to carry coal from the India General Steam Navigation Company in Dibrugarh – the river at that time being the only connection with Calcutta.

A small train on the DSR line took Owain Jenkins to the Muttock Tea Estate not far from Dibrugarh, now amalgamated into the estates of Russell Tea Ltd:

Can you visualise a tea garden? Think of flat land closely covered with a level expanse of evergreen bushes 4 feet high with leaves about the size of a Portugal laurel. Set among them at intervals of 50 yards are tall, single-stemmed trees with grey bark and a small head of feathery leaves to give shade. In the background virgin jungle forms a solid wall of trees and creepers. Beyond, hanging in the sky, is a little twinkling line of distant snows. That was what I saw looking north from the raised veranda of the Manager's bungalow.

'Where are the mountains?' I asked.

'On the left, Tibet. The ones on the right must be in China,' said George.

It was the British who discovered tea in north India. No one knows this better than Derek Perry, whose great-great-grandparents, Rosalie Augier and Louis Delanougerede, arrived at the gateway town to Assam, Guwahati, in 1848. They were pioneers of the 'tea rush', on the coat-tails of the explorer and opium trader Robert Bruce, who had discovered wild tea growing in abundance on land owned by the Singhpo tribe in the far north of Assam. In 1823 he had carried away plants and seeds, and his brother, Charles, had dispatched them to David Scott, the Governor General's agent in Assam; and so to Dr Wallich, superintendent of the Calcutta Botanical Gardens. After much trial and error processing the wild leaf for the domestic cup, but spurred on by the end of the East India Company's tea monopoly with China, Charles Bruce's native bushes from Assam were pronounced by the Governor General in Calcutta, Lord Auckland, to be from the plant *Camellia Sinensis* and capable of producing 'a pot of tea' for the commercial market. In 1838 the British government took over Assam, and the next year a joint stock company, the Assam Company Limited, was formed. That same year Charles Bruce sent 350 pounds of his tea in eight chests to the London auctions, where it sold for between 16 and 34 shillings a pound – a huge vote of confidence.

In 1939 the centenary of this first auction of Assam tea was celebrated in the City of London. Six chests of tea were unloaded at St Katherine's docks and placed on three elephants, which, guided by Sabu the Elephant Boy from the movies, lumbered up to Tower Hill, where the tea chests were transferred to horse-drawn vans, thus symbolising the change from East to West. They were taken in procession to Planters House and hence to the Tea Auction Room. A 2-pound bag of this very special tea was knocked down by the Lord Mayor's hammer for £1,156, the highest price ever paid for tea.

Charles Bruce claimed: 'a sufficiency of seeds and seedlings may now be collected to plant the whole of Assam.' In the 1950s, Derek

Perry drove up the Assam valley and considered this claim by one of
his forebears, for his great-grandfather, Achille Delanougerede, had
married into the Bruce family:

> It was a most prophetic statement! Along a stretch of trunk road for
> nearly 200 miles between the towns of Jorhat, Sibsagar and Dibrugarh,
> between the scattering of rice fields, acre upon acre of tightly knit
> tea bushes merge with the landscape, carefully cultivated to give a
> green table top effect, canopy shaded by tall mature leguminous trees,
> geometrically spaced into neat squares. These many emerald-like
> oases containing the cool thatched managerial houses and large fac-
> tory buildings of smart appearance, stood in stark contrast to the sadly
> impoverished conditions of the general countryside.[2]

As an irresistible footnote to Perry family history, Derek reports that
a later Delanougerede, Louis by name, was a crack shot. 'His hobby
was to take his .22 rifle and "just to keep his eye in" as he would say,
try to nail insects to the walls of rest houses':

> To the Editor of the 'Statesman', Calcutta.
> Sir,
> The account in the Statesman of 17 March 1926 about four tigers
> bagged in 24 hours by I.G. Police in Mysore, recalls an incident which
> occurred some 7 or 8 years ago when my son, Mr L.J. de la Nougerede
> [*sic*] was in the Garo Hills where he managed to shoot 5 tigers in 15
> minutes … I often wonder, as it is several years since the incident
> occurred, whether it was in fact 15 tigers in 5 minutes. There is a great
> element of luck in *shikar* [shooting for sport] as everyone knows, but
> such luck as befell my son is probably unparalleled.
> > Yours etc, A.C. de la Nougerede [Derek's grandfather]
> > Avondale, Shillong.

Derek's parents, Maurice and Dorothy, were both born in Calcutta
of well-established Raj families. Maurice traced his family's ancestry
in India back to 1776 and Dorothy was the second generation of
Irish descent. After marriage they lived in Shillong in a style befitting

the inheritance of great-grandfather Achille, son of Louis, the pioneer tea planter. In fact each of Achille's children had inherited a house in Shillong, known respectively as 'Uplands', 'Hopedale', 'Peachlands', 'Avondale' and 'Acacias'. Derek's parents were conscious of their status as 'domiciled Europeans' as opposed to Anglo-Indians of mixed blood, and the young Derek was often made conscious of it too: 'don't speak with that terrible *cheechee* accent, Derek!' (see Chapter Five). All Derek's parents and grandparents had been educated in England, as befitted their status, and, although he was sent to local schools, his destiny was Home to England as soon as school was over. To reinforce the point, all his immediate aunts, uncles and cousins left to settle at Home either before the war of 1939 or before Independence in 1947. He was the only one of three children to return to India.

Maurice Perry was one of the 'ruling caste', a district officer and magistrate for the British administration in Assam. Photographs show him standing in a group behind the Governor, Sir Robert Reid, a tall, upright figure on his dignity wearing a double-breasted suit, neatly parted hair and round glasses. Seated next to the Governor is Maurice's mother, legs crossed, dark dress well below the knee, sensible shoes and hat. Standing next to her is Derek, a solid little boy wearing sandals, shorts, tie and jacket; he has a slight squint and in one photo is rubbing his eyes.

Derek's upbringing was surrounded by the usual household of servants from *khidmatgar* to *dhobi wallah* (laundry man), and from the age of six he was surrounded by girls at school, because he became a day boy at St Agnes Convent at Haflong, Assam's only hill station in the North Cachar Hills. It was a British education for British and Anglo-Indians only; any departure from King's English was simply 'slang'. From now on young Derek was conscious of the Independence movement. He often took a shortcut to school through an area occupied by the *babu* (clerical) classes, mostly Bengalis working for the railways, and on one occasion the children threw stones at him and shouted 'Go home, white monkey'. This was his first taste of the 'Quit India' movement, although he did not realise it at the time. He thought he was at home. Then, local leaders of

the Congress Party in Haflong stirred up street demonstrations, and
Derek's father, the district officer, threatened them with *thana* (jail).
The question among the family was: 'When Independence comes
will father stay in service or be asked to leave?' Canada was the preferred option.

However, soon after the Perrys' arrival in Haflong in November
1941, Maurice heard on the BBC Daventry radio service that the
Japanese air force had bombed Pearl Harbor. From then on the very
real threat of enemy invasion dominated their lives. Initially, the Perry
family expected that the Japs, 'yellow, slit-eyed upstarts' in the propaganda of the times, would be easily defeated. In fact, even before
the 25th Japanese Army captured Singapore in February 1942, its
15th Army entered Burma through Thailand and advanced remorse-
lessly up country. Soon the first European civilians staggered over
the border into Assam, and Derek remembers his mother responding
to a radio appeal to help cope with an expected flood of refugees.
Arrogance now quickly turned to trepidation. The escape out of
Burma was horrific. Completely unprepared, families had to slash
their way through the thick tropical bush of the Hukawng valley and
slip and slide across the high valley sides. Many fell by the wayside,
sick, starved and exhausted. The horror confronted Derek literally
one morning at Lumding railhead. He and his father were heading for a hearty breakfast in the 'Europeans Only' station restaurant
when they came across a pitiful, numbed group of refugees wearing
what remained of Western clothes:

> Someone called out 'Maurice', my dad's name. We stopped in our
> tracks and this tall man of once elegant stature in scarecrow clothes
> shuffled over with a young lad of about my age in tow. He and my
> father had been colleagues in the Assam civil service until he had
> opted for service in Burma. He had lost his wife and another child on
> this three-month journey through a green hell. The lad opposite me
> and I faced each other. He looked at me with deep, sad, weary eyes,
> his face encrusted with grime and tears. He wore an oversized light
> brown tatty jumper, his shorts were ripped, he wore no shoes. We had
> no words to exchange. We were both lost in private thoughts of our

own with questions that seemed to have no answers. My dad fiddled
in his jacket pocket, pulled out his wallet and slipped the contents of
rupees into the hands of his old chum. With an awkward farewell, dad
and I walked on, the encounter forever etched in my memory.[3]

Perhaps 250,000 refugees escaped from Burma before the monsoon
of mid-May 1942 made movement impossible. A further 40,000
were left behind in makeshift camps until the ceaseless rains were
over; of these only half escaped the following October. Last out was
a British and Indian army of 60,000, which crossed the border just
south of Haflong one week before the monsoon, leaving behind
13,000 dead. It had retreated for 1,000 miles and abandoned Burma.
Crucially for the future, however, the Japanese 15th Army stopped
at the Chindwin River, because it was at the very limit of Japanese
supply lines.

Early in 1944 rumours reached the Perry family that the Japanese
were about to renew their offensive by advancing into Assam and
capturing the British forward positions at Kohima and Imphal just
60 miles away. They also heard that an Indian National Army was
intending to join them. It was led by the Bengali Subhas Chandra
Bose and consisted of 7,000 Indian former prisoners of war whom
the Japanese had freed so that they could 'liberate' their homeland
from the British. Only a few months before, under Japanese protection, Subhas Chandra Bose had 'liberated' the Andaman Islands in
the Bay of Bengal. Derek remembers a sense of foreboding. Would
the Assam defences halt the hitherto unstoppable Japanese? Would
the local population defect also? In fact, the allied army throughout
the Indian subcontinent was now a lot stronger. It had spent the
previous year re-manning and re-equipping, so that, for example, the
town of Silchar, a day's train journey from Haflong, had become a
powerful military base.

Maurice Perry and the extraordinary Miss Ursula Bower, an
adventuress who lived among the Naga hill people, were charged
with employing Naga scouts to bring back intelligence about
Japanese infiltration over the Burmese border. Derek remembers
the 'Naga Queen', as the press called her, giving away the sports

prizes at St Agnes carrying a sten gun and surrounded by her Naga
bodyguards. Then Derek's father put into effect a discreet plan for
the evacuation of civilians. Derek's mother flatly refused to go,
despite the pleading of Bishop Le Pierre, who was already packing
his bags. Nine-year-old Derek was given the option of staying or
joining his grandparents in Shillong. 'Gut-wrenchingly', he chose
to stay, knowing that his father had a desperate last-ditch plan 'if the
balloon went up'.

They could hear the heavy gunfire from Imphal and Kohima;
every evening Japanese planes bombed RAF bases beyond Haflong,
the explosions clearly audible. The local hospital was full of wounded
soldiers, but the market had little food. There was no school, so Derek
reread all his favourite books and wondered whether his father and
Miss Bower were still alive somewhere up in the hills. They had prepared a giant beacon on a hilltop visible from Haflong that was to be
lit only if Kohima and Imphal were lost, but this was the *jhumming*
or slashing and burning season, so there were false alarms that added
to the tension. Eventually, as war histories record in bold, for it was
a turning point in the war, General Slim's 14th Army drove off the
Japanese and pursued them back through Burma.

Later that year Derek returned to St Agnes equipped with heavy
glasses to reduce acute astigmatism. He met a newcomer, a young
teenager called Agnes, who like him was only partially sighted.
They became friends and she told him her tragic story. In 1942 her
mother had died of exhaustion while fleeing through the swollen
streams and blood-sucking leeches of the dreaded Hukawng valley.
Before her death she had given Agnes her jewellery and left her
in the custody of a British officer leading their party. One morning soon after, Agnes had woken up and found herself abandoned,
the jewellery stolen and her glasses crushed. For days she had blun-
dered along the rough trail alone, guided by her instinct for survival
more than her eyes. Eventually she had been discovered by Indian
refugees and handed over to a search party of tea planters. Maurice
Perry was able to get her a small pension because the Japanese had
killed her father, a British civil servant in Burma; but the officer was
never brought to account.

Derek remembers that, just before the war ended, a convoy of American GIs arrived at St Agnes with jeeps full of canned food. The senior girls were allowed to jitterbug unrestrained to Glen Miller's 'In the Mood'. Ten-year-old Derek felt liberated too, and fell in love with Maureen, another pupil. But for all the survivors of war it was but an uneasy prelude before the consequence of peace – withdrawal from India. Maureen's family, like many others, took off to England as soon as they could. Maurice was summoned back to Shillong as district officer, and the family went too, Derek continuing his education at St Edmunds. For the time being Maurice remained at his post and the family stayed together.

In August 1947 Maurice Perry hauled down the Union Jack at the Court House, visibly upset but determined to do his duty. He continued his career in the Indian Administrative Service, now as a Deputy Commissioner working alongside mostly Indian colleagues. During Partition his police force kept the peace between Hindus and Muslims, but remaining Brits said 'I told you so' and became more determined to leave. Most did so over the next three years. Maurice and Dorothy felt differently. After 170 years of Perry domicile in India, they could not accept that 'Home' was somewhere else.

Derek himself left in 1952. Not surprisingly, his new life by comparison was monotone and monotonous. He lived in digs in South London, worked at Gamages Department Store and studied at evening classes in Crystal Palace. He was unhappy. He longed to be back in Assam. Only two years later, aged nineteen, he was recruited by Andrew Yule and Co. of 8 Clive Row, Calcutta, as an assistant manager in one of its tea companies, thereby following in the family tradition begun by his pioneering great-great-grandparents. In the mid-1950s well over 80 per cent of the acreage under tea in India was British dominated and even ten years later Britons held over 500 of the senior tea-garden jobs in Assam. Derek was offered a three-and-a-half-year contract, during which period he was not allowed to marry nor to take home leave. He was on probation, and Andrew Yule's obligation was to return him Home when his services were no longer required. He was given his jabs, boarded the RMS *Caledonia* in Liverpool and eventually presented himself at the Andrew Yule head office. Here he was handed a rupee allowance and a mosquito net, but not much else, and given his orders. He was about to serve his apprenticeship as a *chhota sahib* on the Karballa Tea Estate in the Central Dooars, the hills of West Bengal sandwiched between Bhutan and what is now Bangladesh. The next day he caught the early morning milk-run Dakota that flew from Dum Dum (now Subhas Chandra Bose Airport) up the Assam valley towards the Himalayas, hopping from one airfield to another and delivering cold-storage delights, machinery spare parts and the odd hungover planter from a Calcutta night club.

Six years later, Larry Brown, aged twenty-three, joined the Makum and Namdang Tea Company in Upper Assam. He was a Belfast boy, good looking and happy-go-lucky. He had heard about the tea gardens of north India when he was working for Sirocco of Belfast in the tea machinery design section of the drawing office. He took a ship's passage on the MV *Caledonia*, carrying a guitar and remembering, but not following, the advice given to new assistants by the company director's wife:

> Luscious fruits and salads green
> Harbour deadly germs unseen
> The traveller in the East must not
> Eat anything – unless it's hot.

He flew from Calcutta on a DC3, landed at Mohanbari airfield and was soon on the road to Namdang Tea Estate, marvelling at the exotic birds, banana groves and rice paddies, but squirming with dysentery. He, too, was working for a British Company, for Makum and Namdang was owned jointly by the Assam Railways and Trading Company (AR&TC) and the Kilburn family. The AR&TC had sold land about 10 miles away at Digboi to the Assam (now Burmah) Oil Company, so Larry was joining a sizeable community of over fifty Europeans; this really meant 'white', for it included Americans and Australians. That first evening after dinner he sat out on the veranda of his bungalow: 'The stars were so close you could touch them and in the shrubs surrounding the bungalow a million fireflies pulsed their light. I could hear the sound of beating drums wafting from the labour lines. I was in India.'[4]

Three years later Bob Powell-Jones joined him. Working unhappily in the City of London, he had answered an advertisement in the *Daily Telegraph* he remembers to this day: 'Young assistant manager wanted to work in tea gardens in north east India.' He was interviewed by Jack Kilburn himself and was obviously a 'shoe-in'. Bob had grown up in Africa, where his father worked for Shell in the Congo and Ethiopia, so he spoke French, though with a Belgian accent, and he was self-sufficient. He had been to a public school, Malvern, which in those days was considered an advantage, and then worked for the Forestry Commission in South Wales, which was certainly an advantage.

When he arrived at Makum Namdang, he was taken in a Land Rover on a tour round the five gardens, three that were part of the Makum Company – Margherita, Dirok and Dehing – and two that were part of the Namdang Tea Company – Namdang and Bogapani; in all, 5,000 acres of neatly cultivated tea bushes. He was told he was the Assistant Manager of Margherita and that the Manager, John Moran, expected him on duty first thing the next morning. Like Larry, Bob spoke no Hindi, nor did he know anything about tea, nor was he supposed to see home again for four years. He was twenty-one. The next morning John Moran forgot about him. Bob remembers with mortification standing for three hours in the hot sun not knowing what to do, surrounded by the female tea-pickers who became increasingly cheeky the more he became embarrassed.

For these three, and for others whose memories are on the 'Koihai' website, the 1950s and 1960s were the golden era of the tea gardens, which began after the recovery from war and Partition in the late 1940s and ended with the rapid Indianisation of the industry in the late 1960s. Why was this? For young men out from Britain, the work was physically demanding and managerially responsible, though usually straightforward. For those who did not stay longer than eight years, it was well paid, because salary could be remitted in sterling to a British bank and the employer usually paid the tax.

The tea companies were hierarchical and paternalistic institutions that provided a clear path to promotion and a caring environment.

Social life centred round the Planters Club, but it was the antithesis of Home Counties suburbia. Eccentric characters from the pre-war era stood at the bar next to smooth young Indians just recruited into management and the Anglo-Indian or Bengali administrators. The club provided golf, cricket, drama and dancing too. If all that palled, then outside there was 'the allure of the forbidden', as Larry described it: 'the thickly forested hills, the authentic rope bridges over white-water rivers, the birds, butterflies and people of the North East Frontier Agency' (now Arunachal Pradesh), which was supposedly off limits. Then there were sexual relationships that were by no means forbidden in practice either. The whole environment spelt adventure, and the Khasi women from the Shillong area were particularly beautiful and also Christian; both Larry and Bob have Khasi wives and adult children now who speak two or three languages. A quick plane flight away was Calcutta, the most exciting major city of India. Old planters warned 'what a damned fool career you have chosen', but it was fun while it lasted. That is, it was fun if you avoided the severe labour problems of the Dooar estates that were infiltrated by communist agitators or the severe isolation of remote tea gardens where, said Bob, 'you had to climb on an elephant to cross the river between the bar and your bungalow'.

Planters might say that the unique flavour of Upper Assam comes from its tea, but, if words may suffice, then they come from this description by Jim Robinson, who spent his 1960s childhood on an estate by the Sessa River near Dibrugarh:

> All around us were the tea gardens with their neat lines of shade trees painted white up their trunks to prevent white spider harming the crop of 'two leaves and a bud' that the pluckers methodically collected from May to November.
>
> We had wildlife all around us. A tiger regularly used the gate at the end of the drive as a scratching post. South of the bungalow, a leopard patrolled the *nullas* or drains around the tea bushes. Pythons and cobras basked on the lawn in the sun. Above all there was the magic

of the river. It drew us to it like the cattle that drank from it and the fishermen who threw nets or speared fish with three pronged javelins from their narrow wooden boats. I swam in it, explored its shallows. Below the bridge that the Chinese *mistries* [carpenters] had painstakingly pieced together, large fish swam lazily out of reach. During the rainy season you could barely see more than a few yards. The sandy banks fell like mini avalanches into the swollen water, uprooting trees and carrying away animals.

At festival time, images of the Hindu gods and goddesses were brought down to the river for ceremonial immersion. The clay figures would be escorted with loud drumming and ululations from the women. The upturned faces of Saraswati, Lakshmi or Durga slowly sank as the clay absorbed water and grew heavier and clouds of incense scented the riverbank as the villagers said goodbye and the river carried the gods, in some mysterious way, back to their home, the great Himalaya.[5]

New recruits began by inspecting their new homes, the bungalows. At Makum and Namdang these were approached up neat drives lined with potted plants alongside spacious lawns. Some had corrugated tin roofs while others were thatched. The frame uprights of the bungalows were either *nahor*, the Indian ironwood that termites cannot digest, or steel for the same reason. The white plaster and black beams, verandas and balconies were designed to let in maximum ventilation yet protect from the extremes of monsoon and earthquake. The larger, *chang*, bungalows, as they were called, were built on stilts, with living quarters above and *go-downs* or storage areas below. Some bungalows were relics of a Victorian or Edwardian past, with brass bedsteads and rosewood furniture to match. The *Burra's* (Manager's) bungalow, where Larry Brown spent his first night, was very grand. Outside it were 'tennis courts, flower beds with show standard Dahlias, a wide expanse of closely cut lawn, a gazebo and a large statue of Buddha'. Others were decidedly dilapidated. No. 5 Margherita, a *chang* bungalow lived in by Tony Pickford (who is still in India), had rings and lines marked out on the floor in chalk to indicate where the floor boards were almost eaten through by

white ants. When he arrived, his companion John Barrow-Williams
– bachelors usually shared – pointed out a section of new flooring:

> Damnest thing, I came back from the garden to find a ceiling fan
> on the floor where I parked the car. The bloody ants had got into
> the support beam and the whole lot had given way. The old DC fan
> had crashed straight through the rotten floorboards onto the concrete
> below; brought a nice coffee table with it too.

Larry and Bob both say without fear of contradiction that the
Factory Bungalow at Namdang was haunted. It was shared for a
while by Larry and an Indian assistant manager, Polly Rajpal, who
said at breakfast one morning: 'Something threw me out of bed last
night, and it took me some time to sleep again.' Larry himself had
been more disturbed: 'Out of the corner of my eye I saw a lumi-
nous figure gliding into the room … It leaned on the bedstead end
and peered into my face. I then felt his presence receding – passing
through the closed door. I was absolutely terrified, couldn't move.' It
turned out that the ghost had been a young planter who had died of
blackwater fever in the same bed now occupied by Polly.

The bungalows, of course, had a large Assamese staff, which could
be either daunting or spoiling for a young man, particularly if he
could not speak the language. In fact, a new employee was given a
language allowance and Saighal's *Hindustani Grammar*, which, Larry
Brown discovered, was somewhat out of date. One of the supposedly 'useful phrases' translated into Hindi was 'the postillion has been
struck by lightning'. Under the *bearer* was the *pani wallah* (pantry
boy), the *sweeper* (cleaner), the *malis* (gardeners) and the *chowkidar*
(watchman). The manager or *burra sahib* also had a chauffeur, *syce*
(groom) and *ayah*, even if he was childless. He was the Lord of all,
regarded by the labour force as 'the bringer of rain or sun' and 'the
curer of ills'. *Ab hum log kei mai bap hai* ('you are our mother and
father') said the estate workers with affection as well as submission.
The paternalistic order was brought home to Bob Powell-Jones
when he reported for work that first week at 7.30 a.m.:

This was the time for personnel and labour matters; say a man had let his cow stray, or not done his work. We could deduct wages for that. You see, for a 1,000-acre garden there was a labour force that with family added came to 3,000 people or so, mostly Indians from down south. They lived permanently in lines of huts and indirectly you were responsible for them. When I began, I looked after the east side of Margherita Garden, and that included all the labour and family who worked there, over 1,000 people. It was a big responsibility for a young man, though we had a personnel officer, who guided us on legal matters. Once a week, on a Wednesday afternoon, I held a *bichar*, an open meeting for the airing of complaints. It was quite a spectator sport sometimes, particularly if a labourer accused another of going off with his wife. I took it all seriously. *Ab hum log kei mai bap hai*, we reminded ourselves.

After breakfast, assistant managers bicycled out to the gardens carrying a piece of paper with the lists of labour gangs organised by the *jemadar*, or foreman. 'You were the officer, but he was in charge,' said Bob, 'simple as that, particularly if you couldn't speak the language.' And there were the tea-pickers lined up, section by section, some of them young women with babies. They carried wicker baskets. The plucking season extended from the first rains of March until the start of the dry season in November. It had its cycle. First the pruning or shaping of the bush, then the first flush – the picking of the first growth of leaf that was delicate of flavour – and then the second flush in early May:

> You see [said Bob with enthusiasm undimmed after forty years], you're after a secondary shoot that comes off the stalk of the first shoot. It grows quickly and is plucked every seven days for about ten weeks, because after that the monsoon comes and you're into 'rains teas' and then 'autumnal teas' that are inferior. So it's the second flush you are after. You always pick two leaves and a bud; that's the ideal.

Two leaves and a bud for the finest tea, the pickers discarding *banji* (barren leaf). 'One thing you never do, Perry,' the manager said to the green *chhota sahib*, 'is to refer to any of these women as *banji*, not even in banter.'

Three times a day the pickers took their baskets to be weighed, because they were paid piecework. Then, without delay, the leaves were carted off for treatment in the factory sheds by a process that in essence has not changed for many years. First came the withering troughs, which dried the leaf and reduced it to a flaccid state; then the rolling machines or later the Crushing, Tearing and Curling (CTC) machines, which tore the leaf into small particles; then the fermentation process, which was critical, because it produced the distinctive flavour. Here Bob comes into his own: 'You go by the nose. When there's a rather sweet, pleasant smell you know its ready to be removed for drying. If it's sour or stale, it's overfermented. By the way, there are absolutely no additives in tea. I'm surprised people don't realise it. The whole of the tea manufacture is in the processing.' Finally came the drying, which diminished the moisture of the now minuscule leaf particles to just 3 per cent, the hot air permeating with the smell of tea every corner of the factory. The factory workers were organised in shifts, but, wrote one old hand on the 'Koi-hai' website, 'the assistant could never call his soul his own and had to be on call day and night, like a ship in stormy weather'.

Evenings were spent in the club: the Margherita Club, the Ledo Club, the Digboi Club, the Hilltop Club, or further afield even to the Doom Dooma Club, where ranks kept to themselves. Not so at the Margherita, where the manager of the garden, Peter 'Peewee' Bursnall, ticked off a deferential Bob Powell-Jones: 'don't fookin' Sir me, mate.' He had fought with the 8th Army in North Africa and led the singing of army ribaldry. Back in the bar of his bungalow was a large pottery figure of Venus with a push-down button coming from her head that dispensed gin from her left breast; in his lavatory was a picture of a dowager duchess complete with tiara on her head and her knickers round her ankles – 'The Relief of Ladysmith'. Another old character was Arthur Nuttal, manager of the Bogapani Garden, who was often drinking 'snifters' or *chhota pegs* in one of the bars. Rumour had it that after the war he had bought an American jeep on the black market, and, before the Special Police had arrived on a search, he had dismantled the whole jeep, taken down the hessian ceiling of his bungalow and roped up to the roof trusses the engine, wheels, transmission, body parts, the lot; then he had replaced the ceiling.

The clubs were, of course, for both sexes. Larry and Bob formed a mini dance band, 'The Mudguards', and played on club nights an increasing repertoire for guitar and drums that began with 'Moon River'. Their big night was 'The Bachelors' Ball', a black-tie evening to repay hospitality. Many evenings the clubs became cinemas and sometimes theatres. *Hassan* by James Elroy Flecker was not surprisingly a favourite. It was all so different from before the war.

In 1929 Owain Jenkins had visited the Old Dibrugarh Club and found opposite the main door a separate building with chintz curtains and armchairs. This was the *murghi-khana* or 'hen house', more formally 'the Ladies' Annexe'. Women attended dances by invitation and otherwise were confined to their own building. Separated on arrival, married couples could only arrange their joint departure by exchanging notes.

Memories abound with sporting stories: the time when Derek Perry on the golf course drove his ball in a low, undeviating trajectory up the backside of a straying cow and then had to play his second shot off a thick brown slurry; the time when Bob Powell-Jones fell in the rushing river Tirap because he would not let go of his rod, so Eric Singh dived in to save him, and the next week the same near tragedy happened in reverse; the time when 'Peewee' and his friends commandeered a train and stopped it between stations for a cricket match. 'What time shall I bring the train, Mr Bursnell?' enquired the driver.

In Owain Jenkins's day, up until the war, the sports had been polo and big game hunting. In fact, polo continued into the 1970s, and some new recruits were given an allowance for a pony, *syce* and grass-cutter. The sport of sex never changed. Bob Powell-Jones tells the story of a superintendent still working when he arrived who in his youth had boasted that he would give the plucking season a new meaning by taking more tea-garden girls to bed than any other contestant. By November his score was over eighty, but, said Bob, this was before Independence, when managers were sometimes

magistrates, so the command *hamara bangala jaega* (go to the bungalow) was hard to resist: a nasty plantation story.

When Derek Perry signed on with Andrew Yule and Co., there
was a clause in his contract forbidding sexual relations with garden
girls. His predecessor at Khowang Estate in Upper Assam, where
Derek moved after Karballa, was called by Derek 'Poppet Love-
Smythe', a fictitious name to save his embarrassment. He had been
removed for breaking this regulation:

> Soon after my arrival at Khowang I was standing by a group of women
> tea pickers cajoling them into action and receiving a fair amount of
> cheek in exchange. At this point the chubby figure of Mr Chatterjee,
> the garden head *babu* [clerk], hove into view on his old bicycle, his
> dhoti and shirt billowing in the wind. The women scrambled their
> baskets on to their heads to resume picking. Chatterjee dismounted
> and addressed me, sounding remarkably like Peter Sellers:
>
> 'Mr Perry sah, what I am saying to you? You are one too, too good
> boy. Mr Perry sah, kindly please, you must not go by one wrong way.
> Mr Poppet Love-Smythe, he is also one too, too good boy, but he is
> going by one very wrong way, he is taking girl. Kindly, Mr Perry, you
> must not do this thing. Mr Perry, if you are wanting to take a girl,
> kindly you will pray to your mother first. I am now also praying to
> God for your name.'

With that, Chatterjee Babu mounted his rickety bicycle and mean-
dered over the horizon.

Not that there was a shortage of respectable young women for
the testosterone-charged *chhota sahibs* to take to the swimming pool
or dances. There were the planters' daughters, the Indian or Anglo-
Indian secretaries and clerks and there were the OWs, the 'Old
Women', a chauvinist pre-war phrase still in currency. These were
the Assamese young women who were available as 'housekeepers' for
bachelors. The arrangement could be made by negotiation if not by
attraction, but it often developed into a serious relationship. Larry
Brown married Judy this way, while Bob Powell-Jones pursued his
courtship with Dorothy in Shillong.

This halcyon period of British tea planting in India came to an end all too soon. By the late 1970s there were no entirely British-owned estates left in Assam and very few British tea planters. This was due in part to the government policy of 'Indianising' the tea estates and in part to the economic crisis that hit India in the mid-1960s, but it was also due to the decline in the world markets for Indian tea.

The figures tell their own story. From 1947 until 1970 over 40 per cent of the world's tea came to Britain and 70 per cent of this was imported from India and Ceylon. In fact, tea exports constituted the main trade flow from India to Britain, averaging over £53 million per year. Then unexpectedly the British began to drink less tea, deserting the teashops for coffee bars. As evidence of a remarkable change in drinking habits, in 1960 over five cups of tea were drunk for one cup of coffee, in 1972 less than two. Less tea was drunk and less tea was used because of the rise of the tea bag, an invention of the 1960s as an antidote to instant coffee. The figures here show that for every pound weight of tea the loose leaf provided 225 cups but the tea bag 350, a remarkable 35 per cent reduction in the amount of tea per cup. The tea bag was economic, but it hit the tea garden.

To tell the truth, the British-owned tea gardens in India were not responding competitively enough to changes in the world market. Some of the trouble lay close to home. Production of Indian tea rose only slowly during the 1960s and the percentage of it for export declined by over 10 per cent because of increased consumption in India. Moreover, increasing wage rates in India, forced by labour agitation, were making its tea uncompetitive on the world market, and the new gardens in East Africa took full advantage of this. In some tea gardens the British management was directly to blame. Anticipating the coming Indianisation of the gardens, it underinvested in replanting and sold off land.

The decline in the world markets of Indian tea was gradual, as was the Indianisation of the gardens. The economic crisis of the 1960s was sudden, but by then Derek had already left for more personal reasons. In 1962 the Indian government refused him the right to remit sterling to Britain. Tightening its rules, it judged that, as he now had a daughter born in Shillong (he had married on his second leave home), and his parents had retired there too, he was not an expat but domiciled to India. The same year the Chinese army massed on the North-East Frontier border and plans were announced to evacuate the British from the Upper Assam tea estates. To Derek this brought back bad memories. He had been here before. He persuaded the Catholic Bishop of Shillong to 'launder' his rupees into sterling from the money chests donated by the faithful of Dublin and Milan and embarked his family on the boat back to England. He left, he says, with no regrets and many happy memories. Ten years later he moved to New Zealand and remarried. His parents joined him and are buried there. That, however, was not the end of the Perry odyssey. He and his wife moved to Australia in 1997, where, he reports, 'we have found paradise. We acknowledged this on 30 August 2006 by taking the oath of allegiance at Nambour to Her Majesty. We are now Australian citizens.'

What hit Larry and Bob in 1966 was the catastrophic devaluation of the rupee. Bob remembers the figures exactly; for every thirteen rupees to the pound there were now twenty-one, so that rupees exchanged into pounds for remittance to the United Kingdom lost over one-third of their value. For senior staff needing to educate children back in Britain this meant a crisis that was resolved only if their employer offered an enormous increase in salary, and salaries were now controlled by the Indian government. On top of this, Indian tax rates rose sharply, as we have seen. Some British-owned tea companies now encouraged their British staff to leave because Indian managers were a lot cheaper. From now on, said Bob, it was always Indians who were given the billets vacated by Europeans. Other companies had a policy of 'one to one' – for every European recruited so was one Indian.

For Larry and Bob by the end of the 1960s 'the wind of change' was blowing hard. In fact, had Derek stayed, by 1969 he would no longer have worked for Andrew Yule and Co. Ten years before, in 1959, Andrew Yule and Co. had ceased altogether to hire British assistant managers for the gardens, and when Derek left between ten and fifteen of his colleagues were Indian. Then in 1969 the Indian Companies (Amendment) Act abolished the system of managing companies by agencies altogether. Without doubt, the pro-British attitude of Jawaharlal Nehru, who died in 1964, was replaced by a much more nationalistic approach by his daughter, Indira Gandhi, when she became Prime Minister two years later. Now it was self-interest not sentiment on both sides. Further evidence of this for the tea gardens came in 1971, when the Assam government announced the formation of a tea corporation 'for the purchase, control, development and management of the tea industry'. It said the reason was to prevent 'the making of quick money by selling land and forest products from the reserves of the gardens'. This could only mean the accelerated removal of British firms from the tea industry of India.

Larry Brown and his wife left in 1970. With plans to start a family, he saw no future in Assam, and the tea gardens of Papua New Guinea beckoned. If that venture failed, then he was close to Australia. And there he is today. Bob Powell-Jones was left to face increasing labour unrest in the gardens and the almost complete Indianisation of tea-company ownership.

Labour agitation was worst in the Dooar gardens of West Bengal, where the Naxalite movement began in 1967. A bloody uprising of landless peasants in the village of Naxalbari started the revolt, and ever since the term has applied to communist groups, particularly Maoist, who take the law into their own hands. The so-called Naxalite problem was often an excuse for inter-union rivalry, as it is today for simple banditry. Strikes, walk-outs and *gheraos* or 'surrounds' (see Chapter Three) were common in the Dooar gardens, and they even resulted in the murder of British managers. For some of the remaining few this was the last straw. Bob had a very ugly experience when he was acting manager of Margherita garden in the mid-1970s:

> I was the victim of inter-union rivalry. The trade union came up to me and complained about a particularly uncouth, Assamese, staff member. He used to swear at the workers. I called up this fellow and he denied it, so I said to the union officials 'sorry, unless you bring me proof I can't do anything about him'. Now, the union bore a grudge against this guy and undoubtedly provoked him, but I still had no evidence. One Saturday afternoon during a tea tasting I received a phone

call saying the workers were massing in an ugly mood. I went and saw
the acting superintendent, whose bungalow was in the middle of the
gardens, and soon the whole labour force surrounded us. They barged
into the bungalow, pulled me out physically amid much shouting and
manhandled me down to the factory gate. They made me say that this
fellow was going to be sacked and sign a paper saying so. To tell the
truth, I thought my end had come. The men wanted to lynch me and,
actually, it was the women who surrounded me for my protection.

In 1976 the Makum and Namdang company reduced its British
shareholdings to 75 per cent and set up an Indian Board of Directors
in Calcutta to manage the day-to-day running of the gardens. This
was known as 'rupee-ising' the management. It began to interfere,
and Bob, who was now the Manager of Margherita, resented it:

The trust had gone. That basically was what drove me out. Nothing
racial about it. We all bitched together but I do think the British board
should have helped me more. We had pressure from the unions, we
had pressure from the government to follow the Plantation Labour
Act and we had pressure from our own directors to reduce costs. And
now I couldn't do my job without interference.

By 1982 over half the shares in the company were Indian owned
and undoubtedly the intention was to Indianise fully. In the end I was
pushed out. The Indian directors said they were not going to allow me
to remit my earnings back home. I was the next to last chap to go. The
question of race didn't come into it, but there was the feeling 'it's their
country so we have to accept they want their own chaps in'. Now
there are no Europeans at all working for the tea companies. I didn't
exactly feel bitter but I only just got a pension and I do feel the board
in London let me down. They just saw it all as a sign of the times.

Soon after the company merged into the McLeod Russell group
and that, in turn, has become part of the giant Williamson Magor
group. It is one of the largest tea producers in the world, with
twenty-nine gardens in Assam and the Dooars; British names but
entirely Indian owned.

In Achille Delanougerede's day the journey to Shillong up 4,500 feet from Guwahati took two or three days on horseback. Those unfit for riding were carried on the back of a Khasi hillman in a bamboo seat with a canopy over it known as a *thapa*. Now the journey takes as many hours, the taxis sweeping round the banked corners and overtaking the lumbering Tata lorries like cyclists in a velodrome. As the elevation increases so the climate and vegetation change, from tropical forest thick with bamboo and *sal* trees to the green hills wooded with pine. Now as then the spirits rise as the sultry plain gives way to the gentle winds and clean air of the hills.

Shillong, the 'Highlands of the east', is a disappointment. Here is another Indian city fighting a losing battle against congestion, pollution and urban sprawl. The golf club that boasts it is one of the best in Asia is on the front line. Thinning strips of beautiful *khasi* pine separate fairways down which gangs of teenagers and picnickers wander. The perimeters are protected by barbed wire and warnings that golf balls can be dangerous. Up against the wire is a shantytown of bamboo-framed and tin-roofed bungalows, built that way to resist earthquakes for Shillong is in Zone 5 seismic area.

In fact it was the mighty quake of 1897 that destroyed the first Shillong. According to Derek's grandmother, 'the surface of the land moved like waves', reducing to rubble the cathedral and most of the planters' mansions, including the original 'Hopedale' and 'Avondale.' She escaped with her Christening cup and little else. Shillong was for a time a canvas city, whereas now, over a century later and after complete rebuilding, its centre is a concrete building site for another reason – endless 'modernisation'. The street view from the Centre Point Hotel is of a dispiriting global subculture of jeans and T-shirts, mobile phones and motorised scooters, fast-food stalls and cyber cafés. Kipling would have wept.

Bob and Dorothy live in an earthquake-proof bungalow squeezed between other properties, for Dorothy sold off land to provide them with an income. We sat in front of a fire and drank tea. In fact they drank Bob's own tea, *La Kyrsiew*, which is Khasi for 'the awakening'; 'brewed for 5 minutes until golden', as it said on the packet. I asked for a cup of *chai* (from which the British Tommy in the last war corrupted the word 'char' as in 'char and a wad' meaning 'tea and a bun'), and this was a mistake. Although *chai* has been a favourite Indian drink for ages, it is regarded as a crude station or bus stop tea, in which milk, sugar and spices like cinnamon and ginger are added and brewed together into an aromatic but highly adulterated concoction. It is often called *masala chai*, meaning a 'spicey-sauced tea'. I noticed that Dorothy was unused to making it. We could have been back in Wales, I thought, an impression increased by the dark, almost Celtic features of Dorothy and her two daughters as shown in the wedding photographs on a side table and, also, because there is a strong Welsh connection with Shillong. Welsh missionaries came first to the area in the nineteenth century and converted the Khasis to Christianity. The deserted mission centre at Cherrapunji nearby records that Welsh pastors worked there in continuous succession between 1841 and 1967.

Dorothy kept in the background, which surprised me. Another name for Shillong is 'the land where women reign supreme', for the Khasis are a matrilineal society where the women own the property, pass on their surnames to their children and are responsible for looking after their parents; another reason, said Bob, why he and Dorothy have stayed in Assam.

The twenty years after Bob left Margherita were not easy. He did not receive a golden handshake, and his pension was mean. He bought a 'leaf' (tea) factory and quarrelled with his partner to the point of litigation. Yet he kept his head down, was self-employed and supported by Dorothy – a dutiful couple with their own pew in the cathedral. The British Deputy High Commission in Calcutta 'does not really know I exist. The expats used to have drinks with the Deputy Commissioner when he visited but that's all stopped now.' In fact Bob has no British friends left in Shillong. One of the very last of the real 'stayers-on', Don Papworth, who fought at Imphal and worked in tea, died just forty-eight hours before my arrival. But Bob has no intention of returning to the UK:

I've lived three-quarters of my life abroad and its too late to strike up new relationships. I do what I like here. I love trips to the remote

> villages and above all there's the fishing on the Jia Bharali and Kynshi,
> both tributaries of the Brahmaputra. Catching the mahseer is what I
> like. It's a good fighting game fish and good to eat, though bony.

Through Dorothy's birth in Assam, he is applying for Person of
Indian Origin (PIO) status, and this means that he will no longer
require a visa. 'But I haven't changed my identity. I'm still a Brit.'
So what did he think of the British Raj? Bob was silent and then
came out with the pat answer: 'What the British gave India was the
English language, cricket, the ICS and the railways. A lot of Brits
made a lot of money and they took too much out. So it's a bit of
one and a bit of the other.' It was obviously not a question that he
asked himself often.

The next day Bob took me in his 4x4 to the Tara Tea estate, stopping briefly at the old British cemetery to view the freshly dug grave
of Don Papworth. We travelled off the road to Guwahati, past the
messy Shillong rubbish tip and down through the pinewoods to the
banks of Umiam Lake. Here neat rows of tea bushes covered the
foothills, more reminiscent to me of Sri Lanka than Assam, where the
gardens are normally on flat ground. 'That's why we grew Darjeeling
tea here,' said Bob, 'that and the climate. I can tell the difference from
Assam tea four times out of five with my eyes closed.'

That, in fact, is to be expected. At the tea planters' reunion dinner
in the UK I met the former 'Taster' of Jorehaut Tea Company. He
told me that his first test had been to distinguish the teas of one
country from another – easy – and then from one Assam estate to
another – less easy – finally from one bush to another in the same
garden – very difficult but not impossible. In fact, after one tasting
he had identified such a good taste from the leaves of five bushes
grouped together that he had recommended a new garden should
be planted in which all the bushes were clones of the original five.
This tea, called Hatimari, won the prizes in the 1970s. These days,
he told me, his favourite tea was a Twinings mixture of 50 per cent
Darjeeling and 50 per cent Assam.

Bob showed me a section of garden where the bushes, planted
four years ago, are now reaching maturity: 'They could last at least

100 years and if we did not prune them they could grow to a height of 60 feet,' he said. 'Already we're producing 1,500 kilos of tea a year.' Later he showed me the small factory for which he had designed and built some of the equipment. 'I do everything from bringing soap to cleaning the garden kettle to telling the girls about the style of pruning.' We sat outside a shed looking over the gardens descending in rows of green to the blue Umiam Lake, a few fishermen casting nets in the distance. It was an idyllic scene, further proof that Bob the Planter is in his element. It needed, perhaps, a copywriter's summation, and one is written on every La Kyrsiew packet:

> It has taken almost two centuries for the Khasi Hills to fulfil their early promise. Cultivated in a small tea plantation on the banks of Umiam Lake, at an altitude of between 1,100 and 1,400 metres above sea level, La Kyrsiew, a tea of exceptional quality, combines the fragrance and delicacy imparted by the cool, fresh mountain air with the liquor and body of the finest teas from the steamy plains of Assam.

Chapter Three

TWO OLD DELHIWALAS

In 1988 the historian William Dalrymple wrote an article for *The Tatler*, 'The Last Stayers-On'. In 2006 he told me that only one of his subjects was still alive, and she was Anne Wright (see Chapter One). Of all his stayers-on I am most sorry not to have met Norah Nicholson, because she was a legend in her lifetime, a relic of the Raj who could flourish only in India where spectacular eccentricity is accepted as commonplace. She died in 1989 when she trod on her pet cobra.

In fact one of the greatest legends of all in British India was her great uncle, Brigadier General John Nicholson, known as 'The Lion of the Punjab', 'Black Jack' or 'The Hero of Delhi'. You could say that he was elevated above legend because during his lifetime he was actually deified by a sect that called themselves 'Nikal Seynis'. This hero worship embarrassed 'Black Jack', himself a fire and brimstone Christian, so that he flogged members of the sect who became too demonstrative. He was killed while commanding the British and Indian force that recaptured Delhi during the Mutiny of 1857 and is buried near the centre of action, the Kashmir Gate. Norah was the last surviving member of his family and she lived nearby.

Her home was a dilapidated bungalow, shored up with tin sheets and tarpaulins. According to Dalrymple, peacocks sometimes fell through the roof while she was asleep – 'it's rather a bore to wake up and find a peacock in bed with you' – and pigs nosed around her larder. Norah was proud and obstinate. She had refused to pull strings when she had been evicted from government lodgings without a pension after a bureaucratic tangle. She could have lived in an old person's home owned by St James's church, where she was a faithful member of the congregation for many years, but she preferred her independence. She had the photo album and memories of a titled old 'memsahib' more often found living in Wiltshire. She had been a friend of Lady Mountbatten, an occasional nanny to Indira Gandhi's little boys and a part-time actress for the South East Asia Command in productions like *The Man in the Bowler Hat*. She showed William Dalrymple a photo of herself at the 150th anniversary of St James's church just across the road. In it she was wearing a 1930s cloche hat and shaking hands with an Indian general. 'I call that photograph "India pays homage to England",' she said. 'You know, the trouble with Indians is that they have no sense of humour. I wanted to dress up as a witch for the anniversary, but they wouldn't let me.' She must have worn the title Relic of the Raj with pride, but she was certainly no misfit in modern India. She spoke Hindi fluently, stood content-edly in the milk queue and had many Indian friends. She had been cast out of her home, but she was still a *Delhiwala*, a citizen of the nation's capital (*wala* is an Urdu suffix added to a word that defines its meaning, as in *carwala*, 'the owner of a car'). That is true of the two last – probably the very last – British 'stayers-on' in Delhi who are the subjects of this essay: Nigel Hankin and Father Ian Weathrall. Without moving with the times, how else could they have survived for over sixty years?

Nigel Hankin is a recluse. In fact nobody I have met knows where he lives. He swore me to secrecy even about the location of my letter drop asking for a meeting, and he replied by letter; no phone, no fax, no email, no address. 'I'm still in the steam age about communica-tions,' he wrote. He told me on our third meeting that he lives an elderly bachelor life (he was born in Bexhill, Sussex, in 1920) in an austere flat. In the searing heat of a Delhi summer he is without air-conditioning or running water; he has to get up at 4.30 a.m. to

activate the electric pump that gives him his daily water ration. His
faithful servant of forty years' service brings him eggs and the newspaper for breakfast, 'porridge once a week'. (And it was his faithful
servant who found Nigel dead in bed on 30 November 2007 after
this book had been writtten.) In the circumstances he is an unlikely
guide for tourists wishing to look round old Delhi, but this is how
he earns his money. Our first meeting a few years ago began badly.

His appearance as he unfolded his angular frame from a bicycle
rickshaw outside the hotel was startling. Very tall and gangly, he
began on top with straggly white hair, a bony face and black-framed,
bottle-thick glasses; he ended below with running shoes. In between
he wore, as he always does, dingy brown slacks, a threadbare jacket
and a wool vest. He carried a worn satchel containing the tools of
his trade, ancient press cuttings held together by sellotape and pasted
into his scrapbook and a cheap turban for wearing in holy places.
When I told him about the size and composition of our party, he
became a bit grumpy. He was used, he said, to small groups of VIPs
supplied by the High Commission. When I introduced him to the
group, he spoke to them as if they knew nothing about India, which
was far from the case. I pointed this out to him in a quiet moment,
and he apologised: 'I thought they were American. Some Americans
are completely ignorant about India. I don't like taking them but we
all have to earn a living.' We set off in the minibus, Nigel barking at
the driver *jaldo karo* ('hurry up') and to any beggars getting too close
chalo ('go away!')

He took us first to Coronation Park, a misnomer these days, if
ever there was one, for a desolate flood plain on the northern outskirts of Delhi. We stood before a lone obelisk marking the site of the
1911 *durbar* (an Urdu word introduced by the Mughals for a 'grand
assembly'), where George V declared that Delhi was to succeed
Calcutta as capital of the British Raj. Then we squeezed through
a locked gate to view fallen statues of a few viceroys collected in
a semi-circle on scrubland. Mysteriously, there were more plinths
than statues. Hankin settled under a tree, pulled out of his satchel
the *Illustrated London News* of 1911 and read aloud an account of the
durbar on this very spot, a magnificent pageant of parading elephants

and bejewelled maharajas pledging loyalty to the King Emperor. He
pointed out that the statue of George V had been sawn into pieces
after Independence for removal from the centre of Delhi and crudely
reassembled here. 'He's got a wonderful backside though. His cloak
was ermine you know.' It was a sobering visit for lovers of the Raj:

> 'My name is Ozymandias, king of Kings
> Look on my works, ye Mighty, and despair'.
> Nothing beside remains. Round the decay
> Of that colossal wreck, boundless and bare
> The lone and level sands stretch far away.

Hankin seemed to relish the symbolism of it all.

That afternoon his behaviour became disturbingly eccentric. He
took us to the old Muslim market of Chandni Chowk near the Red
Fort, a labyrinth of congested, polluted streets that can be threatening
to outsiders. Here he increased his pace, darting up the most urine-
smelling, pokey alleys, at one stage leaping on to a bicycle rickshaw
as if challenging us to follow him. He is a tough old bird. He seemed
to be making a statement: I'm an old Delhiwala and I'm going to
confront you with the real India. We followed him through the sari
bazaar, the electronic parts bazaar, the plastic-bottle-top bazaar to the
spice market. By now Nigel was in an excited state. He knew his
spices, as he had been Manager of the British High Commission
Club. He described in detail the aromatic and medicinal properties
of nutmeg, myrrh, anise, pumpkin, sugar and capsicum. He was a
popular figure here and obviously at ease.

Later I read an article by an American tourist that showed Nigel
and the Chandni Chowk in their true light:

> 'Welcome to deepest, darkest Delhi, where no white man doth tread,'
> Nigel Hankin said in mock cadences.
>
> 'We're putting ourselves in your hands,' I gamely replied to the man
> whom diplomat friends had called Delhi's best kept secret.
>
> It wasn't until after braving the 'deepest, darkest' staircase that
> I began to loosen up. I began to trust Nigel. Revulsion turned to

wonder. Suddenly, from inside a stall a boy stretched out his hand, blocking my path and trying to force something on me. I shook my head as I had learned to dozens of times.

Yeh aapke liye hai – 'This is for you,' the boy said, appealing to Nigel.

'He means it as a gift,' Nigel said gently. 'Go ahead, take it.'

The boy poured a dozen green pods into my palm. As I closed my hand over the pods, I thought of the even greater gift my guide had bestowed: without him I'd never have made it here.

'That's green cardamom,' Nigel said matter of factly. 'Very valuable. Crush it up, put it in your cup, and you'll have *masala chai* for bed tea.'

Nigel Hankin arrived in Delhi in July 1945. He had fought with the Second Army in North Africa and was on his way to Burma when the A Bomb ended the War. He decided to stay. 'I just loved it then. The place was so open. There used to be deer so we went hunting and swam in the Yamuna River.' After Independence he worked as a military secretary in British Army HQ and lived an insular life in the army mess. It was a 'stuffy, supercilious life' that cared little about the India outside. Then came Gandhi's murder and funeral in 1948. It opened Hankin's eyes:

> When I saw Gandhi's body on his funeral car and the tears in the eyes of the people as they lined the Rajghat and Governor General Mountbatten seated not on a throne but on a carpet facing the funeral pyre in a dusty piece of scrubland, I realised something of his stature in India. I wanted to learn more about the country and I'm still learning.

He left the army to run his own mobile film company, taking a van of film equipment round India, shooting weddings and festivals and screening black and white Indian movies on a 16-mm projector. It was his initiation into the real India and he loved it. A visit Home in 1951 confirmed his view that the climate and post-war Britain were not for him. He has lived in Delhi ever since, spending most of his career in secretarial jobs at the High Commission. His brother came to visit him years ago, but did not share Nigel's enthusiasm: 'He said there were too many Indians.' Now he is settled into old age: 'I've been over most of India but I don't travel much any more. I'm very happy with Indian beer and hopefully on my evenings with Indian friends we end up with whisky.' He sees little of the High Commission these days: 'There are still people there who are supercilious about India. They stay in that compound and never go out.' But he goes to the annual garden party on the Queen's Birthday.

Nigel Hankin's legacy will be the several editions of *Hanklyn-Janklyn: A Stranger's Rumble-Tumble Guide to Some Words, Customs and Quiddities Indian and Indo-British*. From this arresting title we infer that this is a dictionary of words that have passed between the English and Indian languages, some in complete form and some in semantic miscegenation, during the 400 years of the British presence in India. It is also a guidebook intended, says Nigel in his Preface, 'to provide background information for the stranger residing in India'. Such a one, we learn from *Hanklyn-Janklin*, was once known in East India Company days as a 'griffin' from an eighteenth-century English term for 'newly arrived and ignorant', a word now obsolete. Why the rhyming slang of the title? Hankin is paying homage to his inspiration, the earlier dictionary *Hobson-Jobson: A Spice-Box of Etymological Curiosities and Colourful Expressions* published in 1886. One of its authors was Colonel Henry Yule (the same family as Andrew Yule who started the managing agency in Calcutta), who believed that a catchy title was more likely to sell than a textbook, and Hankin followed his good advice. There is too, says Hankin, a less commercial justification, for Indians are fond of 'jingle or echo words, so that one may give a party-warty, where one may drink a whisky-pisky or a cup of chaiwai': so 'jingle' to 'jangle' to 'janklyn'. He is fascinated with words, particularly the north Indian words from Hindi or Urdu that have passed into Indian English.

In fact this is how he began his dictionary. A newly arrived British doctor at the High Commission gave him a list of twenty Indian words he had read in his English newspaper in Delhi and asked for their meaning and derivation. One of them, for instance, was the word *gherao*, which comes from the Hindi word 'to surround' and was used in the notorious labour disputes of the 1970s as a noun to mean 'a surround of the manager's office'; it is now in *The Oxford*

English Dictionary. So Nigel set to work, and *Hanklyn-Janklin* is the result. He told me he had received 'not a *pice*' (an anglicism for the smallest unit of Indian currency, from the Hindi word *paise* for 'small change') in royalties from his publisher, so that, in Indo-British speak, we might well say his publisher was *picey* (an anglicism for 'mean') and, since a *bandh* (Hindi word for 'a knot', used as slang for 'a strike') was not in Nigel's nature, he should have gathered his friends for a *gherao*. Indo-British compilation is as addictive as crossword puzzles.

Bernard Shaw remarked that Britain and America are two countries divided by a common language. In the same way, India and Britain are two countries uneasily united by a divergent linguistic heritage: Sanskrit. It was the polymath Sir William Jones, founder of the Asiatic Society of Bengal in Calcutta, who first pointed this out in a seminal lecture in 1786:

> The Sanscrit language, whatever be its antiquity, is of a wonderful structure; more perfect than the Greek, more copious than the Latin, and more exquisitely refined than either, yet bearing to both of them a stronger affinity, both in the roots of verbs and in the forms of grammar, that could not possibly have been produced by accident; so strong indeed, that no philologer could examine them all three, without believing them to have sprung from some common source which, perhaps, no longer exists.

The source was the Aryan peoples who lived in the Eurasian steppes in the fifth or fourth millennium BC and then moved west into Europe and east into Persia and north India. Darius the Great, 521–486 BC, called himself 'son of a Persian, having Aryan lineage'. Hence the Indo-European languages, so-called, the discovery of which put paid to the eighteenth-century European orthodoxy that all languages were derived from Hebrew. The earliest literary record of Indian culture is the hymns and chants of the *Vedas* composed in ancient Sanskrit around 1000 BC. 'We are the same people,' Nigel told me with conviction. 'Some went west and some went east. We have different colour skins because some have been out in the sun longer.' He is excited by the etymology of words from the Sanskrit and gave

me a number of examples. 'Look it up, look it up!' he ordered peremptorily. I read aloud from my copy of *Hanklyn-Janklin*: '*Karishma*,
a word from Persian used by both Hindus and Muslims to mean a
miracle or divine action. Closely linked to the classical Greek *kha-
risma* with almost the same meaning, grace or favour from a deity.
Also a girl's name.'[1] 'Take *igg*,' demanded Nigel, 'the Sanskrit word
for "fire"; obviously as in "ignite" and the Indian word is *aglio* meaning "to set fire to". Both *ag* and *igg* obviously come from the same
Sanskrit word.'

Hundreds of years ago the Hindus of North India spoke a regional
language of which the written form had a Sanskrit base. But from
the thirteenth century onwards invading Muslims adulterated this
Hindi with Persian (*farsi*), Arabic and Turkic words, and from this
Urdu evolved, the word coming from central Asia and meaning
'encampment'. Urdu was a linking language, 'the speech of soldiers'.
It became the new vernacular understood throughout north India.
Under the Mughals, Urdu written in Arabic was the language of
government, and, when the British Raj took over, it kept Urdu as its
Indian language of preference, but this time written in the Roman
script. *Hind*, in fact, is the old Urdu name for India, so that Queen
Victoria was *Kaisar-i-Hind* – 'Empress of India'. At Independence
this faced the new Indian government with a dilemma. How could
it use Urdu as the official language when it was appropriated by
Pakistan and both new states were searching for their own cultural
and historical identity?

The new Constitution declared that 'Hindi in the *Devanagari*
[Sanskrit] script shall be the official language of the Union' (Article
343 (1)), and from then on enthusiasts for the new nation tried to
weed out Persian forms and English neologisms, replacing them with
Sanskrit words if they existed and inventing them if they did not. For
example, the name they gave to the state TV system was *Doordarshan*
from the Sanskrit words *dur* ('far') and *darshan* ('vision'). Today's
written Hindi is very different from the Urdu used throughout
northern India in the first half of the twentieth century. The process of Sanskritisation has meant that anyone born before the 1940s
has to make an effort to understand it. The reverse is happening in

Pakistan, where Urdu written in a form of Arabic is the official language (as it is also the language of Muslims in north India). Now the youth of the two countries have difficulty understanding each other unless they speak and write English. No doubt for this reason Article 343 (2) of the 1947 Constitution, which 'provided for the continuing use of English as an official language for 15 years', has been extended indefinitely. Things might have been different if Mahatma Gandhi had had his way. He proposed that the new language should be Urdu written in the Roman script, but Hindu nationalists, who rightly regarded language as the core of identity, rejected this.

As *Hobson-Jobson* did before, *Hanklyn-Janklin* identifies many Indian words for clothing now in common use in Britain that date from the East India Company's textile trade: *pyjama* (a Hindi word), *dungaree* (an English word invented by the East India Company to describe coarse cloth), *shawl* (Persian) and *chintz* (either from the Portuguese *chita* or the Hindi *chint*). Then there are the words brought home a century or so later by the British Army: *dekko* ('have a look' from the Hindi verb *dekhna*, 'to see'), *dixie* (a camp cooking pot) and *doolally* (meaning a bit 'bonkers', from the camp at Deolali near Bombay where troops being repatriated on medical grounds waited to go home). *Hanklyn-Janklin* also lists more recent words now part of British vocabulary that stem from the Western interest in Eastern religion, such as *guru*, *nirvana*, *avatar* and *mantra*, and the Indian or Pakistani restaurant additions to our vocabulary, such as *balti* and *vindaloo*. This last word is the name for 'a strong vegetable curry' that has gone full circle, as the dish originated in Portuguese Goa, where it was called *vinha de alhos* or 'with wine and garlic'. Reversing the linguistic transfer are the many English words in common use in India, particularly those that date from the industrial or technological revolutions. Take the railways, for example: 'train station' and 'broad gauge' have survived intact in Indian usage; 'tram', with a little alteration, has become *tam-tam* in Hindi; while other phrases are reduced to acronym, such as WT, meaning 'without ticket', to counteract which are the TTIs or 'Travelling Ticket Inspectors'.

Simply listing words from *Hanklyn-Janklin* does not do justice to Nigel Hankin's magpie-like mind, nor to his erudition, nor to his humour. In fact Hankin comes alive in the pages of his dictionary. In interview he is brusque, whether from shyness, insecurity or the stupidity of my questions it is hard to tell. 'Look it up! Look it up!' is his usual answer. So I looked up the very first entry of all: '*aagey wala*; the "man in front". On a golf course an Anglicism for the caddy walking ahead with the duty of marking the fall of the ball. Slang for a penis.' Then there is my favourite example of Nigel's lavatorial humour: '*Goli*; a small ball or medicinal pill or testicle, possibly from a railway station vendor between the wars who hawked a well-known patent medicine with the cry *Beecham sahib ke golihan* or "Beecham sahib's balls".' Presumably the cricket phrase 'hit in the goolies' for a painful blow from a cricket ball that strikes the testicles comes from the same source?

The Indian diarrhoea well known to visitors as 'Delhi belly' gives Nigel global scope: 'akin to Gippy Tummy, Rangoon Runs, Montezuma's revenge, Kathmandu quickstep and Turkey Trots. As a pleasantry, Delhi Belly can be the increase in girth often observed on a diplomat after a year's social whirl in the capital.'

Hankin relishes low life in the same way that Henry Mayhew did in his famous study of 1861 *London Labour and the London Poor*: '*Tonga*; an Anglicism from the Hindi *tanga* for a two-wheeled horse drawn vehicle. In action the driver clucks to encourage his pony and loudly addresses other road users to move out of the way in such terms as [a mild example this] *Eh, charas pinewala*, "Oh, drinker and smoker of hash".'

On religious matters he speaks his mind tactfully: '*Harijan* or "one close to God": in spite of the generally used designation given by the Mahatma in the 1930s, many caste Hindus do not accept that the *harijan* is close to God; in fact his position may be thought to be one of considerable distance.'

Hankin cannot be boring. He is in the tradition of idiosyncratic but authoritative word compilers who have given their names to their dictionaries: *Dr Johnson's Dictionary, Roget's Thesaurus, Fowler's Modern English Usage*. How does *Hanklyn-Janklin* compare with *Hobson-Jobson*? Henry Yule and his collaborator Arthur Burnell, who worked for the Madras Civil Service, were the more scholarly and historical. As lexicographers they were concerned with the extraordinarily numerous and diverse cultures that had contributed to Indian civilisation. As Yule put it: 'the words with which we have to do are in fact organic remains deposited under the various currents of external influence that washed the shores of India during twenty centuries or more.' This can make dry reading, but at other times it is irresistible. For instance, the first meaning of shampoo is 'to massage after a hot bath'. *Hobson-Jobson* tells its linguistic history:

> *Shampoo*, v. To knead and press the muscles with the view of relieving fatigue etc. The Hindi verb is *champna*, from the imperative of which *champo* this is probably a corruption. The process is described by Edward Terry, *A Voyage to East India*, in 1616: 'Taking thus their ease, they often call their Barbers, who tenderly gripe and smite their Armes and other parts of their bodies to stir the blood. It is a pleasing wantonnesse, and much valued in these hot climates.' The process was familiar to the Romans whose slaves were called *tractatrix* but with the ancients it was allied to a vice, for which there is no ground that we know in the Indian custom.[2]

Hobson-Jobson then gives six examples of how the British in India have used the word beginning in 1748. This is my favourite:

> There is sometimes a voluptuousness in the climate of India, a stillness in nature, an indescribable softness, which soothes the mind, and gives it up to the most delightful sensations: independent of the effects of opium, **champoing**, and other luxuries indulged in by oriental sensualists – *James Forbes, Oriental Memoirs, 4 vols 1813*.

True imperialists of the late nineteenth century, Yule and Burnell looked down on the Indo-British vocabulary. You can sense their superciliousness: 'Considering the long intercourse with India, it is noteworthy that the additions that have thus accrued to the English language are, from the intellectual standpoint, of no intrinsic value. Nearly all the borrowed words refer to material facts, or to peculiar customs, and though a few of them furnish allusions to the penny-a-

liner, they do not represent new ideas.' Hankin would not agree with
this at all. He acknowledges *Hobson-Jobson* as 'my bedside companion
for at least four decades', but his own compilation is not only more
readable and more useful but also more admiring of India too.

However, the pity is that, unless Nigel Hankin radically revises
the fifth edition, *Hanklyn-Janklin* will become out of date. Not
surprisingly for an old bachelor who admits to being 'in the com-
munications stone-age', he seems scarcely aware of a new adman's
language in North India. This is *Hinglish*, and it is rapidly becoming the currency of the internet, cable TV and advertising. Similarly
there is so-called *Tanglish* in South India (Tamil plus English), and
Banglish in East India (Bengali plus English). *Hinglish* is the hybrid
language of global commerce, of American and British multination-
als, which have a vast market in their sights provided they appeal to
the Indian consciousness. It is the language of the Indianised slogan
that also recognises the trendiness of English. Hence the Pepsi ad
catchphrase 'Ask for More' is turned into *Yeh, Dil Maange More* ('the
heart wants more'). Coke has retaliated with its own *Hinglish* slogan
Life ho to aisi ('Life should be like this'). Domino Pizza asks *Hungry
kya?* ('Are you hungry?') and Macdonalds have the knowing *What
your bahana is?* (*bahana* is Hindi for 'excuse', so 'what's your excuse
for eating MacDonalds?'). There is a buzz about *Hinglish*:

> Before, advertisements used to be conceived in English and then just
> translated into Hindi as an afterthought. But that doesn't work with
> Indians who now have a smattering of English. You may be under-
> stood but not vibed with [as in 'vibration' – a word that is too slang
> for the OED but is now everyday speech among Indian advertisers].
> That's why all the multinationals now speak *Hinglish* in their ads.[3]

Hinglish has spread to the trendy university campuses of India.
Perhaps we should call this *Hindi-Americana*, an offshoot of the
'MTV culture' and the increasing desire of Indian students to enrol
in North American rather than British higher education. The young
émigré Indian asks: Is British English or American English the more
advantageous? A selection of words current on the campuses of

Delhi and Mumbai might include: *batchmate* (a schoolmate of the same grade); *arbit* (slang for arbitrary, as in 'what an arbit ending that movie had!'); *pass-out* (to graduate from college). I would add more speculatively *eve-teasing*, as in the sexual harassment of women, and *prepone*, the antonym for postpone. I recently came across *Mem banke kidhar jaa rahi hai?*, which may be translated as:'Where are you going looking like a *mem*?' Memsahib now means 'white woman' or a girl wearing Western fashion.

Nigel told me that when he listens to AIR (the state-run All India Radio, see Chapter Six) he hears a *potpourri* (from the French,'hotch-potch') of language. This is how it should be, he says, for what did his mentor Yule say about 'the organic remains [of language] deposited under the various currents of external influence that washed the shores of India during twenty centuries or more'? *Hinglish* is a more trendy *potpourri* now found in the newspapers, like this film review of *Namastey* printed in *The Times of India* of March 2007. The Hindi words are in italics and my translations are added in brackets:

> Vipul Shah's celebration of this *sarson ka saag* [local Punjabi dish, a metaphor for 'home food'] versus sauce and finger chips potpourri is essentially a fun film which pitches the *Purab Paschim* ['East–West'] metaphor in muted tones. Troubled by his daughter's wild and *videshi* ['foreign' ways], Rishi Kapoor bundles her off from London to Punjab to find a suitable *desi* ['homeland'] for her … But our girl's quite a shrew and has an ace up her sleeve. She promises her *bhola-bhala* ['innocent'] groom a *subaag raat* ['honeymoon night'] only in London and brings him to foreign shores to declare he's the persona non grata in her life. She's going to wed the *gora* ['whiteman'] who wooes her with vintage wine on his yacht. So what does our never-say-die Indian do? Gives all the *goras* ['whitemen'] a tutorial on India and makes everyone realise; East or West, *Bharat* ['India'] is best.

Not surprisingly, this trendy *Hinglish* does not go down well among the Indian establishment. English is still an official language of central and state government, so that, for example, on AIR the Prime Minister addresses the nation in English and stockmarket reports are always in English. Moreover, this is the formal English as taught in Indian schools from old textbooks like that of J.C. Nesfield (1898), because neither government institutions nor educated Indians who prize 'proper' English consider Indo-British, never mind *Hinglish*, to be 'correct usage'. What is considered 'proper' other eyes may well read as archaic. The influence of the *babu* or government clerk since East India Company days means that letters are still signed 'please do the needful' and 'you will be intimated shortly'. Apparently, an attempt by the Oxford University Press to publish a dictionary of Indo-British words was a failure because customers preferred the 'proper' English dictionary. British writers like P.G. Wodehouse and Enid Blyton are still popular in India, although their views express the racist attitudes of the 1930s and 1940s.

Whether English should be an official language of government has always been a contentious issue. Mark Tully (see Chapter Six) wrote in *No Full Stops in India* (1991): 'The best way to destroy a people's culture and identity is to undermine its religion and its language. We, the British, as India's rulers did that.' The British-born educationalist James Gibson, who stayed on in India for over forty years after Independence, quoted in his diary for 1968 from a letter he had just received from a former pupil: 'I feel that Hindi should become the national language as soon as possible and that English should become a foreign language taught as such. We must evolve a post-Independence Indian identity, not a half-baked Anglo-Indian one.' The trouble was, Gibson replied, that India has so many mother tongues. In 1963, when he had been headmaster of the famous independent school Mayo College, he had asked the boys to welcome the chief guest for Speech Day in their first languages, and they did so in twenty-three different languages or dialects. English was the only language they had in common. When Mrs Gandhi's government tried to force Hindi on south India in the 1960s, the Tamil speakers rioted in the streets. In 1996 the Indian Prime Minister was a Tamil who spoke no Hindi, so that, when he delivered the traditional Independence Day speech to the nation in Hindi, he did so in a language he did not understand, reading from a script that made no sense, as it was written in Kannada, or Tamil. The gap between the English-speaking elite in India and the majority of Indians who speak no English at all – Nigel Hankin estimates that number as well over 600 million – is exacerbated by the English-speaking TV and IT global world we live in. The Indian middle class is signed up to it, while the vast mass of Indians are excluded: another of the contradictions of India.

I asked Nigel Hankin if he regretted that English was still the official language of India, but he was not disposed to discuss the matter at all sympathetically:

> *NH*: Why should I regret it? It's so convenient for me. The whole world finds in convenient. They can come here and talk English, which is something they can't do in Japan.
>
> *Me*: But surely, it divides Indian society?
>
> *NH*: It does. Those who are English speakers and those who are not. Yes, if you don't know English, it's very hard to get on.

It was time for Nigel to get on. We walked to a shop in the local market and tried to use the photocopying machine. He peered at the smudgy grey print through his thick glasses: *Bekar kaam hai! Acka namin hai*! ('It's no good'), he barked. Eventually we found one that worked and then he said, 'You won't be needing me any more.' It was a statement and I watched him loping off into the crowd by the Kashmir Gate, an old Englishman with his white hair bobbing up and down into the distance. I can imagine him reading this essay and saying 'Look it up, Look it up': '*Chapati* school of writing: a term referring to the habit of some English authors writing about India of inserting in their texts as many local words as possible with the intention of adding ethnic colour.'

'O for a thousand tongues to sing my dear Redeemer's praise' began the first hymn. I wish! Joining the Sunday congregation of the Cathedral Church of the Redemption in New Delhi and listening to the self-conscious, tuneless singing that is heard in most Protestant churches these days, I longed for a Welsh choir. The slip of paper in front of me, its edges stirred by the ceiling fans, encouraged us to 'Come join the Fun' at the annual sale of the Missionary Society, but the invitation surely fell on deaf ears. The cathedral was built in the Romanesque style of Edward Lutyens in the 1920s with the intention, in Viceroy Hardinge's words, of testifying to 'the ideal and fact of British rule in India', yet now it seemed more like the mausoleum of the Raj.

Appearances, however, were deceptive. As the congregation queued up to take Communion, I counted over 200 people from many different countries, so that I was reminded of my Sunday School book in the 1950s with pictures of 'the family of man'. Indians and Africans with their colourful national dress dispelled the gloom; several British couples took Communion too, showing that the Raj connection had not been totally severed. I wondered if everyone would take Communion or whether some would be given a blessing, because it is not unusual, even in the Cathedral Church, for non-Christians to expect to receive the sacraments. After all, visitors to Sikh *gurudwaras* or Hindu *mandirs* are offered *prasad*, food that is blessed, and it is an insult not to accept it. India is a multi-faith country with give and take between religions, and offence may be caused when ceremonies are not shared. I heard afterwards that a priest here had a prayer book thrown at him when he refused Communion to a non-Christian.

My attention, however, was on the priest at the altar. As old and British as the church itself, he still possessed a vigour that the church, perhaps, did not deserve. There was something monumental about him; tall but stooped, his brown face, balding head and deep-set eyes weathered by heat and glare and his features sharpened with age, he looked down at his congregation like a living statue. I noticed that under his surplice he wore a heavy-duty white cassock and below that his feet were bare. He was the remarkable Father Ian Weathrall, aged eighty-five.

Afterwards I waited for Father Weathrall to greet his congregation outside and for it to be replaced inside by hundreds of Tamil Christians from south India waiting for their vernacular service. Surprisingly to me, Christians make up the third largest religious grouping in India, after the Hindus and Muslims but before the Sikhs, Buddhists and Jains. I waited for some time. The good Father knew his flock, and there was much small talk over orangeade and biscuits as the sun began to beat down. It was definitely a cathedral congregation, I noticed, made up of a sprinkling of diplomats and tourists and then the prosperous Delhi middle classes wearing in many cases European clothes and with their Maruti cars parked nearby. I wondered whether many of the families were Anglo-Indian. Then we went off in a little taxi that was booked for Father Weathrall every Sunday. He squeezed in without effort and continued his small talk uninterrupted. Despite his age he is a man who likes to keep in touch and drop a few surprises:

> I'm reading three books at the moment. There's Willy's on the Mutiny (William Dalrymple, *The Last Mughal*) that makes it out to be more of a *jihad* than I thought. Apparently all the Indian Christians were murdered on sight. Then there's a new book by Edward Luce (*In Spite of the Gods: The Strange Rise of Modern India*). He really understands this country. I've been reading about your father too [in the 1960s my father was a Canon of Worcester Cathedral – not the sort of reputation to be remembered in New Delhi many years later]. I'm addicted to religious biographies and he's in a book about Bishop Kemp. I knew him of course.

We chatted about the service as if we were still in a coffee bar in Winchester, where we had met a few months before:

> Some of those Victorian hymns are quite dreadful. You didn't hear what the choir sang during communion? Thank goodness! There was one line that went 'Take time to be Holy'. What do those words mean? You see, you get this American music that comes in quite cheaply, whereas English hymnals are more expensive. There's that lovely hymn 'God be in my head and in my understanding' but they don't know it here. We've never sung it. We have this cheap American music instead and some of it's quite dreadful.

Father Weathrall nipped out of the taxi and, speaking fluent Urdu, which he told me he had learnt in the war serving in the 9/16th

Punjabi Regiment of the Indian Army, bought eggs and fruit for our breakfast. When he climbed back in – he was wearing sandals now – he became more sombre:

> Did you notice that very tall person sitting opposite you wearing *kurta pyjama*? I've never seen him in the Cathedral before and I'm not sure about him. You see Indians are very touchy about outsiders saying something insulting about their faiths. From time to time people drop in to watch what's going on. You have to be a little careful, that's all.

The taxi drew up at Number 7, Court Lane, a grey stone house that, apart from the wide arches of the veranda, could have been in a town like Huddersfield where wealthy industrialists built their villas a hundred years ago. But sunk into the terrace floor outside the front door was a design that created quite a different impression. I made out the ancient Christian sign of the fish with a line of its body transformed into a conch shell, the Eastern call to worship. On either side of the fish were two large footprints, the ancient sign of pilgrimage. We had arrived at the monastery of the Delhi Brotherhood of the Ascended Christ founded as far back as 1877 by Bishop Fosse Westcott of Cambridge University. One of its aims has always been to learn from eastern religions, hence the conch shell, and perhaps because of this it is the only Protestant monastery left in India.

Three of the four monks are now Indian, so Father Weathrall is the last of the long line of British Brothers who have committed their lives to India. He is without doubt the longest-serving Christian missionary in India and quite probably the only permanent one left from abroad. The Indian government has always resented Christian missionaries and since 1967 it has denied them residential visas unless they held them before that date. Even so, residential visas expire after a few years, and in 2006 the good Father found 'inquiries had been made' before his visa was renewed – this after sixty years of selfless service. In fact, although Article 25 of the Indian Constitution guarantees every citizen 'freedom of conscience and free profession, practice and propaganda of religion', several states have laws making religious conversions a criminal offence. The conversion of Hindus to Christianity is a particularly touchy subject, and the current practice of some visiting missionaries on tourist visas who make instant conversions, believe it or not paid for by an American foundation on a per capita basis, is much resented. Perhaps it is for this reason that recently Christian churches have been burnt down and old cemeteries desecrated. In one shocking incident that is frequently recalled an Australian missionary and his two sons were torched to death in their car in Andhra Pradesh. All this makes the good Father anxious.

Ever since British missionaries arrived in India, there has been a tension between fundamentalists who believe that Christianity is the exclusive, only true, religion, that only Christians may be saved, and liberals who believe that Christianity must coexist with other faiths in this most religious of countries and that salvation needs to be left to the Almighty. Father Weathrall belongs firmly to the latter, liberal, persuasion, and the Cambridge Brotherhood, as it was called initially, has done so from the beginning. Now all the main Christian denominations accept that the price of survival is to accept India's pluralist traditions and not press for conversions. This even applies to the Jesuits. A priest told Mark Tully, the former BBC Correspondent in India: 'The Church does not convert; God does and God does not seem to regard this is a high priority.' It was not ever thus.

A perfect example of this Christian dichotomy between the fundamentalists and the liberals, between the Old Testament and the New, may be seen in St James's church at the Kashmir Gate, where Father Weathrall was the chaplain between 1951 and 1976. It is more familiarly known as Skinner's church after its founder Sir James Skinner. He was an Anglo-Indian with a Rajput mother and Scots father, and because of this he was not entitled to serve in the East India Company army; so he founded his own regiment instead, Skinner's Horse. His men became known as the Yellow Boys after the colour of their uniform. Converted to Christianity and at one time lying badly wounded on a battlefield, he vowed to build a church if he recovered. St James's was consecrated in 1836 as the first Christian church in Delhi. Skinner also renovated a mosque in honour of his chief wife, a Muslim, and built a temple for his Hindu mother, so he was definitely not a Christian hard-liner. 'Wherever there is God there is religion,' he said expansively. After his death his children, 'of all hues and colours' from his wives and a dozen concubines, became an extensive Delhi family. Many of them are buried in the dry, dusty churchyard of St James's. Skinner's Horse still serves in mechanised form in the Indian Army.

At the time of the Indian Mutiny in 1857 the chaplain of St James's was the Revd Midgeley John Jennings, an uncompromising evangelical who saw himself as 'Missionary to the Heathen'. His God-given task was to purge the false beliefs of the Indian, if necessary by force. 'The roots of ancient religions have in Delhi, as in all old places, struck deep and men must be able to fathom them in order to uproot them,' he preached. Instead the heathen should be converted to the Christian faith, 'the pearl of great price', the 'greatest blessing of the British Empire'. Jennings and his daughter were slaughtered by the mutineers as soon as the rebellion reached Delhi on 11 May 1857, and St James's was quickly sacked. One of the British congregation recorded: 'It was riddled with cannon balls, the marble-slabs and wooden altar rails were smashed and the bell ropes cut so that the bells crashed to the ground.' Today there is a memorial in St James's to Jennings and his daughter. It does not say 'Vengeance is mine sayeth the Lord', but that is the clear message. Close to it is another memorial to a Chinese convert, Dr Chaman Lal, who was also murdered that day. His plaque does carry an inscription: 'Lord, lay not this sin to their charge.' The Old Testament and the New, a doctrine of conquest and religious superiority next to the message of forgiveness, love and peace. The Jennings' bigotry that contributed to the Indian uprising of 1857 is as alive today among Christian evangelicals as is the pure Christianity of Dr Lal, personified in Father Weathrall and the social work of his Order.

Father Weathrall and I ate a simple breakfast sitting on benches at the long refectory table. On the walls were paintings by Indian Christian artists, showing, for example, the Virgin Mary wearing a sari and the ascended Christ floating above the Delhi rooftops. We moved to the threadbare common room, English magazines on coffee tables and easy chairs that sagged, the walls lined with dusty bookcases and the Brothers' rooms leading off, looking austere through their open doors. There were no other Brothers present. I got out my tape recorder, and Father Weathrall lay back so that his long frame and his chair sagged towards the floor.

'In India', he began, 'everyone believes in God. Divinity varies but everyone believes in a supreme being and Hinduism has all sorts of lesser deities. The West has given up on the idea of God at all.' He sighed. It seemed to me that there are so many Hindu gods and Hinduism is so all embracing that it might absorb Christianity, particularly with this trend in Christian worship towards Indianisation, or 'enculturalisation', as it is called. 'Oh, dear,' sighed Father Weathrall again:

Father Ian: What makes Christianity unique?

Me: That Jesus is the Son of God?

Father Ian: No! We've got plenty of sons of God. There are plenty of avatars about. No. Hindus also accept the austerities of Lent. They've got plenty of gurus or swamis who are being austere. No. It's the Resurrection. That's the thing. It's not Good Friday, because there are plenty of martyrs in Hinduism and Islam, but it's the Resurrection. That cuts straight across the idea of being reborn – the doctrine of *karma*. The fact that Christ was resurrected meant that he was absorbed in to the divinity and that's what makes Christianity unique in India.

Me: Do you think any believer may be saved, or only Christians?

Father Ian: Oh no! You've got to remember that the Holy Spirit works where it will and is not confined to the Christian faith. Bishop Westcott was one of the great pioneers of that. We must believe that the Holy Spirit is not confined to the Christian church.

Me: What do you think then of the evangelicals who believe that salvation is only for those who are baptised in the Holy Spirit?

Father Ian: That is wrong, erroneous, a sort of religious fundamentalism. Just go back into history a minute. It was religious

fundamentalism whether practised by Christians like the
Revd Jennings or Muslims preaching *Jihad* that caused
1857. It is dangerous and wrong.

Father Weathrall was probably thinking – and I certainly was – of churches like the Evangelical Church of India, the Assembly of God and the New Life Fellowship, all relatively new to India and all fast growing. According to some, this is where the future of Christianity in India lies. They have in common a strong emphasis on personal salvation, available only to believers, and a belief that the second coming of Christ is imminent; also a fundamentalist approach to the Bible and a belief in charismatic forms of worship such as spiritual healing and 'speaking in tongues'. It is heady stuff, particularly attractive to Hindus, because they do not have a corporate form of worship.

To young Indians it must seem light years away from the gloomy Victorian gothic churches built during the Raj and the half-hearted intonation of Victorian hymns. Father Weathrall, however, urged me not to judge the Indian Church by the Cathedral Church of the Redemption, for example. The future for him was in the countryside and south India, where services are far more Indianised both in art forms and in liturgy; where the congregation sit bare-footed on the floor of a purpose-built church, sing *bhajans* based on *bhakti* or traditional devotional music and take part in a service conducted in their own language. The Delhi Brotherhood has always been in the forefront of adapting Western Christianity to Indian conditions.

Bishop Westcott wrote in the beginning: 'The West has much to learn from the East and the lesson will not be learned until we hear the truth as it is apprehended by Eastern minds.' When the first six members of the Cambridge Brotherhood arrived in India only twenty years after the Mutiny, their overall aim was to set up a mission as a means towards founding an independent Christian church in India, 'a self-governing, self-supporting, self-propagating Church', as they put it. Their hope was to do this in an environment where the great faiths could mingle. As the first Head Brother, Edward Bickersteth, wrote: 'Indian Christianity can never be cast in the same mould as English Christianity. We must become Indians if we would win India for Christ.' This was an extraordinarily radical statement, the significance of which was pointed out by the historian Percival Spear, who taught in India for twenty years from the 1920s:

> Missions in the 19th century were mostly the ecclesiastical form of colonialism. Their object was to collect converts as imperialists collected subjects and they were as convinced of the inferiority of other world religions as imperialists were of other civilisations. This declaration that the West must learn from the East was therefore regarded by many missionaries as almost heretical and by many officials as seditious.[4]

The work of the early Brothers was hampered by the unforeseen requirement of taking over the administration of the Society for the Propagation of the Gospel (the SPG) and building up the Christian community in a devastated city. Nevertheless, their first achievement was to found St Stephen's College with five students, not one of them a Christian. As early as 1907, in the high noon of Lord Curzon's British Raj, the Brothers controversially elected an Indian Principal of the College, Susil Rudra. Now St Stephen's is a prestigious College of Delhi University.

Rudra was a friend of Charles Andrews, who joined the Brotherhood in 1904. He became the most radical and questioning Brother in its history. Such was the effect that India had on his life that he later called the date of his arrival 'a second birthday so that in a very real sense I am a *duvija* or twice born'. Through his struggle we can see the dilemma of the truly Christian priest working within the context of the British Empire. He wrote: 'I shall not soon forget the strangeness of my first few days in Delhi, the policemen saluting, the people salaaming, the Indian soldiers standing to attention, everyone making way. It was due to the simple fact that I was a Sahib.' He soon came to regard his status as pernicious: 'The position of Sahib is one of extraordinary danger for one who is to represent the poverty and humility of Christ, to live the life of the Crucified, to imitate Him who came "not to be ministered unto, but to minister". Yet the position of Sahib in the past has been almost forced upon the missionary.'[5] Moreover, the message of the Indian religious life was clear:

That true religion means renunciation is the strongest religious instinct among educated and uneducated Indians of all creeds. Poverty is the most suitable environment for spiritual growth … Christ commands us to cast off the Western leading strings, for it is neither our money nor our organisation that is being weighed in the balance. It is the intensity of our religious life.

Father Andrews's increasing unease with his status at least had a clear political resolution. Deeply affected by the so-called national movement, which he described as a 'heaving ferment like volcanic lava cracking through the surface of the soil', and disgusted by the racial undertones that separated British from Indian Christians, he became an outspoken advocate of total, unqualified Indian Independence. This was some time before most nationalists had reached that position.

In 1912 Andrews met the great Bengali poet, Hindu mystic and opponent of British colonialism, Rabindrath Tagore. They became friends. Andrews visited his ashram at Santiniketan and pondered how to fuse Western with Indian philosophy. Through him he met Mahatma Gandhi and travelled with him to South Africa to investigate the plight of indentured Indian labourers. Inevitably, he moved away from the Brotherhood and his Christian faith. What had begun as an empathetic wish to learn from Indian faiths now resulted in his questioning the basic tenets of Christianity like the Virgin birth and the Resurrection itself. At a Christmas Day service in 1912 Andrews heard Indian choirboys chant the *Quicunque Vult*: 'Whoesoever will be saved; before all things it is necessary that he hold the Catholick Faith. Which Faith except everyone keep whole and undefiled, without doubt he shall perish everlastingly.' It was an emotional tipping point. He was revolted that these dire threats should be put into the mouths of choirboys; shocked by the realisation that even Tagore would be consigned to hell. In a more modern and accommodating age like the 1960s these doubts might have been accepted or excused as metaphors but not in 1912. When he resigned from the Brotherhood and from the Christian ministry he left with affection but relief on both sides.

Eventually Andrews returned to the Christian faith. In the late 1930s he frequently wandered into 7 Court Lane, where he was well received. One Sunday he attended a service at St James's, after which an entry in the Church Record Book stated: 'Charles Freer Andrews desires to return thanks to Almighty God for being allowed to renew his ministry after many years.' In 1935 he was appointed a lecturer in Divinity at Cambridge University. He died in 1941 aged sixty-nine and was buried, as he wished in his will, 'in the Christian faith at St Paul's Cathedral, Calcutta'. He seems to have led a life of personal anguish, but the verdicts of history are definite though diverse. To British Christians in India he was a dissident. Had the Brotherhood followed his path, it would have cut itself off from the British Establishment and ceased to exist. But to many Indian Christians Andrews was a saint and to them his initials CFA stand for 'Christ's Faithful Apostle'.

Ian Weathrall arrived at Brotherhood House just a few years after the death of Father Andrews. He was born in Lancashire into an Anglo-Scots family in 1922. He followed both his father and grandfather into the Indian Army and was commissioned in 1943 into the 9/16th Punjabi Regiment. At first he was in a reserve battalion and taught jungle warfare prior to the invasion of Burma. He remembers a visit from the famous hunter Jim Corbett (see Chapter Four): 'I felt privileged. Extraordinary man. He loped like a wild animal; same speed whatever the terrain. In the evenings we would sit round the campfire and he would call up the wild animals. Once a tiger responded and lurked in the trees. You must have read his book *Jungle Lore*?'

Then he was sent to the North-West Frontier, which, as in the days of the Great Game, was vulnerable to infiltration and invasion from hostile powers; in this case the fascists. In fact nothing happened, and Ian Weathrall's different memory is of Dr Muhammad Jinnah's car being towed through Peshawar by enthusiastic supporters.

At the end of the war, Weathrall attended a selection weekend for ordinands at Brotherhood House. This was his first experience of a monastic order and it appealed to him. After studying theology at Kings College, London University, and serving his curacy in Winchester diocese, he returned to Delhi and took the vows of celibacy and life membership of the Brotherhood. He has kept the vows for fifty-six years and remained in Brotherhood House.

The same year, 1951, he also became chaplain of St James's church, still with a large congregation of British and Anglo-Indians. It was not long before his uncompromising Christian faith revealed itself from behind his smooth social manner, which was so useful on the expat party circuit. In those days a group of lepers gathered outside the church to beg for alms, and in 1957 some of them asked him to visit their slum dwelling at Jumna Bazaar near the cremation ground by the Yamuna River. One of them, a Tamil Christian, had died and needed a Christian funeral. Weathrall obliged, taking the service through an interpreter. Then he invited the Christian lepers from the colony of about 400 to come into St James's and take Holy Communion whenever they liked. 'This was considered quite a revolutionary act,' says the official history of the Brotherhood tactfully. Moreover, he took regular services for them in their slum dwelling over the next five years until the government moved the colony out.

From this beginning the Brotherhood under Father Weathrall, for he became Head Brother for the first time in 1969, moved from pastoral care into professional social work. In 1973 it set up as a Charitable Society with the name of the Delhi Brotherhood Society (DBS) and established a new base, the 'House of Hope', first in the re-settlement slums of Seemapuri and then in the squatting slums of Shahidnagar, both areas on the outskirts of east Delhi towards Uttar Pradesh. In the 1980s the latter was a vast area of reclaimed rural slum devoid of even basic facilities like electricity, running water, health services and schools. Here lived a population of perhaps 50,000, many of them Muslim immigrants. Now the DBS with aid from other charities employs a team of social workers to run community health projects, schools and practical training schemes. These include a novel street theatre project under Brother Solomon George to alert the community to the dangers of communal violence, environmental pollution and so on. In fact, very few of the inhabitants of these slum colonies are Christian, and the Brotherhood does not see proselytising as one of its purposes. This deeply impresses the SPG in

London: 'It is unconditional love in action,' the librarian told me, admiringly. I put this to Father Weathrall. Did the Brotherhood make any distinction as to the faith of those who wanted help?

Father Ian: Oh no! Of course not. No. No.

Me: But isn't there a temptation to preach The Word?

Father Ian: You do it discreetly, when the opportunity occurs. I call it divine intervention. But you musn't go out aggressively, not that kind of thing. Hindus particularly do not like dogma.

Also under Father Weathrall's headship, the Brotherhood fulfilled the wish of the founding fathers by taking a new lesson in Eastern spirituality. A French Benedictine Monk, Henri Le Saux, now using his Hindu name of Swami Abhishiktananda, befriended one of the Brothers, James Stuart, and introduced him at his ashram to silent prayer and meditation. Several of these Schools of Prayer were held at the Brotherhood in the 1970s. Stuart wrote:

During the day there were many periods of silent prayer, for which people sat in a still position they could keep for forty-five minutes without moving. They practised deep breathing. Each period began with the singing of a short Sanskrit mantra, starting in a natural voice and then fading away altogether. This was the path into silence. At the end of the period the same mantra was sung softly, gradually increasing again to the natural voice. At the end of the silence we were asked to take the spirit of silence with us as we left the chapel, not to hurry and not to engage in conversation unless it seemed the right thing to do, for five minutes.

The main aim of the founding Brothers was to use the mission as a means of establishing an independent Christian church in India. As Indian Independence came closer, so the move throughout India from 'Mission' to 'Church', as it was called, gradually advanced towards that goal. The old foreign missions withdrew, consigned to the colonial past. In 1947 the Church of South India was established, and in 1970 the six Protestant churches of North India – that is, the Anglicans, British Baptists, Congregationalists, Methodists, Brethren and Disciples of Christ, united into the Church of North India, the CNI. A new Book of Common Worship was agreed and translated into Urdu, Tamil and Hindi. It was Father Weathrall and another Brother, Christopher Joshua Robinson, who were asked to design the service of unification. And so the vision of the first Head Brother, Edward Bickersteth, was made real by his successors almost a century later.

Father Weathrall designed a solemn and elaborate service that culminated in a declaration of duty and the singing of the hymn 'Glorious things of thee are spoken, Zion, city of our God'. Yet when I asked Father Weathrall about it he reverted to the conversational banter of our first meeting and selected a well-honed anecdote:

> It was a day never to be forgotten, perhaps for the wrong reasons. The service was held in the open air on a wooden stage. I went to get the wine for the offertory and my heart sank like a stone. We had put the altar wine into old beer bottles and the stoppers didn't fit and the ants got in. Brother Joshua, who was later Bishop of Bombay, just crept round with me and we had a messy and sticky job of digging the ants out of the offertory wine. Luckily, it was a long service.

In 1975 Father Weathrall was awarded the OBE for 'confirming the links between the Christian churches in India and in the UK'.

He seems indestructible. He is now Head of the Brotherhood for the second time. Yet that Sunday morning in an empty Brotherhood House he seemed a man alone. The ethos of the Brotherhood is exacting: 'Each member has accepted and followed a call from God ... to seek the reality and power of the love of Christ in their common life and share its blessedness and compassion with others ... to put the will of God before everything.' Never to leave, never to marry: it seemed to me a heavy price to pay for one so convivial and so suitable for the comfortable life of a cathedral close in, say, Winchester. After sixty years of service in the heat and discomfort of Delhi, would he not like to come home to

end his days? His reply was one I heard many times from the last of
the stayers-on:

Father Ian: If I went back to Britain who would know me? Where
would I go? What would I do? All my contemporaries
have dropped off like leaves from a tree and now there's a
different generation with different values.

Me: Do you ever feel lonely?

Father Ian: I'm the last of the expats. In the 1950s and 1960s it was
very different. I had lots of friends, some at the High
Commission. There was a time when I took matins there
once a month, but no one's interested in that any more.
The present High Commissioner has decided that the
Commission is secular. There's still the annual carol service that I shall take, and everyone will say how wonderful
it was. But it doesn't add up to much. The oldest friend I
have now is Mark Tully, of course.

Me: Do you think the Raj has disappeared entirely in just
half a century?

Father Ian: Oh, yes, it's part of our colonial past. And that's well and
truly gone.

It was time for the good Father's midday rest. I left the sanctuary
of Brotherhood House marvelling that unconditional love had out-
lasted a mighty empire.

Chapter Four

TIGER HUNTERS

It is the eve of Colonel John 'Papa' Wakefield's ninety-first birthday. He is in his customary chair next to his customary glass of whisky on the veranda of the Viceroy's Hunting Lodge at Kabini near Mysore. Although he is seated with his walking stick to hand, he has an unmistakable military appearance: a 'toothbrush' moustache once popular among army officers and a face that would suit a monocle though in fact he has large round glasses, a camouflage jacket and khaki trousers. He has the manner to go with it, somewhat peremptory to his Indian bearers and used to giving orders. Surrounding him are colour photographs of tigers – one with a paw caught in a trap – and celebrities who have visited, including the film star Goldie Hawn. He refers to her mischievously as 'golden horn'. Outside are photographs of celebrities of another age: the Prince of Wales and Lord Louis Mountbatten with HH the Maharaja of Mysore in 1933, the Russian Grand Dukes' breakfast party in the jungle some years earlier. Fourteen years in the Indian Army and a big game hunter before and after that, Colonel Wakefield looks like a relic of the Raj. He has the pedigree too. His Uncle George was the author of *Recollections: Fifty Years in the Service of India*. Two generations before George was the extraordinary Edward Gibbon Wakefield, who was sent to Newgate prison for abducting a fifteen-year-old girl and afterwards became a driving force behind the early colonisation of South Australia, New Zealand and Canada.

Once again appearances are deceptive. 'Papa' is adamant that he is Indian. He was born in Bihar. He has always had an Indian passport and his employers have nearly all been Indian. Only recently did he sign another five-year contract with Jungle Lodges and Resorts, 100 per cent owned by the Government of Karnataka, as 'Brand Ambassador.' He has not returned to England since 1932, and his second wife was the widow of a maharaja. The only time he wished he had been British, he said, was when he was refused entrance to a Calcutta swimming pool in the 1950s for not producing the right passport. Were it not for his name, he added, no one these days would even raise the subject.

The truth is that Colonel Wakefield's universal name now is 'Papa', whether to the Commander in Chief of the Indian Army or to his family. He is the elderly patriarch to whom further questions of identity do not apply. 'Welcome Papa' proclaim the banners when he visits other wildlife centres. The Raj ended in the last millennium, and to the Indian families staying at Kabini Lodge the question of whether the old man who knows the surrounding jungle like the back of his hand is British or Indian probably never occurs.

John Felix Wakefield was born on 21 March 1916 at Gaya in the state of Bihar. He is the oldest of four children, and his father was the General Manager of the Tikari estate. It was a *zemindar* estate, meaning that the owner, although a maharaja, was more a large landowner in the eyes of the British than a hereditary aristocrat who owed his allegiance directly to the British Crown, for *zemindars* had acquired the freehold of the land in return for collecting the taxes. This had serious implications for the Wakefields after Indian Independence.

John is the fourth generation of Wakefields in India, for his great-grandfather, John Howard, joined the Bengal Army in 1825 and became a colonel during the Sikh Wars of the 1840s. Like his brother, Edward Gibbon, who eloped with a young girl before founding the British Empire, he too had an eye for the ladies. According to another family memoir, *Past Imperative*, he successfully wooed a Rajput girl 'of singular loveliness and high birth' after he had disguised himself as a camel driver and stared at her over the garden wall. They married, and she converted to Christianity with the name of Maria Suffolk.

John Howard and Maria had three daughters, one of whom married into the British aristocracy and another into the Prussian. Their son, John's grandfather, in 1857 was the assistant in Peshawar to the hero of the Indian Mutiny, John Nicholson, alias 'The Lion of the Punjab' (see Chapter Three), and he himself played a significant role in preventing the spread of the Mutiny to that area. According to *Recollections: 50 Years in the Service of India* written by Uncle George:

> My father was riding home from court one evening when he noticed a new Fakir sitting under a tree by the roadside. It was no remarkable sight but an inner consciousness kept on urging him to speak to the man … He took him to the Court Room and had him stripped and searched. Suddenly noticing that the man who stood stark naked had his arms suspiciously glued to his sides, my father ordered his arms to be lifted and from one of his armpits fell out a small leather-bag which was found to contain a long strip of closely-wrapped paper, upon which was written a message from the would-be mutineers in Meerut to the Indian troops in Peshawar, calling upon them to rebel and join forces 'with offerings of fruit in baskets'. This was later found to mean the heads of their British officers.[1]

The conclusion to this brief glimpse into the branches of the Wakefield family tree shows, first, that John is of Anglo-Indian descent and, second, that the Wakefields led exciting lives, a tradition that John has continued.

I asked 'Papa' about his childhood. To him that meant his first steps as a hunter. First he showed me a photograph of young John aged three carrying what looked like an airgun and standing on a dead tiger. He was rehearsing early for that iconic photo of the hunter with one foot planted on the head of the king of the forest. The next photo showed a cheetah on a lead in the back of a truck. 'The cheetah is a hunting leopard,' explained 'Papa'. 'We trained him to hunt black buck.' Then he got out a truly incredible photograph of a shooting party of seven in the Kashmir in the 1920s sitting among rows and rows and rows of dead ducks. In fact seven guns had shot 2,136 birds in five hours, which means that on average each member of the party had downed one bird every minute. 'It was a world record,' said 'Papa'. 'That's me' (he pointed to a small boy), 'next to HH Hari Singh [the ruler of the then independent state of Kashmir] and next to him is the Nawab of Hyderabad.' His Uncle George, who was Diwan (Prime Minister) of Kashmir at the time, said that two two-and-a-half-ton lorries were required to carry the birds to Srinagar, where they were given away. 'Papa' put away the photo album and began to talk:

> My father was a hunter and I was brought up as a hunter. He had to look after the forests owned by the Maharaja of Tikari. He organised shoots for British guests like the collector, the district magistrate, the governor and so on. They all wanted to shoot a tiger and the forests were full of them. We never organised a shoot without a kill. The training you get hunting you could never get from books because when you are hunting it's a question of life or death. Before I went to school I could follow animal footprints in the sand and tell if an animal was limping and why. The gun came with it. As soon as you were old enough you used it.

A well-known story about young John was told by Sir Maurice Hallett, who became Governor of United Provinces (UP). They were out hunting when a tiger charged down a hill towards them. John, aged seven, tapped Sir Maurice on the back and whispered: 'Don't be afraid, Mr Hallett, I am here.' I asked 'Papa' about his first kill:

> My father was standing behind me when I shot my first tiger aged 9. What happened was that we needed to keep a big male tiger so that it could be shot by Sir Henry Wheeler, the Governor of Bihar, but a female tiger with cubs was attracting him. So my father shot the female and that meant the cubs had to go too, although the one I shot was three-quarter grown. The only thing my father taught me about shooting was to squeeze the trigger, after that it was all coordination and speed of reaction. At that age even I was probably a better shot than he was.

At the age of ten 'Papa' was uprooted from the life of adventure that most boys can only dream of and sent thousands of miles away to boarding school at West Buckland in Devon. He saw neither his parents nor his home for six years and spent the holidays with a childless couple who thought that daily immersions all year round in the English Channel were a good idea. This lonely and cold experience was not particularly unfamiliar for sons of the Raj, but no doubt these days a psychiatrist would pick up on it. He preferred to tell me an amusing story:

> When I arrived at school, I was asked my name. 'Wakefield' I said. 'Not any relation of WW?' I thought, well, there are so few Wakefields that I probably was, so I said 'Yes, sir'. The master said, 'Right, straight to the rugger field', although I had never seen a rugger ball in my life. W.W. Wakefield was captaining England at the time.

'Papa' said that he never passed any exams but excelled, predictably, at shooting. In fact he was runner-up to the winner of the Ashburton Shield at Bisley in 1931, aged fifteen, which was the shooting equivalent of getting to the final of Junior Wimbledon. The next year 'Papa's' father was very ill with rheumatic fever, so he returned to India. He has not been back since that time, when Ramsay MacDonald was Prime Minister. 'Why should I? What would I do? I'd be punching tickets on the buses.' Occasionally his long absence shows.

When 'Papa' returned from England aged sixteen his father told him to manage the eleven villages the Maharaja of Tikari had given him in lieu of an income. As a *zemindar* estate owner, the Maharaja had the overall tax revenue owed to the government assessed as a total, and how he collected it and how much he added to it for his own purposes was up to him; so the tenants of these eleven villages, sublet by the Maharaja so to speak, became the responsibility of a teenager, both as a collector of revenue and as landlord. 'Papa' found himself with a responsibility way beyond his years, settling disputes, collecting money and protecting the villages from predatory wildlife. Today when 'Papa' speaks of the India he loves it is this traditional India of the villages amid the forests, an India akin to Kipling's *Jungle*

Book or the *My India* by the tiger hunter Jim Corbett. Half the year 'Papa' spent organising shoots, and the same regime applied when he moved north in the mid-1930s to manage another *zemindar* estate at Tajpur on the banks of the Ganges north-east of Delhi. It was here that he met the famous Jim Corbett and it was now that wildlife became his life until the disruption of war in 1941.

Jim Corbett lived near the Kumaon hill village of Naini Tal, and both hunters organised shoots in the *terai* (moist land). This is a belt of marshy grasslands, savannas and forests at the base of the Himalayas; above lies the Bhabhar, a forested belt of rock and gravel eroded from the high mountain range, and below lies the great alluvial plain of the Yamuna and Ganges. 'From Naini Tal', says a guidebook, 'magnificent views can be obtained of the vast plain to the south, or of the mass of tangled ridges lying north, bounded by the great snowy range which forms the central axis of the Himalayas.' It was an area abounding in wildlife.

Me: What was the point of tiger hunting, John?

'Papa': Originally, pride. I shot my first ten, then I shot my first twenty. I didn't feel guilty about taking life in those days. Now, you feel, there's been a change. There was a ruler in Bihar who died at the age of 85 who shot a thousand tigers on his estate during his lifetime and there were still plenty left, because all these rulers protected tiger better than they are protected today. In my day, on land owned by the British but copied by many princely states, you were given a permit from the Forest Department that allowed you to shoot only one tiger in fifteen days.

Me: Will you describe a day's hunting?

'Papa': We would take a forest bungalow or shooting block for fifteen days, either in Tikari or in Tajpur. We would send our own elephants and *shikaris* (trackers) out four days before we arrived to see what tracks the tigers were using. Then we would tie up buffalo as bait. Every morning we would get up before dawn, go out on the elephant and inspect the bait. If the tiger was still on it, having killed it, we would take a shot.

If it had eaten half and left it we would find where the tiger was lying up for the day. Then we would arrange a beat with the elephants. We would sit up a tree and get the elephants to drive the tiger towards us. But we had to be out of the forest by night. 'Sun-down, gun-down' was the rule, and that applied to all forests. It was very dangerous to shoot at night and very easy to wound the prey and lose track of it. Today, 90 per cent of the public tiger sanctuaries are in the state forests that used to be part of the princely estates. These are the only places where tigers are saved.

Me: Will you describe one kill that stays in your mind?

'Papa': In Tajpur we were in a valley following a river and as we came up to the head of a valley we saw a tiger walking down the path towards us. I was on the lead elephant so I levelled the gun, took a shot and hit the tiger right up its tailbone. This paralysed its back legs but it still came charging at us, roaring and screaming – A-a-a-h-h-h-h – dragging its back legs along the ground. The elephant began to panic. It began to shake. I had the option of either breaking the gun and putting another bullet in or waiting until the tiger got closer with only one shot in the barrel. That would have to be the death shot. Luckily, the chap on the elephant behind shot the tiger and it dropped two yards from my feet. I couldn't light a cigarette for a few minutes after that.

Me: I must say I sympathise with the tiger.

'Papa': In those days one didn't worry about the tiger, just oneself. I never had any attachment to a tiger but plenty to elephants.

> Tiger, tiger, burning bright
> In the forests of the night
> What immortal hand or eye
> Could frame thy fearful symmetry?

The lines came back to me listening to 'Papa's' matter-of-fact description. It was not that I was expecting to hear anything poetic, but I was hoping for something about the beauty of nature at least.

Later I bought Jim Corbett's *My India* in a Mysore bookshop and found this redemptive passage, straight out of Isaiah 11:6: 'The leopard will lie down with the goat, the calf and the lion and the yearling together':

> I once saw a tigress stalking a month-old kid. The ground was very open and the kid saw the tigress while she was still some distance away and started bleating, whereon the tigress gave up her stalk and walked straight up to it. When the tigress had approached to within a few yards, the kid went forward to greet her, and on reaching the tigress it stretched out its neck and put up its head to smell her. For the duration of a few heartbeats the month-old kid and the Queen of the Forest stood nose to nose, and then the queen walked off in the direction from which she had come.[2]

I remarked to 'Papa' that Corbett had the reputation for shooting only tigers that were endangering human life. He was sceptical: 'Everyone wanted to shoot tiger in those days. I can assure you he shot plenty that were not man killers or eaters. The Jim Corbett books were written by his sister Maggie. He was a very quiet fellow. I can see him now walking down the track in front of me with his dog, Robin.' The number of tigers shot in the 1930s was huge and we know this from the meticulously kept record books of India's main taxidermists, Van Ingen and Van Ingen (see later in the chapter). They record that in the seven years 1933–9 Van Ingens alone cured the skins and sometimes mounted 3,634 tigers (and 3,834 panthers).

When Japan bombed Pearl Harbor in December 1941, the war was on India's doorstep. Twenty-five-year-old John Wakefield was commissioned earlier that year as a lieutenant in the Armoured Corps of the British Indian Army, and he left the Indian Army fourteen years later in 1954 as a colonel. During his service he was engaged in the offensive that pushed the Japanese Army back through Burma to surrender in Rangoon in May 1945; then in the bloodbath of Partition in 1947 and in the war over Kashmir that followed in 1947–8; and finally in Operation Polo, which kept Hyderabad within the new India, also in 1948. Throughout this period he witnessed the changeover from a British Indian Army to an independent Indian Army with all the continuity and discontinuity that entailed. He said that, when it came to the traditions, the uniforms, the regimental ethos of the army, he hardly noticed the difference between the two, and still does not. On an officer's uniform the Indian emblem of the three squatting lions under the *chakra* (wheel) has replaced the Crown and the four-pointed star of the British Indian Army, but the visible continuity is very evident: a legacy of the Raj.

At the beginning of the war the strength of the British Indian Army was 144,000 men and by the end it was over 2 million men, the largest volunteer army known in history. Under the pressure of defence and then offence it radically altered in character. In 1939 the British Indian Army was formed in no small way according to the posthumous prejudices of Lord Roberts VC, who had fought in the Indian Mutiny and ended his career in India in 1893 as Commander in Chief; *Forty-One Years in India* was the title of his autobiography. In other words, he was a nineteenth-century soldier whose seminal views moulded the British Indian Army up until the Second World War.

His first prejudice was a racial distinction between 'the martial races' of India and the others. 'No comparison', he wrote, 'can be made between the warlike races of northern India … and the effeminate peoples of the south.' He instigated a policy of Punjabisation, so that in 1914, the year of his death in fact, half the infantry battalions in the British Indian Army came from the Sikhs, Jats, Dogras, Hindus and Muslims of the Punjab, and from the Pathans and Baluchis of the North-West Frontier Province; and a further quarter from the martial races of Nepal, primarily the Ghurkas. The successor soldiers to the old Madras Army that had stood firm under Clive at the battle of Plassey and marched north to defend the East India Company during the Mutiny a hundred years later were no longer valued, nor were what Roberts called dismissively the 'so-called fighting Mahrattas of Bombay.' As for the old Bengal Army that had mutinied in 1857, it had been disbanded, and its successor soldiers found themselves bottom of the list. British officials in Calcutta regarded Bengalis as *challaki* or 'too clever by half', and this prejudice was confirmed in a revealing report of 1930 that stated 'broadly speaking one may say that those races that furnish the best *sepoys* [footsoldiers] are emphatically not those which exhibit the greatest accomplishments of mind in examination'. The composition and size of the Indian Army was little different in 1939 than it had been in 1914.

The second prejudice of Lord Roberts was that Indian soldiers, however brave, did not make good officers. Being an officer himself, he did not mince his words:

> It is the consciousness of the inherent superiority of the European which has won for us India. However well educated and clever a native may be, and however brave he may have proved himself, I believe that no rank that we may bestow upon him would cause him to be considered an equal by a British officer. Native officers can never take the place of British officers. Eastern races, however brave and accustomed to war, do not possess the qualities that go to make good leaders of men.[3]

In 1914 every officer in the British Indian Army was British, from subaltern to Commander in Chief. The loss of British officers on the western front, together with political pressure from the Congress Party, necessitated a policy of Indianisation that reluctantly dragged the British Indian Army into the twentieth century. The very concept of Indianisation was anathema to Congress Party leaders like Motilal Nehru (father of Jawaharlal Nehru). He spoke out in the Legislative Assembly in 1928: 'I may say at once that the word Indianisation is a word that I hate from the bottom of my heart. I cannot understand the word. What do you mean by Indianising the Army? The Army is ours and we have to officer our own Army. There is no question of Indianising there. What we want is to get rid of the Europeans of the Indian army.'[4]

Neverthess, in 1939 there were still only 400 Indian officers in the entire British Indian Army, that is only 10 per cent of the officer cadre. Further, they were mostly confined to eight Indianised regiments in which the Viceroy's Commissioned Officers or VCOs (that is junior officers known as jemadars or risaldars) had been replaced by British warrant officers, supposedly to make up for the inadequacies of their

Indian superiors. None of the Indian officers held a rank above
company level and most were platoon commanders. Many British
regarded Indianised regiments as 'pariah' regiments, thus proving the
continuing prejudice of Lord Roberts. It is interesting to note the
observation of the last Commander in Chief of the British Indian
Army, Lord Auchinleck, writing in 1946: 'There is no doubt that
Indianisation at its inception was looked upon as a political expedient
that was bound to fail militarily. There is no doubt also that senior
British officers believed and even hoped that it would fail.'[5]

The war put paid to 'pariah units' and the notion that British
soldiers should not serve under Indian officers. Only the Ghurka
regiments retained solely British officers, until 1947. John Wakefield
was one of 8,000 soldiers recruited in India who were granted
Emergency Commissions during the war into all regiments of the
British Indian Army, and by the time the war was over forty Indian
officers had reached the rank of lieutenant colonel; two were briga-
diers. A small number of aristocratic Indian officers had attended
Sandhurst since 1918, and the Indian Military Academy (IMA) at
Dehra Dun had provided a similar high-fliers' course since 1933, but
all the instructors before the war were British.

One recruit to the IMA at Dehra Dun in the 1930s was D.K. Palit
(eventually Major-General), who was asked at the selection interview about his political ideas. His father, who was also in the British
Indian Army, had warned him against 'showing any great enthusiasm for being a nationalist'. So, when he was asked what he thought
about Gandhi, he replied that he was 'a saint', which presumably
elevated him above politics. Most of the Emergency Commission
Officers were fresh from schools and colleges, where they had been
exposed to the Independence movement, and no doubt this changed
the outlook of the army. This sharpens the question: how could an
army fight for the freedom of others when it was not free itself,
when it was ruled by a colonial power? The question is even sharper
when one remembers that Governor General Lord Linlithgow
committed India to a world war in 1939 without so much as con-
sulting Congress. This was bitterly resented and strengthened the
Independence movement. Jawaharlal Nehru complained: 'There was

something rotten when one man, and a foreigner and representative of a hated system, could plunge 400 million human beings into a war without the slightest reference to them.' A further question stems from the first. Since Independence, why has the Indian Army always stayed loyal to the civilian government, when, in the late 1980s, for example, over fifty former colonial powers were military dictatorships or were dominated by the military?

There are many answers to these questions, but one concerns the regimental structure of the British Indian Army. Traditionally, battalions were formed on a 'class-company' basis, meaning a race and religious basis, so that a typical battalion from the Punjab would consist of two companies of Punjabi Mussulmans (Muslims, or PMs), a company of Sikhs and another of Jats. This made easier proper observance of religious and caste distinction, neatly expressed early in the century by the famous iron ration, the Sheikhupura Biscuit. This was identical for all rankers but came in different wrappers: those for Hindus certified that Brahmins manufactured them under priestly supervision, and those for Muslims certified that Islamic mullahs approved them. The lesson of the infamous Enfield cartridge that 'caused' the Mutiny of 1857 had been learned well. The 'class-company' structure broadly pertains today among the old infantry regiments, although the PMs have gone to Pakistan and the Sikhs have declined in number from about 20 to 10 per cent of the Army. This laid the basis of a communal identity.

Moreover, what gave a British Indian Army regiment its unique quality was its family character. Men in every company were drawn from specific areas, as were their VCOs and NCOs. They knew each other, and in many cases belonged to the same family. Their British officers identified with them too, often taking leave in their soldiers' villages. When D.K. Palit joined the 5/10 Baluch (King George V's Own) Battalion in Peshawar just before the war, he joined a regiment in which most of the officers were British, but all spoke Urdu and Pashto, the local language of the troops. In fact, they appeared more at ease with their rank and file than with their brother Indian officers:

One day I happened to go into the adjutant's office and saw him looking through a pile of sheet roles (other ranks' records). He had just joined the company and he was trying to get an inkling of the family background of the men, so that he knew what they would be talking about. When a chap came up to ask for leave and said 'Sahib, my house has fallen down', it would come out that his brother, in the same platoon, had built a house a few years before. Officers quite frequently spent their leave with the villagers and got to know the parents of their men. This was a great part, a rewarding part of being in the army.[6]

It was more than that. The platoon was the focus of a soldier's loyalty, then ultimately the regiment, but not the British Raj nor the Indian government in power. This was drummed into the VCOs of the British Indian Army, and then into the Junior Commissioned Officers (JCOs) of the Indian Army, who were the vital links between officers and men, as described by K. Subrahmanyam, Director of the Indian Institute of Defence Studies, in 1989:

The British conditioned him [the VCO] to be totally apolitical. He was not in the Army to fight for either the country or the King Emperor. He had chosen the army as a career as generations of his forefathers did. He had sworn an oath of loyalty on his religious book and participated in the traditional salt-taking ceremony, and his duty was to uphold the honour and glory of his platoon, then his company, then his battalion and then his regiment.

While credit must be given to the British for having correctly evaluated the Indian (mainly Hindu) ethos and having raised the British Indian Army according to it, the ethos itself goes back to millennia-old concepts of Hindu society. The bearing of arms was a profession and loyalty to the oath undertaken and the honour and glory of the unit were all that mattered, so long as there was an assurance that the social values and framework would not be changed.[7]

Hence, Subrahmanyam continued:

The officers and men of the Indian Army did not find any contradiction between fighting for the Allied cause and their innate sympathies for the Indian Freedom struggle. They felt the political settlement on India's future was up to the Nationalist movement and the British. They waited for the day when they would become the Armed Forces of Independent India.

This explains the statement of Gandhi in 1942: 'India's soldiers are not a national army, but professionals who will as soon fight under the Japanese or any other if paid for fighting.' He was wrong to suggest that they were simply mercenaries. Nevertheless, the disapproval of the Indian Army for the 50,000 of their fellow soldiers who joined the Indian National Army (INA) and fought under Subhas Chandra Bose for the fascists was because they had broken a religious oath and taken a political decision. After the war INA soldiers were offered jobs in civilian life, but they were not allowed back into the army. They had broken with tradition.

In this respect John Wakefield was a typical officer of the British Indian Army, despite his dual identity:

> I was accepted by Wavell [Commander in Chief, later Viceroy of India] because he thought I was a British officer and I was accepted by the Indians because I was an officer. My aim has always been not to disturb either side. I thought Nehru and Gandhi were simply doing their job and if they didn't do it who else would have done? The Japanese? I accepted the change of government completely

What interested him more was the continuing regimental ethos handed down from the British to the Indian Army;

> Up to 1947 there was only really one army, whether British Army or British Indian Army, we fought as one. After 1947 the traditions of the old British (Indian) Army have continued to this day. The mess dinners are 100 per cent British rituals. The colonel sits at the head of the table and the pipers play 'The Last Post' – Indian pipers but originally trained by the Scots. The only difference is we toast the President of India and not the Queen.

'Regimental spirit could be seen at its best in the old British Indian Army,' wrote General M.L. Chibber in 1989. 'It was essentially a warrior tribal affair, sometimes even an affair of villages. A young soldier knew that, if he did not do well in battle, he had to face the scorn of his village. This tradition is alive today. It is based on pride in the regiment.'[8] The traditions of the regiment are taught at *mandir* (Hindu temple), *masjid* (mosque), *gurudwara* (Sikh temple) and church parades, and, of course, on mess nights, when new recruits are expected to recognise each trophy and piece of silver. The family ethos of some regiments is so strong that an officer about to marry has to ask permission of his commanding officer in the presence of his 'brother' officers. By now some families have five generations of service in the same Indian regiment.

Tales abound about the lengths regiments go to in order to preserve traditions. For example, in 1954 the commander of the 5/5 Gurkha Rifles, Lieutenant-Colonel J.T. Sataravala, found in Calcutta a 6-metre-high statue of Lord Roberts VC lying by the side of the Maidan, in the process of being carted away by the Marxist city government. 'Bobs Bahadur' had been the first colonel of the 5 Ghurkas. Lieutenant-Colonel Sataravala summoned his officers to the mess to tell them of his discovery and read from the *Regimental History*. Lord Roberts's coat of arms was:

Dexter – A Highlander of the 72nd Regiment
Sinister – A Ghurka
Both habited and holding in their exterior hands a rifle

The soldier who devised this powerful symbol of unity had to be respected, even in death. Discussion took place about how to purchase and then remove his colossal piece of statuary to the parade ground of the Regimental Centre of the 5 Ghurkas in Dehra Dun. It took twenty years to accomplish the mission, and then the statue ended up in the Artillery Centre at Deolali because Lord Roberts had been a Master Gunner.

According to General Chibber the strongest cohesion in a regiment is the closeness of officers to men, and therefore the regimental system of the Indian Army inherited from the British continues to be a strong link between India and Britain. He wrote this in 1989 and an appendix to his article, 'Names of British Officers and their Relatives who Participated in Regimental Events in India', lists 184 ex-officers and wives, all of whom must have been at least in their sixties, who visited their old regiments between 1985 and 1988. The UK branch of the Indian Army Association held its final reunion in 2005, sixty years after the end of the war.

Wakefield's War may be briefly told. Although he joined the Armoured Corps, the Japanese captured his own regiment at Singapore in February 1942 before he could join it, so he spent the war years attached to the Royal Indian Army Service Corps (RIASC). In 1943 he was sent to instruct the Jungle Warfare Training Divisions at Chindwara in the Central Provinces, where the 14th and 39th Indian Divisions were sent on two-month training courses in jungle warfare to prepare them for re-entry into Burma. Here he met up again with fellow instructor Jim Corbett and specialised in teaching the drivers of motorised transport to convert from the deserts of the Middle East to the tropics of South East Asia. 'Most of the troops were more afraid of the forests than they were of the Japanese,' he said.

In December 1944 Captain Wakefield entered Burma from Imphal with the 14th Army and followed it through to Rangoon, where the Japanese surrendered in August 1945. Here he transferred to the Civil Affairs Services Burma (CASB) and found himself the following year with Mountbatten's South East Asia Command in Singapore with the unlikely job of President of the Courts' Martial Appeal Court. 'I did all sorts of odd jobs,' he said vaguely.

I sensed that 'Papa' did not really want to talk about the war. He was more interested in wildlife, so I asked him about his time in 1942, when he had been pig sticking with General Wavell. Pig sticking was a blood sport of the Raj much enthused over by the arch-imperialist Major-General Sir Robert Baden-Powell, who believed that 'the boar enjoys it too'. This seems unlikely, as the boar ended up speared to death. In the famous Kadir Cup Meet near Meerut, however, the winner of three horsemen or 'spears' in each heat was the one who

simply drew first blood on the boar after it had been flushed out of
a thicket and chased through the scrub. The skill, said 'Papa', was to
keep the boar on the right side of the horse, because you held the
long lance under your right arm, and obviously at a fierce gallop
you could not change over. The Kadir Cup ended on the outbreak
of war, but three years later the new Commander in Chief, Lord
Archibald Wavell, agreed to pig stick against some of his junior officers on the same pitch. Of course he had to win. The trouble was,
said 'Papa', that 'we discovered Wavell's right eye was made of glass
[an injury in the First World War] and he could not see on his right
side. Luckily his horse, called Misfire and Squeaker [*sic*], had won
the Kadir Cup on three occasions and knew exactly what to do. So
Wavell got first blood and we all pulled up.' (This makes a good story,
but actually it was Wavell's left eye that was glass.)

'Papa' was an admirer of Lord Wavell as Commander in Chief in
India but less of him as Viceroy at the end of the war supervising
the promised transfer to Independence: 'He could not manage the
political part of it and he never had the support of the politicians
at Westminster.' Wavell was replaced by Lord Louis Mountbatten,
whose hugely controversial decision to divide the Indian subcontinent on religious fault lines between India and West and East
Pakistan has been disputed ever since. Not only did he decide on
Partition, but he also imposed a rigid, drastic and arbitrary timetable
on it – seventy-three days from the announcement of Plan Balkan,
or Partition, to British withdrawal on 15 August 1947. Asked at a
press conference when the Raj would end, he plucked out of the
air the second anniversary of the Japanese surrender. 'Was it too
quick?' asked Prime Minister Attlee afterwards, and that must be
one of history's big unanswered questions. John Wakefield thought
Mountbatten was right:

> I had every sympathy with him. He had no alternative. You see he
> could not keep British troops in India. They had had enough. [Prime
> Minister Attlee agreed with that, giving it as one reason for the pre-
> cipitate withdrawal.] It was only his diplomacy that persuaded most
> of the princely states to go with India. You see they were really

British colonies owing allegiance to the British Cown, and it was
Mountbatten's diplomacy that got them to go with India.

'Diplomacy' here was an unintended euphemism. In fact many of
the 500 or so princes were planning to transform their states into
constitutional monarchies, and it was only by arm-twisting, lies
and intrigue that Mountbatten persuaded all but the rulers of the
Kashmir, Hyderabad and the tiny state of Junagadh to opt for India
by 15 August. Commenting on this unedifying spectacle years later,
Lord Templar said to Mountbatten: 'You're so crooked Dickie, if you
swallowed a nail you'd shit a corkscrew.'

Partition divided the Punjab. In all, 5.5 million Hindus and Sikhs
fled to India from the new Pakistan during the autumn and winter
of 1947 and nearly 6 million Muslims fled the other way. It was
the largest forced migration in history. On one day, 14 September,
it was calculated that 1.25 million non-Muslims were on the move
to East Punjab, while 890,000 Muslims were heading the other
way to West Punjab. In all, over a million people perished, though
Mountbatten said the number was far less. The violence began well
before Partition; indeed sectarian violence was one of the reasons for
Partition, and it was almost impossible for the British Indian Army
and then the separate Indian and Pakistan Armies to cope. After all,
the majority of the army came from the Punjab, so many soldiers'
families were on the move too. Mixed regiments had to be separated
and the whole post-war army divided one-third to Pakistan (140,000
men) and two-thirds to India; the same applied to arms, baggage and
supplies. Most of the army cantonments were in Pakistan, although
most of the army was in India.

When the Commander in Chief of the British Indian Army,
Lord Auchinleck (who had succeeded Wavell), was asked by Viceroy
Mountbatten how long it would take to split his army, he replied
'possibly five years'. He was given four weeks to prepare a plan that
included the replacement of 11,000 British officers so that only 2,500
remained. Most of the Indian officers had served for seven years or
less and very few in senior ranks. Claude Auchinleck had joined the
Indian Army in 1904 and loved it. He found the business of disbanding

it 'the most painful and distasteful episode of my career'. In fact, he never got over it. He retired to Marrakesh and told an interviewer in the 1970s: 'The English never really cared. I don't think they cared about India. I think they used it. You felt your life's work was finished, you see, when what you have been working for all along was just torn into two pieces.'[9] He called Mountbatten 'pretty Dickie'.

Major John Wakefield was one of the officers who remained. He was sent to work for the Indian Military Evacuation Authority under General Chimni escorting Hindus out of Pakistan:

> Do you want to know the horror side of it or the pleasure side of it? There were both. I have seen women carrying small babies and covered with flies because their breasts had been cut off. You could not see a tree with bark or leaves as far as the eye could see on both sides of the road because thousands and thousands of Hindus were coming out of Pakistan with nothing to eat. The whole area looked as bad as Germany after the Allied bombings. And I've seen the other side as well. You get to a Hindu camp in the desert and you find that Muslims have been looking after them and cooking for them. They were sorry to let them go but they said 'we can't carry on, the pressure's too much'. We evacuated as many as we could with a transport unit. We had a fleet of buses and my protection unit from the Garhwali Rifles sat on top armed with machine guns so we never had any trouble. We took them down to Lahore and then to Amritsar, where they were put on trains going to Delhi.

Immediately after Partition, Major John Wakefield was involved in actions that determined the fate of the two states that had not opted to join either India or Pakistan at Independence: the two largest and richest states, in both natural beauty and wealth, of Kashmir and Hyderabad. The former had a Hindu ruler, Maharaja Hari Singh, but a population that was Muslim in the majority, while the latter (known then as the 'Nizam's Dominions') had a Muslim ruler, the Nizam Osman Ali Khan, while most of his people were Hindu. This complicated matters, but the strategic importance of both states meant that independence was not really an option.

The fate of the Kashmir was decided by the British in extraordinary circumstances, although by then Pakistan and India were independent nations. It was the epilogue of the Raj after the curtain had come down. The crucial players were three Britishers: Lord Mountbatten, now reincarnated as the First Governor General of India; Lord Auchinleck, now promoted to Supreme Commander of both the Indian and Pakistan armies; and General Douglas Gracey, Commander in Chief of the Pakistan Army. It is important to remember too that both new nations were British Dominions and remained so until 1950 (India) and 1956 (Pakistan).

Only ten weeks after Independence, up to 10,000 tribesmen from the North-West Frontier led by ex-members of the Indian National Army invaded the Vale of Kashmir, pillaging and looting. Maharaja Hari Singh fled south to Jammu and, making up his mind in a hurry, signed an Instrument of Accession that renounced his princely kingdom in favour of India. Rumour reached Delhi that the raiders were backed by the new Pakistan government and that their aim was to capture Srinagar Airport. This would have prevented an Indian army from retaliating, because Partition had given Pakistan the main road access to the Kashmir and therefore by this *coup de main* Pakistan invaders would hold the state. The rumours were accurate. A quickly summoned, largely airborne, Indian force managed to defend Srinagar and then take back the town of Baramulla, after which it ran out of supplies.

Then the President of Pakistan, Dr Muhammad Ali Jinnah, acted officially. He summoned his Commander in Chief and told him to send the full Pakistan Army to occupy the Kashmir. Gracey consulted Auchinleck, who faced down Jinnah in Lahore and told him this amounted to a declaration of war, as the Kashmir had acceded to India. Jinnah angrily agreed, but now the belligerent boot was on the other foot, as the Indian government, incensed by what was happening, demanded that its army clear the Kashmir of Pakistan-backed raiders and establish a demilitarised zone.

The extraordinary situation now arose of two armies that until a few months before had been brothers in arms sizing up to destroy each other. They were still commanded by British officers who were both answerable to a British Supreme Commander. Mountbatten acted with one of his high-handed and questionable assertions, telling the Indian Cabinet that its military aims were impossible to achieve. Auchinleck, backed by Prime Minister Attlee in London, told both sides that, if war ensued, no British officers would take part in it. They would 'stand down'. That settled the matter, and Nehru referred the conflict to the United Nations. A tenuous ceasefire came into effect on 1 January 1949.

Wakefield witnessed this from Srinagar, where he was stationed from 1947, sending supplies to the front line at Baramulla:

> It was extraordinary. One minute we were best friends, then we were fighting. I always supported the ruler of Kashmir. Remember my uncle had been his Diwan. I think if there had been a plebiscite in 1947, most Kashmiris would have supported Hari Singh's decision to go with India. The raiders threw it away with all this rape and pillage. They were terrorists. If they had not wasted two days ransacking Baramulla at the beginning, they could have taken Srinagar airport and then things would have been very different.

The Hyderabad action of 1948 saw a similar confrontation between former brother officers, and this time it was witnessed in person by Lieutenant-Colonel Wakefield. The Nizam, whose dominion in size was equal to a sizeable chunk of west Europe, was pro-Pakistan and provoked India by banning Indian currency and lending Pakistan a large sum of money. An aggressive Muslim organisation within Hyderabad called the 'Razakars' terrorised Hindus despite warnings from the Indian government. It was rumoured that the Nizam wanted to join Pakistan by buying Goa and forcing a land corridor that would extend his state to the Arabian Sea. The Nizam was courting disaster. In the words of Lord Mountbatten's biographer Philip Zeigler: 'Extravagantly rich, spectacularly mean, resolutely doleful, this Indian Ghetty, Muslim ruler of a Hindu state, was from the start destined for eventual disaster.' By August Nehru had enough and ordered the 'liberation' of the Hyderabadi people. He launched Operation Polo.

The Armoured Division went in, commanded by Major-General Chaudhury, and from the outset the result was a foregone conclusion. For a start, Hyderabad was entirely surrounded by India. After minor skirmishing and the loss of life of 800 or so Hyderabadis, the Nizam's army surrendered on 3 September. Wakefield was there as part of Chaudhury's staff:

> The Hyderabad commander was General El-Edroos, who had been five years senior to Major-General Chowdhury only a few months earlier. But he had to go through the protocol of surrender. He had to get out of his jeep and walk fifty yards to Chowdhury, who was sitting in his tank with the Indian flag flying and gun trained. Coming up, El-Edroos said: 'Oh, hello Chowdhury, nice to see you.' Chowdhury said 'Cut out the familiarity and sign here!'

In 1946 John had married a British nurse, Betsy Rawlinson, whom he had met during the war in Burma, when she was working for the Queen Alexandra Imperial Nursing Service. She soon gave birth to two girls, their names indicating where the parents were at the time; Sarah Bernadette Anne (South Burma Area) and Jacqueline Angela Katherine (Jammu and Kashmir). The girls grew up on the family property outside Gaya in Bihar, and Jackie has memories of her father shooting a cobra lying under her cot, although surprisingly she cannot remember if she was in it at the time! He also raised a black panther from birth and kept it round the property long after it should have been released. When guests came, he had the panther put in a cage in the living room. Typical of his sense of humour, he would surreptitiously click his fingers, at which the panther would roar, as it had been trained to do! The little girls went to the St Nazareth's Academy convent school, where, says Jackie, the teaching nuns wore wimples and flowing white robes. Now a family man, Colonel Wakefield had had enough of the army. With a wife and two children to support, he said he was earning no more than he had with the old army as a lieutenant in 1941. In 1954 he resigned.

The next decade was out of character and, it seems, best forgotten. Colonel Wakefield found a job as public-relations officer with the

firm of Surujmal Nagamal Jhalan in Calcutta, and, definitively, his
family left him. One reason for this was that he had 'taken to the
bottle', as he put it, a result of the temptations of public relations and
the seductions of Calcutta. In 1955 the girls left for England with
their mother, and they did not see their father again for thirty-four
years. As if this was not enough, during the same period his mother,
formerly Queenie Murphy, and his two sisters, Zoe and Sheila, also
emigrated, either to the United Kingdom or to the United States.
They thought that India 'was going to the dogs', said John, and
wanted no more part of it. This was a familiar expression among
the British left behind in 1947, and John has his own answer to it:
'If India's gone to the dogs, then I would be a dog myself living
here. Mention any place in the world and I couldn't get what I'm
getting here.' So all the women in John's life left, but the men of the
family stayed. John's brother Arthur died in Gaya as recently as 2006,
and their father, John Gurney Wakefield, who once asked Queenie
'what's wrong with being buried in India?', died in Gaya in 1958.

Life changed irredeemably for the worse on the Tikari estate too.
The old Maharaja had died some time before and been succeeded by
his son, Kumar Amar Singh, but throughout the 1950s the government of India had been working to abolish the *zemindari* estates. By
the end of the decade the proprietary rights of the large estate holders had been transferred to the state governments, so that the great
barons of the Indian countryside, many of whose properties went
back to the earliest days of colonial rule, were left with no more than
their titles. Kumar Amar Singh died in 1965. Long before this, John's
father had sold on the landlord rights to the eleven villages sublet to
him by the old Maharaja.

Now John and Maharaja Kumar Singh had grown up together.
They had gone off to England together for their education and
returned together. They had been close friends for many years, so
when the Maharaja died and Bihar was beset by drought and famine
at the same time (the mid-1960s), John tried to help the family of the
late Maharaja's fourth wife, Rani Ram Kali Devi. In 1972 he took
the family away from Bihar to live in a Tikari property in Dehra
Dun, that favoured town of the Raj nestling under the Himalayan

foothills with the hill station of Mussoorie looking down on it, and here he married the Rani. He was told to do so by her daughter Lakshmi, who had been nine when her father died, and 'Papa' did not hold back, although he still had a wife in England.

When John left Calcutta in 1964, he returned to Tajpur and formed the Kumaon Hunters Safari Company, one of the first groups in India since the Raj to organise hunting safaris. They were primarily for rich Americans, who were charged $2,000 for a fifteen-day shoot, but otherwise the hunting was much the same as thirty years earlier. Perhaps the fee paid required a new obligation: 'We always had a second gun positioned just behind the client firing the same kind of bullet. They would shoot at the same time. We always told the guest he had shot the tiger, even if his bullet had gone wide.' Other tricks were more traditional:

> In the old days a big tiger had to be at least eleven feet in length for a VIP shoot, so we had a tape measure made with eleven inches in a foot. Sometimes we would go as far as making the tiger an opium addict. The tiger would always start eating from the buttocks of a bait, so we would get opium, make a paste of it and put it on the buttocks. After the third buffalo the tiger would become addicted and would only eat buffalo that was tied up, because then it would get more opium.

Anne Wright estimated that during the 1950s perhaps 10,000 tigers were shot in India. She remembers shops in Delhi where the skins for sale were piled up for display like blankets.

John's life changed completely in 1972. A census of that year revealed the shocking fact that only 1,800 tigers were to be found in the whole of India. This discovery devastated conservationists, including the Prime Minister Indira Gandhi, and it became a call to action. The Wildlife Protection Act of 1972 was hurriedly enacted. The tiger was listed in Schedule 1 of the Act, which meant it was an endangered and strictly protected species. Only proven man-eaters could now be killed, and this required a decision by a district magistrate. Heavy fines and even gaol sentences were imposed on tiger hunters, in theory anyway. The next year Project Tiger began. Nine sanctuaries and national parks were made Project Tiger reserves, which protected, so it was estimated, 268 tigers between them. They received funding and staffing from the central government. The boast 'I bagged a tiger' became the slogan 'Save the tiger'.

Colonel Wakefield, the last of the *shikaris*, had to find a new job, and new professional opportunities opened up. Straight away he pioneered wildlife tourism with a leading US adventure travel company, Lindblad Travel, and took the first groups to Project Tiger reserves such as Ranthambhore and Kanha. At the same time he became a consultant to the British TV company *Survival Anglia* and worked on several series of wildlife films. He swopped his gun for a camera; wildlife-killing clients for wildlife-watching clients. The skills learnt during his youth seem much the same, but the end result was the opposite, from destroying to conserving. Did the old hunter feel a sense of guilt? Did he change in his heart? My attempts to extract from him any kind of *mea culpa* were brushed off irritably, but unless he was wholeheartedly committed to his new role it would never have become the vocation it has for the last thirty-five years. Army officer that he was, 'Papa' is too stiff upper lip to display his feelings, nor does he have the Jim Corbett gift of describing sensitively what his eyes see. Luckily, in Kanha National Park on 23 May 1974, he had with him Anne Wright's daughter Belinda, also a tiger conservationist. Her description of watching a large male tiger, a tigress and two cubs lying on the sand conjures up an irresistible vision that must have confirmed to the watching Wakefield that his conversion was in a good cause:

When the sun grew hot, the tigers, one by one, roused themselves and padded to the nearby water hole. The male cub drank briefly and rushed off before the big tiger arrived. The tiger strolled up to the tigress and affectionately made a gentle swipe at her with his paw. Then he bounded into the water, sat on his haunches, and with a perplexed expression pawed the water surface. We think he was bothered by his reflection. After a while we noticed the female cub looking round mischievously. Slowly she swam to the end of the pool and then sneaked up behind Arjuna. She pounced on him. Instantaneously

he leapt around and bared his teeth – water flying everywhere – but
the tigress was unperturbed. The little cubs bounded out of the pool
followed by the tigress and Arjuna went to sleep.

In 1977 John moved his second family to Delhi, but he spent much
of his time in the Himalayas. In 1978 he joined the famous Tiger
Tops Jungle Lodge (TTJL) in Chitwan National Park in the *terai* of
Nepal, first as a consultant and then as General Manager of its operations in the Kashmir and Ladakh. These included a travel company
in Srinagar in the Kashmir, where he developed a fish protection
programme and the distinctive Ladakh Sarai outside Leh, a tourist
camp with Mongolian-style canvas tents. TTJL was modelled on
the Treetops Hotel in Nyeri, Kenya. Jim Corbett moved to Nyeri
in 1947, and here Princess Elizabeth was staying on the night of 6
February 1952 when she heard that her father, George VI, had died.
Corbett's entry in the hotel register must be in a class of its own: 'For
the first time in the history of the world, a young girl climbed into
a tree one day as a princess, and having had what she described as
her most thrilling experience, she climbed down the next day as a
Queen – God bless her.'

TTJL calls itself 'the pioneer wildlife safari lodge of Nepal and
Asia where "Responsible and Sustainable tourism" was initiated long
before Ecotourism became a buzzword.' That same year, 1978, the
Tourism Minister for Karnataka, Gundu Rao, stayed at TTJL and was
inspired to start a similar enterprise in his pristine jungles. If tourists
were prepared to go to Kathmandu, then why not to Karnataka?
Eventually a deputation of advisers from TTJL travelled down to
Mysore. One of its number was John Wakefield, who cannot have
realised that this first visit was the start of a new life aged sixty-two. A
joint venture was agreed, and so was born Jungle Lodges and Resorts,
Karnataka, with Colonel Wakefield as a director. A first location was
chosen at Mastigudi on the banks of the river Kabini in the heart of
the Nagarhole jungle. Tents were pitched. For various reasons the
Mastigudi Jungle Lodge failed, not least because Nagarahole was
declared a National Park and that meant that commercial activity
was off limits.

It was a blessing in disguise, for John tracked down just outside the park the 125-year-old Hunting Lodge of the Maharaja of Mysore, with the old Viceroy's Bungalow next to it. They were in semi-ruins, broken glass and tiles littered about. To John the site was the ideal fusion of his old India with the new as he wished it to be, his past with his future. In 1984 the renamed Kabini River Lodge opened, and John became its first Resident Director. Twenty-two years later and aged ninety he was 'promoted upstairs', as he put it, to become 'Brand Ambassador'. But his future is assured and his home guaranteed in a small part of the former Viceroy's Lodge. Few lives in a century of revolutionary change can have had such continuity. As a small boy John Wakefield tracked wildlife for a maharaja and his Raj guests; as an old man he lives next to a maharaja's residence and does the same for the Indian raj and wealthy British tourists.

At the entrance to Kabini Lodge is the Estate Office with a board of Current Wildlife Sightings:

> Sunday; leopard and sloth bear.
> Wednesday; tiger seen from the boat.
> Daily sightings: wild elephant, gaur [Indian wild ox], deer and wild boars.
> Birds: woodpecker, brahminy kite, ibis, egret, sandpiper, cormorant and serpent eagle; crocodiles.

The track winds down past a variety of trees: rosewood, tamarind, peepal and a 'tabubea argenta' planted by Goldie Hawn, to the carefully modernised Viceroy's Lodge. Here, it is said, 'Papa' is sitting on his veranda behind the bougainvillea observing everything that moves and occasionally reaching for his catapult to scare off crows and monkeys. The path crosses the lawns down to the circular, open-sided dining hall with a thatched domed roof called a *Gol Ghar* (a feature brought from Tiger Tops) and then to the tourist bungalows on the edge of Kabini Lake. In fact it is a river, but a dam 20 kilometres downstream gives rise to this placid expanse of water over which the birds of Kabini swoop and skim. Monkeys swing through the trees by the bungalows; lizards crawl lazily over the paths. It is tempting to sit and luxuriate in this tourist resort, but that is not what 'Papa' has in mind. He hates the very word 'resort'. This is a wildlife sanctuary, and every morning, early, and every afternoon, late, the jeeps depart with their guides to enter Nagarahole National Park for serious study. Nature films are shown before supper and an early knock on the door before it is even light begins the next day's regime.

One of 'Papa's themes is the tension between conservation and commercialisation. Jungle Lodges is a state-run enterprise, and over the years many managing directors and chairmen have been 'posted' here who have been tempted to maximise profits by introducing picnic spots, ayurvedic medicine treatment, a swimming pool. An empty houseboat offshore is mute witness to another scheme – a floating restaurant – and visible across the water are the bungalows of a private resort built without planning permission. 'Papa' views all this with scorn but also with vigilance, as it makes nonsense of the concept of a wildlife sanctuary. He told me that at Ranthambhore tiger sanctuary in the early days only the Maharaja of Jaipur owned a resort; today there are 2,500 beds round the periphery of the park, some of them costing $1,000 a day. Too many jeeps piled too high with tourists charge round the sanctuary expecting the tigers to provide photo opportunities. 'Papa' fears that when he goes the same could happen at Kabini. He wins awards for Best Maintained Eco-Friendly Tourist Project 'synonymous with the name of Colonel John Wakefield', but is that enough?

One evening I entered the park in a jeep with a guide. The track went through thickets of scrub and woodland, mostly teak, rosewood and strands of bamboo. We were silent, occasionally stopping to photograph wild birds and slowing by salt licks and artificial water holes in the hopes that bigger wildlife would be there. Eventually we came out by the meandering Kabini River. Sprouting grass in the meadows had attracted wild elephant, gaur and deer to graze. Wild boar snuffled about and crocodiles lazed on the mud banks. It was a peaceful scene in the evening sun, the wildlife equivalent of the Garden of Eden.

It is said that 'Papa' has a rapport with the wildlife, an intuition that will find a tiger if one is around. If an elephant blocks the path, he shouts and it moves away. 'Nothing to do with my voice,' says 'Papa', 'after twenty-five years here the animals recognise my smell.' On the way back our guide suddenly gestured to the driver. He stopped the jeep. About 150 metres away, prowling from a water hole into the woodland, was a young male tiger. A 'blaze of tiger' is the phrase I recognised at that moment. Out came the digital cameras and for a full minute we watched, spellbound. Afterwards we shook hands as the hunters of the Raj did years ago, although like them we had no reason to congratulate ourselves. Instead of standing by our prey, we looked at each other's digital pictures.

'Papa' knew we had seen a tiger before we told him. That evening we discussed the future of the animal that has been so much of his life for nearly a century. Nagarahole covers 640 square kilometres, and the tiger population has remained constant at about 55 for several years. In other words, there is one tiger for every 10 square kilometres and, with a healthy prey population, that is the right number. 'Papa' is very proud of this. In India as a whole the numbers are dwindling, despite Project Tiger, so that there are fewer tigers now than when the project started – just over 1,000 according to the latest figures. 'Why?' asks 'Papa' rhetorically. His answer is poaching. It did not exist in the old days, but it is the Chinese, Korean and Tibetan markets that want Indian tiger now:

> What is the price of dehydrated tiger bones and tiger meat? $50,000 – $60,000 per tiger. And what does the poacher here get? Not much, but enough to keep him alive for a few months. If you order tiger penis soup in Korea, it will cost you $100. It's supposed to have aphrodisiac properties. In my day the carcass of a tiger had no value at all. In Tibet the skins are supposed to have magical properties, but, after Belinda Wright made a film with a hidden camera about all that, the Dalai Lama stopped it; said it wasn't Buddhism. That trade has stopped, thanks to Belinda.

So does 'Papa' have a solution? He gives two radical answers. The first is that only carefully controlled tourism will protect the tiger from the poachers. His guides work in collaboration with the wildlife protection force, radioing through anything suspicious. He makes sure that all his local staff, jungle people from the Kuruba tribe, are paid properly from the profits of tourism, so that they are not tempted into poaching. His second answer is related and a contradiction of official policy. The Wildlife Institute at Dehra Dun recommends that 'core' zones must be reserved for tigers from which humans are banned even from collecting firewood. 'Papa' is against this concept. Although 'core' zones are patrolled by the Forestry Department, he claims that they are a 'poacher's paradise'. Tigers are not hard to find, he says, particularly with powerful torches and 4x4 vehicles. The temptations to poach are too hard for poor villagers to resist. That is why, per head, there are more tigers now in tourist areas where they may be protected than in the tiger 'core' zones. This is particularly true of places like Nagarahole, where there is a pro-active policy to attract them with salt licks and the like.

Belinda Wright believes that poachers kill over 250 tigers each year and that Project Tiger is not doing nearly enough to catch them. An Indian government report recently concluded that poachers were killing three out of every five Indian tigers. Can the tiger in India survive, I asked 'Papa'?

Man has lived with tiger for thousands of years. Man did not disturb the tiger and the tiger did not disturb man. Now we are encouraging tribals to disturb the tiger by poaching. Apart from poaching, what we need is to stop man from expanding into the tiger areas. Ten or twelve tigers die round here – natural deaths, fighting for territory – because there is no more land for them. It is only the common people living along the fringes of the forest who are going to save the animals. The biggest problem is democracy. Politicians are influenced by the man with the vote, but the animal has no vote.

Some years ago a leopard appeared from nowhere and padded up to where Colonel Wakefield was sitting outside the Viceroy's Lodge. It stopped about 10 metres away, took a long hard look and then padded away again. Perhaps it was making sure that 'Papa' had changed his spots. Col. John 'Papa' Wakefield died on 26 April 2010. His ashes were scattered at Kabini.

In Mysore I called in at Bissal Munti ('sunny rock'), the family
home of India's last and most famous taxidermists, the Van Ingens,
who practised until a few years ago. As recently as 2005, twenty-three
Van Ingen tiger skins were sold in British auction rooms along with
a selection of their leopards, gazelles, jackals and a bear. They were
trophies, of course, consisting in most cases of skin and head only. If
you wanted your tiger skin to hang on a wall, the Van Ingens fixed
the head so that its eyes stared at you when you looked up, whereas, if
you wanted your skin to cover the floor, the Van Ingens would supply
a flatter head so that you would not trip over it. Sometimes they supplied head and shoulders or full body mounts, the skin stretched over
a papier mâché frame. You could choose from a catalogue the tiger's
expression, open-mouthed or with a snarl, for instance, and also its
pose, pouncing, lying, whatever. Clients liked bears on two legs,
because they were used as dumb waiters with plates in their outstretched paws. Perhaps some of these were auctioned too. You can
tell a Van Ingen animal trophy by its tongue and eyes. The tongues
are handcrafted from thin sheets of lead tapped with a hand punch to
create the surface details; the eyes are glass blanks purchased in bulk
from Germany and handpainted with Windsor and Newton paints.
Nothing but the best for 'Van Ingen and Van Ingen'.

There were three Van Ingen brothers who ran the business and
a fourth who lived on a coffee estate. Their Dutch father, Eugene,
who came to Mysore at the turn of the last century from Sri Lanka,
named them after generals in the Boer War: de Wet, Botha, Joubert
and Kruger. Apparently he wished to spite the British. With an eye
on his new business, he made the eldest, de Wet, his manager, sent
Botha to the National Leather Sellers' College in London to learn
the latest science of skin preservation and dispatched Joubert to a
college for sculptors in Berlin, because he was going to make the clay
models on which the taxidermy was based. The boys' mother, Patti
Wheal, was British but born in India, the daughter of a vet. A fierce
matriarch, she forbade her sons to marry, so de Wet and Joubert lived
all their long lives as bachelors in Bissal Munti, together with a wild
pig that had the run of the house. Joubert lives there still, the last of
the brothers, now in his ninety-fifth year.

The house breaks all the Indian rules, with small windows up under Gothic eaves, no veranda and many doors painted black and shut; a gloomy, defensive place. The high central corridor is creepy because the walls are covered with animal trophies: mounted heads, splayed skins, body parts. The Van Ingens were hunters themselves. Here are the skins of the first tigers that de Wet and Botha shot and next to them is the head of Joubert's first wild pig. There is at least one trophy that defies identification unless you are in the know. It is of a huge mahseer fish (de Wit holds the record for a catch weighing 120 pounds), but all that is mounted are the pharyngeal bones from the back of its throat stuck on a board. Why there is no plaster cast of this remarkable catch I do not know. Outside Bissal Munti is the former Van Ingen factory that Joubert was forced to close down a year or two ago, and until recently piles of skeletons lay about – a monkey head, articulated dog skeleton, sections of an elephant skull, that sort of thing.

Joubert cuts an elegant figure. He is still as slim and straight as a spear, with his skin stretched thin and tight over his frame, as a taxidermist might view it. We sit outside, and his eyes dart over the garden, missing nothing that moves. All his life he has lived for hunting as a sport. In the 1930s he was Club Secretary of the Mysore Pig-Stickers Club and wrote in *The Hoghunter's Annual* how sorry he was not to be able to spear bears and tigers too. He still lives for his hunting and fishing and makes no secret that he pursues his quarry illegally. He does not want to discuss anything with me except the taxidermy and here we are helped by a recent book, *Van Ingen & Van Ingen, Artists in Taxidermy*,[10] for which the British authors photographed the factory. We look at it together.

It occurs to me that, of all the 'stayers-on' I have met, Joubert is the one relic of the Raj. Killing animals and preserving them gave acceptability to the Dutch burgher Van Ingens among the snobbish British Raj set of Mysore, particularly when they were appointed taxidermists to the Maharaja. When the Raj withdrew, there was less demand for their work, and then the Wildlife Protection Act of 1972 finished it off, though only gradually, for museums and zoos still wanted Van Ingen trophies for a few years, as did illegal hunters. 'We were pestered by inspectors,' said Joubert. Living for taxidermy in the family house, the elderly bachelors de Wit and Joubert, unworldly and untravelled since their young days (except during the war, when Joubert was a prisoner of the Japanese on the Burma railway), were left high and dry. Michael Van Ingen, de Botha's son, said to me: 'The whole basis of Joubert's self-esteem and social standing were based on the fact that he could shoot tigers and preserve them. Suddenly that became a very undesirable thing to do and Joubert's never got over it. He has no other identity. Even the family recognises that.'

When a tiger skin plus head arrived at the factory in the old days, the skin was taken to the Fleshing Shed, where twenty or so employees would scrape and pare down the skin to remove any meat; then it was soaked in a patent Botha Van Ingen chrome tan solution to preserve it. Meanwhile, the skull of the tiger was measured and matched for size with one of thirteen different-sized moulds of tigers' heads in the Mould Store. 'I could tell at a glance', said Joubert, 'what size the tiger was. Most were 5 or 6, a really large tiger was 13.' Then a 'manikin' was selected from the Manikin Store for the right-sized head – that is a papier mâché model made by stuffing what Joubert called 'paper mash' inside the hollow mould and then removing it, if necessary by breaking the mould. This might not fit exactly the skin of the particular tiger's head being mounted, so when the skin was still wet it was stretched over the manikin and clay added to fit the contours. The skin was then removed, the manikin sealed with pitch or varnish and the skin replaced, stuck on with glue. The process was similar when a whole body mount was required. If no manikin was available on the shelf, then one had to be made bespoke, so to speak. This was where Joubert came in. He would make a model in clay based on photographs of the many skeletons of tigers in the sheds and from this a mould was made. The resultant manikin would be reinforced by light wooden spars fitted inside, for, as may be easily imagined, a springing tiger could not be made of 'paper mash' alone. Then the finishers got to work, painting, whiskering (nylon bristles from old brooms were used if necessary), eyeballing, false teeth (made of porcelain) and tongue fitting. It was quite likely that eight craftsmen would work on a taxidermied tiger: skin scraper, tanner, manikin maker, carpenter, eye-painter, modeller, finisher and packer. Joubert was proud of the whole production line.

It all seemed ghoulish to me, particularly the moulds and manikins. Pink in colour and lacking individual features, particularly eyes, they reminded me of aborted foetuses. Sometimes it was hard to recognise even the species from the over-smoothed features, yet, disturbingly, they were based exactly on creatures that had once been alive. Was that really a mould for a baby giraffe? Where had that snow leopard 'MC No. 5' (mouth closed, size 5) padded the Himalayan wastes? The nilgai head looked peacefully asleep, but the cranial portion was a cavity into which a wooden block would be inserted for screwing on the horns. I had hoped that, as Joubert had been the sculptor of tigers, he might talk of them like an artist. But no, imagination and taxidermy do not go together.

My sense of looking at an art gallery for veterinary butchers was increased by a photograph of a Van Ingen exhibition of tiger skulls badly damaged by gunshot wounds. Over fifty such skulls were in this macabre display, which had once been mounted in the factory as a warning against poaching. Joubert told me how the display had started:

We had the skin and skull of a tigress that had killed 100 people. It was very cunning, and villagers had tried many times to kill it. Eventually they shot it and sent the skin and head to us, and we found that someone much earlier had shot the tigress in the face and removed the whole of her front jaw. It had ossified so the poor tiger had lived entirely on eating people because human skin is so soft it's easy to get at the flesh. We kept the skin, but we had to use another skull. Many man-eaters were simply wounded tigers from gun wounds, broken legs, broken jaw. The electric torch made things worse. No animal had a chance, from hares to tigers. Many of our skins were made from wounded animals.

The actual collection is now in the Regional Museum of Natural History in Bhopal.

I asked Joubert if one particular Van Ingen commission came to mind, and he told me that the brothers had mounted the original white tiger. This is how it had come about:

> The Maharaja of Rewa shot about 1,000 tigers. He would sit up a tree reading a book and he had a pet monkey in the top of the tree to tell him when they were coming. Once he saw a tiger with four cubs running along, and one was white, so he asked his men to catch it. It was a young male. It grew up in his palace gardens and he mated it with an ordinary tigress. The cubs came out dark but when the Maharaja mated the white tiger again with one of its own offspring, the cubs all came out white and that is how it started. They sold many of them. Now there are white tigers in every zoo.

Old Joubert told me that he felt no affinity with tigers. Nevertheless, he realised they were a very special animal. On the subject of breeding he told me about his old employer, the fabulously wealthy previous Maharaja of Mysore, who had many daughters but no son and heir. So, said Joubert, 'the priests and stuff told him "you must shoot 100 tigers before you have a good son". It worked and that's how we got this present fat fellow.'

Writing about British India of the twentieth century, I am constantly reminded of how much attitudes have changed. The older generation who grew up under the Raj admit to their children of multiracial Britain that yes, they were racist in today's terms then; that yes, they shot tigers for the fun of it; that yes, they never learnt to cook and clean, because they always had servants. This is often said with a note of apology, but none of this would occur to old Joubert.

1. '2 K.G.' The High Commissioner's residence in New Delhi, painted by Sir David Goodall.

2. 'Raja' and Anne Wright at Tollygunge Club, 1989. (Photograph by Lord Drogheda)

3. Bob Powell Jones in his Shillong tea garden, 2007.

4. Derek Perry wears his 'Bombay bloomers' and shows off his Ford Prefect, New Dooars tea gardens, *c.* 1960.

5. 'Two leaves and a bud.' Pickers in an Assam tea garden, November 2005. (Photograph Romash Bhattacharji)

6. The late Nigel Hankin in expansive mood, 2006.

7. Father Weathrall with two sahibs, outside St James Church, Old Delhi, 2007.

8. The logo of the Delhi Brotherhood. The ancient Christian sign of the fish becomes a conch shell, the Eastern call to worship; either side are the feet of the pilgrim.

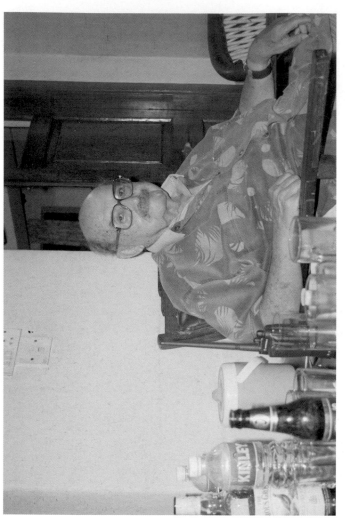

9. The late 'Papa' Wakefield enjoys his 91st birthday at Kabini Lodge, 2007.

10. To the victor the spoils. Wakefield, father and son with tiger, c. 1924.

11. The last of the taxidermists. Joubert Van Ingen with his trophies, at Bissal Munti, Mysore, 2006.

12. 'Our Apostolate: Roman Catholic Unification Founder and Director.' Melvyn Brown in front of his altar, Kolkata, 2007.

13. The Bannisters of Bethlehem Villas, Chakradharpur, 2007.

14. Kitty Texiera shows her daughter Yvonne the family history. McCluskigunge, 2007.

15. 'Something Understood.' Mark Tully with Muslim imams, 1994. (BBC photograph)

16. 'From Our Delhi Correspondent'. Mark Tully on the Pakistan border, 1982. (BBC photograph)

17. The late Frank Courtney MC and Bar, OBE, reading the lesson at the Remembrance Sunday service, the Afghan Church, Mumbai, 2007. (Photograph Lt-Col Graham Tullet OBE)

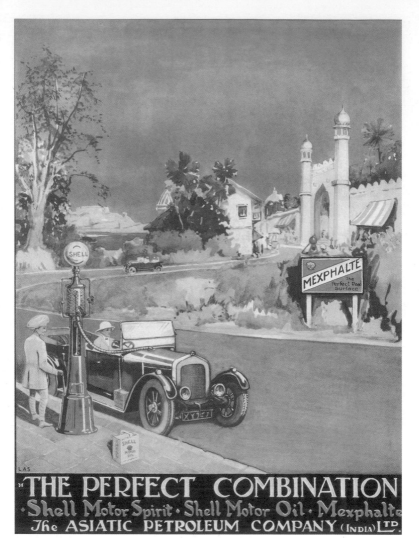

18. A British view of India in the 1930s, for sale in Mumbai.

19. Farida Hoosenally surrounded by British Indian tables in her Mumbai warehouse, 2007. (Photograph Deepak Haldankar)

20. Clues to the treasure. Foy Nissen with his family pictures. Mumbai, 2006. (Photograph Deepak Haldankar)

21. 'The liveliest society in Britain for the deadliest subject.' The late Theon Wilkinson and Dr Rosemary Llewellyn-Jones of BACSA, 1996.

22. The rich man in his mausoleum, the poor man at the gate. South Park Cemetery in the early 1970s before its renovation by BACSA.

Chapter Five

KITTY'S STORY

In 1912 Marjorie Roberts was born at Shillong in Assam and christened in the Welsh Presbyterian chapel down in the valley at Guwahati. Her Welsh grandfather had served in an East India Company regiment, but she was of mixed blood, an Anglo-Indian. She grew up, became a nurse in the war and married another 'half-caste', to use an ugly contemporary description, an Indian Portuguese from Goa called Texiera. After the war they moved to McCluskiegunge, a settlement in the wilderness of Bihar founded in 1933 as an intended homeland or *mulk* for their race. One of her friends who loved growing roses said: 'I am a hybrid, and here among my fellow hybrids is the only place I can feel at home.' In 1952 Marjorie gave birth to Kitty, but then disaster followed disaster. The Texieras had invested all their savings in the company running McCluskiegunge and, when it became clear that the homeland concept was doomed to failure, lost the lot. Then Marjorie's husband died. Imbued with a sense of being more British than Indian and feeling out of place in the new India, she was left to pine for a Britain she had never seen and lament her fate. Her bookcase contained her childhood reading, novels like *Little Women* and *What Katy Did*, and she quoted meaningfully to visitors the lines from Shakespeare's *As You Like It*: 'And so, from hour to hour we ripe and ripe, and then from hour to hour we rot and rot. And thereby hangs a tale.' She died in 1989, but not before she had become a grandmother.

Kitty had spent her childhood, uneducated, playing in the woods and hanging round the station. Not surprisingly in those circumstances she had 'gone jungli' and produced four children by a 'tribal' (the local aboriginal people). After Marjorie died she brought them up on her own, working the while by selling fruit down at the station, from which she earned an income of under 100 rupees a day (just over £1 in today's value). The hut where she had been born was still, in the 1990s, without running water or electricity or even a gas cylinder to cook on. Goats wandered in during the day and chewed what remained of the furniture.

I visited Kitty in 2007. She lives in the same hut, now with a stand pump outside, beside a small orchard of mango trees. She was dressed in threadbare clothes, but she spoke English with a refined accent. The original Welsh patriarch looked down severely on the poverty below from a painting that shared a wall with a photo of his granddaughter Marjorie, a self-possessed young lady in European clothes looking levelly at the camera from out of a cracked glass frame. Kitty introduced me to three smartly dressed and polite Indian-looking girls called Linda, Sylvia and Yvonne. They are her daughters. 'Kitty Mem' is marooned in McCluskiegunge, still illiterate and without any contact with the world outside, even a radio, but she is a survivor. She has found her answer to the plight of many of her people, including her mother, who still feel stuck in a country that is no longer the home of their choice.

Not surprisingly there are more Anglo-Indians in Kolkata than in any other Indian city, perhaps 20,000 families by the latest count. The founder of Calcutta in 1686, Job Charnock married an Indian widow he had saved from *suttee*, the burning alive of a widow on her husband's funeral pyre, so their three daughters must have been the earliest Anglo-Indians in the city. In fact, they were called Indo-British then and Eurasians later, for 'Anglo-Indian' meant something else – namely, a Briton returned home after many years in India. In those days there were fewer than 100 British women in Calcutta, and throughout the eighteenth century it was perfectly acceptable for British men to take Indian wives or concubines; mistresses were *bibis*, sometimes 'sleeping dictionaries', as pillow talk was considered a good way of learning English. 'Going native' was not a pejorative term then, and mixed relationships did not constitute a separate community. An advertisement in the *Calcutta Gazette* of 1809 showed how usual, and expensive, the maintenance of a *bibi* could be: 'To be sold by private sale, a garden house and grounds situated at Taltolah Bazar, which to any gentleman about to leave India, who may be solicitous to provide for an Hundostanee Female Friend, will be found a most desirable purchase.'

It was only when the British realised that they were outnumbered in Calcutta by Eurasians that they passed laws barring Eurasians from military and civil positions (1791) and forbade them from moving out of the towns. They also barred them from receiving a British education. That is why so many of the best Indian private schools, like La Martiniere College in Lucknow, were established for Eurasian boys. At the same time, the East India Company began its imperial phase of conquer and rule. From now on an attitude of cultural and political superiority prevailed, simply racism in fact. Marriage with 'half-castes' became socially unacceptable, so that, in 1835, 'to be seen in public with, or to be known to be intimate at the houses of Indo-Britons [Eurasians], was fatal to a new arrival in Calcutta; there was no possibility of emerging from the shade, or of making friends and connections in a higher sphere'.[1]

The Eurasian community grew up separate and inferior from this time. And then far more memsahibs came out, further isolating the British from the Indo-British. Later the term 'Domiciled Europeans' was given to Indian-born Europeans who only married or bred among their own race, but there can have been few of these over the generations.

Nevertheless, a campaign by prominent Eurasians in Calcutta forced the British government in 1833 to open middle-ranking government jobs to their community. From the mid-nineteenth century until the end of the Raj Anglo-Indians held most of these jobs on the railways, in customs, the post office and police. No wonder they were called 'the cranks, the levers of the Empire building machinery'. Their communities today are in towns with railway terminals, of which Kolkata is the largest. Here many 'A-Is', as they call them-

selves, live in Chowringhee, round Park Street, Bow Street and Elliot
Road. One Sunday morning, as the bell of St Mary's Catholic church
rang for Mass, I called on Melvyn Brown.

Melvyn is a self-important person. For a start he is the self-titled
'*Anglo-Indian Chronicler* in Calcutta'. He is also the editor of the
Anglo-Indian Newsletter, 'a non-profit, non-political effort to preserve, promote, propagate our history, heritage and culture'. He goes
about his work with zeal, even organising and presenting himself
the annual 'A-I Awards'. One of his small campaigns is to rename
his road 'Stephen Smith Road' in honour of 'the first Anglo-Indian
rocket expert'. Wearing his other hat, he is also a fervent Catholic
who has founded his own movement, Ambassadors for Jesus. In
this connection he calls himself 'Our Apostolate: Roman Catholic
Unification Founder and Director'. His multi-colour card ends,
in red print, 'Come and meet Melvyn Brown – An experience to
remember'. And so it was to prove.

A tiny man, as sharp and pointy as a needle, he sat in a chintz-
covered armchair with white antimacassar, dwarfed by an altar that
takes up the whole of the end wall of his living room. I became
mesmerised by this altar during our interview and at one point I
imagined Melvyn hopping onto it and squatting there like a gnome
beside all the other statuary. Down one side of his small front room
was a large bookcase with 2,000 VHS tapes, for Melvyn helps the
students of nearby Loretto College with their Film Studies. On the
opposite side wall were clocks giving the time round the world, con-
spicuously in the UK and Holland, where his son and daughter now
live. Melvyn yearns to be with them, though he knows it is too late.
He is an A-I, of course, though reluctant to talk about his parentage,
for he was handed over to an orphanage as a baby during the last
years of the Raj.

I asked him first to define an Anglo-Indian, and he put in his own
words the Indian Constitution, Article 366, 1950: 'A person whose
father or any of whose other progenitors in the male line is or was of
European descent but who is domiciled within the territory of India
and is or was born within such territory of parents habitually resident therein and not established there for temporary purposes only.'

This definition is based on the notion that all Europeans were *sahibs*. In the early days Portuguese mixed race were known as *mesticos*, Dutch as *olandis* and, wonderful to relate, in Bhopal still today are the Indo-French Bourbons, descendants of a younger brother of Henry of Navarre. The Government of India officially recognised the term Anglo-Indian in 1911, thereby replacing all previous definitions and applying it to all European–Indian mixed marriages or relationships of male descent. It is not a definition that finds favour with many 'true' Anglo-Indians – that is, by British descent through the male line. Nevertheless, Melvyn was proud because 'we are the only minority specifically referred to in the Constitution'. He spoke English in a slightly sing-song voice but with perfect elocution. I congratulated him. He replied: 'I want to say something very important. For Anglo-Indians English is the mother tongue and we are unique in that respect. All the other communities in India have their own language, but an Anglo-Indian is born with English. Even in the orphanage no one spoke to me in Hindi or Bengali.'

English is the distinguishing characteristic of the A-I. It is impossible to recognise an Anglo-Indian by appearance, so mixed are the genes, although in the racist days of the Raj various methods were attempted. A memsahib who suspected a young woman to be Eurasian might lift the girl's upper lip to check for blueness in the gums, just as horse owners inspect the teeth before buying. But language is a giveaway. A-Is used to be called *cheechees* because, says *Hobson-Johson*: 'It is a kind of onomatopoeia, indicating the mincing pronunciation that often characterises them [Eurasians]. It should be added that there are many well-educated East Indians who are quite free from this mincing accent. It is supposed to come from the way English is taught in the convent or Brothers' schools.'

I did not notice anything *cheechee* about Melvyn's English, though the slight lilt sounded a bit Welsh? Apparently that is a characteristic of Kolkata A-Is – an attempt in the past, some say, to disguise the racial origin.

The English language was the passport to Anglo-Indian success. For the men it eased the way into middle-management government jobs, and for the women it led the way towards emancipation.

Crisply dressed, efficient and discreet, the hallmarks of their race, Anglo-Indian women found work in British companies as secretaries and typists, in hospitals as nurses and in schools as teachers. The first air hostess in India was an A-I. It is well known that several film stars in the West were Anglo-Indian, such as Vivien Leigh and Merle Oberon, for A-I women are celebrated for their beauty, but it is less well known that Renée Smith (*Sita Devi*), Ruby Myers (*Sulochana*) and others became stars of Indian movies too. Film stars, band soloists, dancers and hotel receptionists – the sort of jobs that can give a girl a bad name; and they did. More deserved is the reputation that Anglos like having a good time, and they are happy to admit this. It was 'sugar in the morning, sugar in the evening, sugar at suppertime', remembered one, recalling the years when American sailors roamed the bars. Another admitted 'we enjoyed today because we thought there would be no tomorrow'; the angst of the Anglo-Indian.

Melvyn assured me that the other distinguishing feature of the A-I was the Christian faith. He had the dogmatic manner of the teacher:

> That's something I'd like to clarify. All Anglo-Indians are Christians, but not all Christians are Anglo-Indians. That's very, very important in preserving our heritage. There are many Bengali Christians who wear a cross around their neck and have an English name just because they've been converted. I had a man walk in here who said he was an Anglo-Indian and wanted a letter of introduction for a job. He said 'My name is Shane McGregor'. I said 'Who gave you that name?' I saw he was Nepali, 100 per cent, a Nepali from Nepal. He said: 'I was a Hindu but when Father baptised me he said "from today you are Shane McGregor"'. I told him to go and read the Indian Constitution. Actually, I've never met a Hindu Anglo-Indian. We are all Christians.

Whereas during the Raj the Anglo-Indian home might well have had a picture on the wall of the King Emperor, now it is more likely to be a picture of Christ or the Virgin Mary. I found this to be the case wherever I went. One day I arrived in the town of Chakradharpur in Jarkhand to see an old Anglo-Indian couple named the Bannisters, who lived in Nazareth Villa, and just then the nearby mosque called the faithful to prayer with the *azan*. 'That's my call to Angelus', said Pat, 'we have to rely on the mosque now.' I asked Kitty if she went to church? 'Well,' she said, 'I do go to the Catholic church, but I don't really like it. I am an Anglican.' In the circumstances her delicate sectarianism seemed a little incongruous. The church has taken over from the club as the centre of Anglo life. In Kolkata the A-I Ranger Club still exists, though in a state of dilapidation, where young men play billiards until the small hours and eat free chips with tomato sauce to go with their Kingfisher beer. It is largely a sporting club now, for the A-Is have always excelled, particularly at hockey.

I asked Melvyn if he felt more British than Indian or the other way round? 'That's a very tricky question you know. I do like the fact that I'm half English, but I'm very pleased about the other half too, because it puts me in a very flexible position.' As a matter of fact, Melvyn's wishful thinking extends to the claim in his literature that he is British. His booklet 'All about Melvyn Brown' says: 'his mother, Iris Sarah, was the daughter of a British boiler maker and his father, Eric James (Clifford) Brown was an English civil servant.' When I pointed this out to him, he admitted he could not prove it. Clearly he is Anglo-Indian, and this affectation is simply another example of how some Anglos yearn to be British in the same way that they regard Britain as Home.

The A-Is pride themselves on being good mixers, and, of course, their success in government jobs under the Raj was because they could act as subordinates of the rulers while understanding the ruled. Then Melvyn went on: 'having said that, it's in our genes to be very loyal and dedicated to the British. That's why after Independence we felt kicked in the teeth. But the Anglo-Indian is very loyal. You can kick him, bruise him, but he will still come back for more.' He was referring to the common assumption that, when the British went Home in 1947, they left their partial kith and kin behind. Melvyn feels very strongly about this: 'One of our first leaders, Frank Anthony, wrote a book called *Britain's Betrayal in India*. It was outlandish, shocking, what is the meaning of this? But I've looked into the matter. The British did desert us. It was 1947, the time of the bloody Partition. That was the time the British should have given us a hand.'

Exactly what this hand should have been Melvyn did not say. In fact, the assumption is surely more a state of mind than the truth? Although the British Nationality Act of 1949 removed British nationality from Anglo-Indians, it did not restrict their right to immigrate into the United Kingdom, because they were regarded as Commonwealth citizens with unrestricted right of entry. This right lasted until the Commonwealth Immigration Act of 1962. Although they were not offered assisted passage, they were given a special dispensation, if they wanted to leave, of the free repatriation of capital. It is, however, still a sore point. I was once shown round Lucknow by a former pupil of La Martiniere School, and together we met another Anglo-Indian, a CNI priest. The guide received a frosty reception when he announced he was about to immigrate to Dubai. Afterwards I asked him why? 'The vicar still hasn't forgiven you British for not taking him with you, so he's jealous of me.'

The image of doglike devotion unreciprocated by the master runs through Anglo-Indian history. In the early days the *bibi* had no choice but loyalty to her master, because she had often been rejected by her Indian family. In the Indian Mutiny, Eurasians supported the British at great cost to themselves, particularly as the mutineers killed all Christians out of hand, but were still mocked as *eight annas* (half a rupee) or *tar brushes*. The nominated leader of the Anglo-Indians in the Constituent Assembly, Sir Henry Gidney, said in 1928: 'Let me inform the Government that like faithful dogs we have followed the bone but today it is meatless. And what have you done for us?' The truth was that under the Raj many Anglo-Indians identified with Britain far more than with India but felt they were mocked for doing so.

This is one of the themes of John Master's novel *Bhowani Junction*, written in 1954 about the time immediately before Independence. The beautiful A-I heroine, train driver's daughter Victoria Jones, has a crisis of identity. With Independence coming, she thinks she has to decide whether she is British or Indian because the new India will have no place for the 'cranks and levers of Empire'. Her A-I boyfriend, Patrick Taylor, calls Indians 'Wogs' and always wears a solar *topi*, rain or shine, a sunhat that was so much part of the British uniform

that the British were called *topi-wallahs*, 'the hat people'. Realising
that he will soon be an anachronism, she decides to make her future
with a Sikh suitor, and is thrown out of the British club for wearing
a *sari*. But she feels no more at home in the Sikh *gurdwara* (temple)
than wearing a *sari*, and this is when the third character in the tri-
angle, the arrogant Lieutenant-Colonel Rodney Savage, enters the
scene. He ignores the Sikh, Ranjit Singh, and mocks Patrick Taylor's
cheechee accent and *topi*. He soon seduces the vulnerable Victoria,
knowing that Patrick will still admire him. She says to Patrick of a
previous affair: 'He thought because he was a British officer and I
was a *cheechee* girl I'd do anything. And – Patrick, do you understand
this? – he was right. Slowly, slowly, I did feel I had to do it.'

Victoria's dilemma has a most powerful catharsis in two juxtapos-
ing scenes. The first is when she is persuaded to convert to Sikhism
by her new boyfriend, Ranjit Singh. At the height of the ceremony,
numbed by the chanting and strange rituals, the words of the guru
'beating down like steady hammers, merciless, emphatic', she is given
the new Sikh name of 'Kirat'. This shocks her to her senses: 'But my
name was Victoria. I was a *cheechee* engine driver's daughter. I am
Victoria Jones.' She runs headlong out of the *gurdwara* until, her mind
in automatic pilot, she finds herself in Bhowani Junction station. The
Ninety Eight Up, driven by her father, is just pulling out and she
jumps onto the footplate:

> Woof! The platform began to slide back. The safety valve shut down
> with a click as the steam entered the cylinders. Out in front of us
> the rails stretched like tangled snakes between the yards and the Loco
> sheds. I hugged myself with pleasure, even in a *sari*, and muttered the
> names of the signals I knew by heart, 'Up Yard Approach–clear, Up
> Loco Shed–clear ...'

Victoria is numbed by different sounds 'beating down like steady hammers, merciless, emphatic', but this time she is intoxicated. Afterwards
she thanks her father, who says 'the other thing was all wrong, but
now you have found that out for yourself.' But she soon finds out that
the Raj culture, as personified by Colonel Savage, is 'all wrong' too

and will become even more wrong if she goes Home with him. She throws in her lot with Patrick again and decides to stay. But whether they will find a new home in India is left a question mark.

In 1947 many Anglo-Indians did not, like Victoria and Patrick, give the new India a chance. They did not just feel out of place; they felt fear that they would be persecuted for having supported the Raj against Indian nationalism. Indeed, some were. They found the 'Quit India' slogan daubed on their doors, and in Bombay, where the Indian Navy had mutinied against the British, some were spat at in public. Moreover, some felt despised by both Muslims and Hindus because they were illegitimate, the result of British and American soldiery in recent years. Many thousands left in a hurry for the ABC of Australia, Britain and Canada. Melvyn told me his earliest memory that recurred to him as a dream was of busloads of A–I's racing to the port of Calcutta in 1947, where a big ship was waiting, but he could not get on it. Another giveaway.

In fact, said Melvyn, this was 'a fear phobia that was misplaced. Those who remained discovered that the Indians had a Sahib complex. The British had ruled them for 350 years so that after the British left they transferred this complex to the Anglo-Indian.' He added with satisfaction: 'they were drawn to us like magnets.' Earlier I asked him why so many Anglo-Indians had worked on the railways. His reply was revealing:

> MB: In the first place because the Anglo was very close to the Indian. He knew all the languages and we needed them to work on the railways, because they could manage the thousands of Indians needed to build this huge system.
> Me: You say 'we' needed them. 'We' being …?
> MB: Ha, ha, ha, you've got me there! You see the loyalty is still there. You've got me trapped!

Melvyn seems to have his own crisis of identity. Indians say *desai murghi*, *belati bath*, meaning 'local chicken, English talk'.

The second mass exodus of Anglo-Indians was in that decade of change, the 1960s. Impoverished by the economic slump that led to devaluation and depressed by the withering-away of Raj sentiment symbolised by Nehru's death, many felt in Melvyn's words 'now look, we're not part of your problems'. There was a more specific reason too. The Indian government of 1947 had continued the Anglo-Indian reservation of jobs on the railways and in other public services from one generation of a family to the next, provided the applicant was of the right standard, but only for one more generation. So son followed father until the 1960s. Then, under competition, he found that he was no longer superior. Melvyn knew why: 'The Anglos are epicurean. They live one day at a time. Just like Alcoholics Anonymous.' He meant that they did not have the determination to study and better themselves, which perhaps is not surprising, if so many jobs were handed down in the family. In any event, the British government once again mocked Anglo aspirations by closing the door with the Immigration Acts of the 1960s. That left the United States, Commonwealth and the Middle East.

From then on for another two decades the living standards of the Anglo-Indian declined, so that many in Calcutta, as elsewhere, were reduced to a genteel and isolating poverty depicted poignantly in the film *36 Chowringhee Lane*. The gap between income and lifestyle widened, for A-Is are well known for keeping up appearances. Morale fell, and many girls 'married out', because they looked down on the Anglo boys. Some thought that only the dregs of their society remained. Marjorie Roberts of McCluskiegunge was not the only one with a pathological desire to leave. When India celebrated its fiftieth anniversary, a popular song among the Anglos was sung by one of their sons, Arnold Dorsey of Madras, alias Engelbert Humperdinck: 'Please release me, let me go, for I don't love you any more.' Another sore point is that Harry Webb, alias Cliff Richard, apparently does not mention in his autobiography his A-I upbringing in Lucknow. Both Melvyn's children left. His son is now working with a church in Southall outside London: 'I advised him to go, yes. I said "Son, it was always my dream to go to England" and he said, "What you can't do, I'm going to do for you."' He is relieved, nevertheless, that his son has married an Anglo girl, for anything else would be 'marrying out', even in the UK. Now there are perhaps 400,000 Anglo-Indians left in India.

Before I left I asked Melvyn about his altar, the very size and gaudiness of which in that small front room had overwhelmed our conversation. Actually, according to Melvyn's publicity, 3 Elliot Road is not really a private home and the altar is something else as well. He calls the altar THE HOME OF DIVINE MERCY and his home THE AMBASSADORS FOR JESUS CENTRE. No one could accuse Melvyn of the Anglo-Indian inferiority complex. He holds a Ladies' Prayer Circle in front of the altar regularly, the aim of which is to speed on their way petitions, handed over in advance on a piece of paper with the relevant boxes ticked: 'good health, family unity, safe journey, peace of mind, peaceful death' and so on. But his main aim is Catholic unity, as he explained to me:

> I wrote a 30-page letter to the Holy Father, Pope John Paul II. I explained to him 'Look here'. I got up one morning and I realised there should be a lay Catholic movement working inside the church to bring about unity among Catholics. I realised that the breakaway brethren, as we call Protestants, were more educated. They could quote directly from the Bible – whole lines and passages – and we could not. The Protestants know their Bibles inside out and upside down. Also, Catholics are not very polite. If you go to a Catholic house and knock on the door, the owner will bang the door in your face, whereas when you go to a Protestant home and knock on the door, the owner is very polite. The Holy Father took six months before he sent me a reply. It just said 'Deus Vult'. It's Latin.

Melvyn pulled a sad face at this recollection. It seemed to me a bit of a put-down, but I needed a translation. 'It means "If God Wills",' said Melvyn, and we left it at that.

I wanted to pay homage to the 'railway Johnnies', because without doubt they had operated the largest railway system in the world and probably the most idiosyncratic. Figures in India are always staggering, as if an extra zero has been added, but these statistics from 2002 seem correct: 37,000 miles of track carried 7,000 trains every day on which over 3.7 billion passengers travelled every year, the whole system serviced by a colossal staff of 1.6 million. The trains may be slow and overcrowded by Western standards, but they seem to leave and arrive mostly on time, without mishap, and cover vast distances measured by days sometimes more than hundreds of miles. The 'vade mecum' for train buffs is a Byzantine, 200-page book of timetables called 'Trains at a Glance'. Proof to me of the efficiency of the railway system is a miraculous piece of paper called the Carriage Passenger List, for it proves that out of chaos comes order.

Arriving after dark at a large station is disconcerting, sometimes threatening. A red-badged porter seizes your case, like it or not, places it on his head for recognition, and takes off through a crowd of humanity. You are forced to follow, assailed by beggar boys who crowd in from all directions (Howrah station in Kolkata is home for 3,000 children who roam in gangs), while you step round families or groups of pilgrims, for that matter, who are sleeping or eating on the platforms. On the tracks the trains wait. Through the dirty carriage windows or the bars of the open-sided cars carrying third class or lower you can see in the semi-dark countless limbs and faces of passengers squeezed together. You are aware that this may soon be your fate. Sweat sticks your shirt to your back, above you myriads of insects buzz round the dirty neon lighting and you cannot avoid the smell. Then you see what you are looking for, Carriage Second Class A/C (Air-Conditioned), Three Tier, on the, say, Coromandel Express from Kolkata to Chennai leaving at 00.30 hours. Stuck to the side is a computer print-out of the names, ages and sex and berth numbers of all passengers travelling therein. No matter that there are thirty-six of you, one on top of the other separated by little curtains, and your porter has disappeared inside with your case. You have been exactly identified as an individual among this crush of humanity. It is with a feeling of relief and excitement that you heave yourself aboard.

Thirty years ago, in 1957, the BBC radio reporter Gerald Priestland recorded a memorable edition of *From our own Correspondent*, which he wrote while waiting for a train near Kolkata:

> Railway India is an India all its own. And, unlike any of the other Indias, it embraces the whole country. The man who loves the Punjab may be miserable in Madras. But the man who loves Indian railways

can be happy anywhere in the subcontinent. Together with the English language, they are probably the most useful gifts the British left here. As I see it, he who is tired of Indian railway stations is tired of life, for they're not merely places of transit – life goes on in them.

Since 1957 the trains have changed. No longer do the first-and second-class compartments look like Victorian waiting rooms with their own private bathrooms. No longer are there warnings like 'Beware of thieves asking for permission to sleep on the floor'. But what Priestland called the 'timeless Indian railway spirit' still exists:

> It's given me a new emotional – one might say almost spiritual – experience, a sort of romantic railway melancholy. It is only to be found on long journeys in the dark and comes during poignant halts beside stale-scented platforms whose names, if one could read the language, might well be Lethe or Limbo. Or it comes as the engine trundles its way through the night, as if it had lost its way and suspected it might be in the wrong country.
>
> At moments like this, the enormous questions of the universe seem to come crowding into one's compartment, like Indian ticket collectors, to demand: 'Who are you? Where do you come from? Where are you going?' Well, on an Indian railway – who knows?

No doubt many people travel by train because the roads are so dreadful. With the exception of new trunk roads connecting the metropolitan bases of Delhi, Mumbai, Kolkata and Chennai, they are in calamitous condition and overwhelmed with a variety of traffic found nowhere else. Express buses and private cars force their way through 'as if', said a friend, 'there is no tomorrow and for some of their passengers there probably isn't'. Heavy lorries belching fumes and staggering under outsize loads follow them. Weaving in between like minnows among whales are auto-rickshaws (known as *tuk-tuks*) and bicycles. In the rear, sometimes blithely stationary in fact, are sacred cows and bullocks pulling carts that seem to have a blind faith in their survival. Only two rules seem to apply: right always gives way to might, and, just as nature abhors a vacuum, so drivers abhor an empty space. Within seconds a vehicle has manœu-vred to fill it simply to keep moving. I travelled on one such road from Ranchi in the new state of Jharkhand to the railway junction town of Chakradharpur, there to meet a community of retired 'rail-way Johnnies'.

I was a passenger in the car of Joseph Galstaun, a prominent Anglo-Indian who has Armenian, Dutch, Portuguese, Irish and Indian blood coursing through his veins. He is, in fact, the local member of the state parliament, the Legislative Assembly, for Jharkhand is one of the states where the ruling party, in this case the Bharatiya Janata Party (BJP), may nominate two Anglo-Indian members. With us were his private assistant and bodyguard, and over the next few days I never discovered whether their presence was more a comment on the state of politics in this corrupt state or on his own personal status. In 2005 the Chief Minister of the neighbouring state of Bihar was the wife of a former Chief Minister, Laloo Prasad Yadav, who had corruption charges pending against him. He himself was Minister of Railways for the whole of India and possibly responsible for the neat legal dodge called 'anticipatory bail'. *Hanklyn-Janklin* defines it as 'a provision, unique in the world's judicial codes, whereby in anticipation of a criminal accusation, a person may apply to a court for bail: if granted and the charge is made, he will be exempt from police custody'.

In the car Joseph handed me a sheet of notepaper printed with a shield on the top. Quartered into stars and lions, it read round the edge: 'The All India Anglo-Indian Association, Courage is Destiny, 1876'. Pinned to it was a file containing details about the thirteen railway families that I was about to meet: the Bannisters, Greens, O'Learys, Vengeances, Jennings, Samuels, Wilsons, Pentons, Paynes, Godfreys, Smiths, Reids and Van Haeftens. Here was the Christian caste of railwaymen and proof, if any were needed, that A-Is descend through the male line. Seven of the thirteen families had served on the railways from the 1940s onwards through two or more genera-tions, and most of the old railwaymen had been drivers, inspectors, instructors or supervisors – that is, the senior NCO-type jobs.

Their community in Chakradharpur was clustered round a Catholic church; small bungalows with two rooms front and back, cement facia walls with tiled roofs and neat gardens. I noticed that, when we arrived, Joseph kissed the wives on the cheek, a recognition signal that ostentatiously distinguishes Christians from Muslims and Hindus. The bungalow interiors were similar, displaying the identification symbols of the Anglo-Indian – that is Catholic paintings of the Virgin Mary or the crucifixion, sometimes a UK calendar or a copy of a Constable rural scene and photographs of relatives long since departed abroad.

The leader of the community, Keith Godfrey, stood by a picture of his grandfather, Ernest Stanley Godfrey, who had been the British stationmaster at Chakradharpur and obviously the first of the line. He looked something of a dandy, with a waxed moustache and a wide lapelled dark blazer with white braid. Keith had worked at Chakradharpur for forty years and graduated as a driver from steam through diesel to electric locomotives. Like all the others I met, he was immensely proud of his time on the railways as a driver and said that even today, if a VVIP (a Very, Very, Important Person) was a passenger, then an A-I driver was found if possible for the loco. Like the others too, he wished he had emigrated to Britain or Australia in the 1960s, but he had left it too late and could not get a visa. So now it was charity work for the church, housey-housey (Bingo!) evenings and a big Christian Christmas. His daughter had married an Indian, because Anglo boys are lazy – 'they're dropouts, plenty of brain but not enough effort' – and by now he felt more Indian than British. Nevertheless, he was proud to be an Anglo-Indian: 'I can recognise an Anglo by his behaviour. He is a good mixer, no discrimination. All are equal but we are better than Indians. We take responsibility. We always do our job. We are reliable and efficient. That was our reputation and I think it still is.'

My favourite was Pat Bannister, an English teacher from 1959 until retirement, who was married to hard-of-hearing George, one time 'Chargeman, Loco Boiler Department'. She handed me a glass of her home-made marigold wine when I arrived and showed me her address book that contained thirty-seven British addresses for Christmas cards. She was in a gay Sunday mood and started to trill: '"Que sera, sera, whatever will be, will be, the future's not ours to see, que sera, sera." Of course I wanted to leave India, and my daughters still reproach me, but George wouldn't budge. He said he liked the railways too much. "Better the devil you know" was his view.'

She spoke and sang with a clear voice, a twinkle in her eye and, as far as I could see, just one tooth in her mouth. She used many English catchphrases and quotations, as Anglo-Indians do:

> We were happier under the British, so when Independence came we were sad and glad. The British gave us a lot of opportunities, though they did look down on us a bit. We hoped things would work efficiently under the Indians, and they did to start with. All our nurses were Anglos. Our trains were never late. Our men were called 'the sahibs'. I never thought we didn't belong and I've never felt superior to Indians. I'm very proud to be an Anglo. We have the culture of both. We can dine with the king and also the beggar.

Pat was an optimist and the first Anglo I met, though not the last, with a positive view about the future:

> Our boys and girls are doing well now, after a slump. In fact they are getting better jobs than our sales girls in Australia. We go into Indian homes and mix a lot. This is new. We are adapting. Indians are ready to help us and we to help them. You see 'Que sera, sera', and whatever is past, is past. We are here to stay.

Joseph Galstaun, MLA, took his cue: 'We have put our stamp on Indian society and we still do. After a depression we are starting to take up the challenges and our young people are getting educated. Now we are ready for everything.' Joseph embraced Pat and we said goodbye, rejoining his personal assistant and bodyguard, who were waiting outside Nazareth Villas. We drove back through the afternoon sun, and I tried to imagine Victoria Jones and Patrick Taylor living as an elderly couple in Bhowani Junction.

The next day Joseph was going to take me to McCluskiegunge, but he said it was unsafe. One of the so-called Naxalite bandits had been murdered nearby, and his supporters were refusing to remove his corpse from the road unless the police paid them compensation. Instead we talked in my hotel at Ranchi, which, to provide a pointer, is about seven hours by rail due west of Kolkata and roughly two hours equidistant between McCluskiegunge to the north-east and Chakradharpur to the north-west. Galstaun came in looking every inch a powerful public figure; stocky build with swept-back silvery hair and black-framed glasses, wearing a dark blue Nehru waistcoat over collarless white shirt and trousers, with black shoes. His retinue remained in the lobby.

Joseph told me that he had been a teacher until retirement with a reputation for helping Anglo-Indians like himself, so the BJP had nominated him for one of the two MLA posts reserved for his community. This causes him some embarrassment, because the BJP is adopting an anti-Christian stance provoked by missionaries in Jharkand who are paid, said Joseph, on a *per capita* basis by an American foundation for conversions to Christ. He has been given an education portfolio and is determined to obtain state funding for Anglo-Indian Christian schooling. In 1982 he founded the Dominic Savio High School in Patna, which now has over 5,000 boys and girls, and for years he has paid out of his own pocket for poor A-I children to attend. The more Joseph talked, the more I realised he is one of the rare politicians in India with a concept of public service and the drive to be effective. He has kind eyes behind those power spectacles.

Joseph was born in Patna in 1939. His great-grandfather had fled from Armenia to India via Holland, and his maternal grandmother had been *pukka* Irish, he said. One of his earliest memories was of hotheads from the Quit India movement coming to their home to drag her away, because her fair complexion and inability to speak Hindi made her an enemy. She hid in a clothes chest. Later, when the Union Jack was pulled down outside the Collectors House, his grandmother cried and so did all the servants; but the family decided to stay. They sent Joseph to St Michael's School in Patna, where 80 per cent of the pupils were Anglo-Indians, mostly children of railwaymen. The teachers were Irish Christian Brothers. Joseph then reached into an inside pocket of his waistcoat and pulled out a photograph. It was labelled 'St Michael's Reunion September 2006' and showed a group of thirty-two prosperous-looking late-middle-aged alumni, hardly a brown face among them, standing in a garden in Croydon, south London. It took some time for the significance of this perfectly ordinary looking photo to sink in. At least half of them (for wives were in the photo too) had been children in the same school, at the same time, in a small town in India; all had migrated to England. Remarkable! Not surprisingly, St Michael's is now entirely Indian and the Irish Brothers have left too.

The leader of the Anglo-Indians in 1947 was a lawyer, Frank Anthony. Alarmed at the mass exodus of his community, he made his position clear: 'Let us cling and cling tenaciously to all we hold dear, our language, our way of life and our distinctive culture. But let us always remember we are Indians.' Joseph stressed the second sentence when he quoted this to me. Frank Anthony was a member of the Indian parliament, the *Lok Sabha* ('House of the People'), as well as a lawyer, so he was able to get the Anglo-Indian community constitutional safeguards the British had always refused – two nominated seats in the *Lok Sabha* and about ten in several state Legislative Assemblies. More importantly, the new Indian Constitution singled out the Anglo-Indians as a community, the only community mentioned by name, and safeguarded both the Christian religion and the English language. Yet Joseph thought this was insufficient. He thought that the 'replacement employment' practice in public jobs should have extended for another decade, 'to give Anglos more of a chance'. That was history, but his campaign now is to extend the rights of the scheduled castes and tribes who are given 15–20 per cent of all government posts to cover Anglo-Indians too. 'Why shouldn't we have this minority treatment?'

Joseph Galstaun looks to the future. Not for him the yearning to be 'Home', the subconscious assumption of being British caricatured by Melvyn Brown. He quotes the Anthony dictum 'remember we are Indians'. He finds the McCluskiegunge concept of living in a ghetto and clinging to a unique identity completely out of time. 'India is a pluralist society and we must embrace that.' Moreover, he told me, there are many signs that this new positive attitude is winning:

We are staging a comeback. Most Anglos have decided they do have a future in India. Indeed, some are returning from abroad. Also, now that India is much more concerned with women's rights there are many women who think they should be eligible for Anglo-Indian descent if it's passed through the female line. After all, whether you are a boy or a girl if either of your parents is of European heritage then you should be treated as an Anglo-Indian. It shouldn't matter that you've lost your name.

As with many things, it is the economic boom in India that is changing established ways of life. The growing middle class in India, said Joseph, is adopting Western lifestyles in clothes, furnishings and food and becoming far more familiar with them through television. Thus the Anglo should be moving from a relic of a past culture to membership of the growing Indian middle class. Moreover, with Westernisation come also new job opportunities for the young Anglo male: 'He should be going into an office and saying: "Look, I speak both languages, English and Hindi. I have the right appearance and the right name for dealing with America or Britain." Our Anglo women were never backward in any way. They brought respectability into the office, and now it's the boys' turn.'

Positive to his fingertips, Joseph sees another advantage for the Anglo male in this new world, he has the right walk:

It's a peculiar trait. If you are used to wearing a *pyjama* (loose cotton trousers with a draw string) or a *dhoti* (a Gandhi-like loincloth wrapped round the waist and thighs and tucked between the legs), you are always hitching it up and you stoop, whereas the Anglo who walks with a pair of pants walks properly. He doesn't stoop; he's upright.

I asked him whether the Indian-Anglo was contributing to this new age – an outcome of the Indians in Britain rather than the British in India. After all, 'onelayer urban communities', as sociologists call places like Hounslow or Southall in the London suburbs, are now Indian-Anglo in lifestyle, including intermarriage. Disappointingly, he did not accept this: 'No, it hasn't affected our community in any way. Actually, I have observed that Indians who marry abroad and bring their British wives home here don't get a very good reception from the Indian community.'

The next day I left for McCluskiegunge with the bodyguard in a hired car. He wore civilian clothes so as to avoid attention and tucked his gun inside his shirt. Come what may, Joseph Galstaun ordered, we had to be off the single-track road through the forest before dark. This struck me as so incongruous. In my mind throughout the journey was a Sunday colour-supplement article about McCluskiegunge that had caught my eye in the late 1970s. The photos showed a sort of Tunbridge Wells in an Indian wilderness. At least, the insides of the houses and the people who lived in them could have been in Tunbridge Wells: quite grand retired folk from the armed or civil services taking tea and reading back copies of *Country Life* in their chintz-covered armchairs under a picture of the Queen, probably with a dog at their feet. *Chhota England* in fact. Home Counties smugness did not go with bandits hiding in the woods. Come to think of it, nothing in McCluskiegunge seemed to go with India at all. It was not even an anachronism; it was a fantasy, and that was its attraction.

The car turned off a tarmac road and wound up the Chhota Nagpur hills to a plateau at about 1,500 feet. Either side of the track was thick woodland, where lived in small villages the Adivasi tribal people; and supposedly some bandits too. It seemed an unlikely place to found a *mulk* or homeland, but that is what happened in the 1930s, when an Irish-Indian estate agent in Calcutta, T.E. McCluskie, persuaded the Raja of Ratu to donate 10,000 acres to the cause. Perhaps McCluskie saw himself as another Theodor Herzl, the founder of political Zionism, for the Anglo-Indians compared themselves with the Jews as an abused and wandering people. A homeland in India seemed a better option to McCluskie and 350 or so Anglo-Indian families than either going Home with the British or finding home amid the new India that everyone knew would shortly be born. Other locations were spotted too, like Whitefield near Bangalore, and another community came into being at Tangaserri in Kerala. McCluskie and his followers set to with energy, and, being a real-estate man, he knew what to do. He set up the Colonisation Society of India Ltd, which lent money for the construction of spacious, *burra sahib* bungalows complete with high ceilings, verandas, fire-grates, et al. As with other pioneering settlements, the dream was pronounced true when the church was built, and in June 1940 the *Colonisation Observer* recorded the event. It said: 'We see in McCluskiegunge the beginnings of what the Muslems call Pakistan, but what we call Anglo-India: a place in India where we can foregather and mix freely.' By that time other features of the British dream were reality too: a public garden with a fountain, a club of course, and houses called Retreat, The Hermitage and Dunroamin.

But from the beginning the rural idyll was not practical, except for rich second-home owners from Calcutta who wanted to hunt wild pig and make marmalade from the newly planted orange trees. It was cut off, apart from a twice-daily steam train. It lacked reliable supplies of electricity, and, critically, there was nothing for the young people to do. They left almost from the start. During the second Anglo-Indian exodus of the 1960s, the insecurity reached McCluskiegunge too and turned into a small panic. Some fled with the 'For Sale' sign still hanging from the gatepost, while others sold for throwaway prices. By the 1970s the vibrant energy of the early years had been replaced by the listlessness of a geriatric community. The society went into liquidation and the club closed. The trains no longer arrived with any frequency. And that was thirty years ago.

The road stopped climbing and levelled out onto the plateau. Scattered among the thin lines of trees were large bungalows behind overgrown gardens, empty and boarded up. Only twenty-three families remain in the Anglo-Indian part of McCluskiegunge. We drove past the Don Bosco Christian Academy founded in 1997 and stopped outside School View Hostel. No one was about except a large dog behind a heavy barred gate reinforced with chains and a padlock. Then I recognised from a photo that, behind the dog and recumbent in a wicker chair, was old Captain Mendonca. Standing next to him was a scared little boy, who, after gruff orders and much effort, opened the gate. The bodyguard remained outside looking vigilant and I sipped tea with the old sailor. He had little to say except that once his merchant ship had anchored in the port of London, so we sent out the frightened little boy, who was boarding at the hostel and about to start at the Don Bosco Academy, to bring back Mrs Mendonca from her shopping. I sat on the wall looking at a poor yard that seemed to belong more to a depopulated Irish village than to salubrious Tunbridge Wells. Then Mrs Mendonca appeared, much younger than her husband and wearing a *sari* with a blue scarf. Her pale complexion gave her away, and then that unmistakable voice, refined but slightly stilted: 'How do you do, I'm Judy Tip-Top,' she said, extending her hand. 'Not Dorothy?' I said without thinking. 'She was my mother,' Judy replied, and then I realised a generation had passed since that Sunday supplement article in 1979.

It was written by the British journalist Ian Jack, whose wife's aunt and uncle lived in Calcutta and had bought a second home in McCluskigunge. He visited several times until 1991, fascinated by this marooned community pretending it was in the Home Counties: 'McCluskiegunge is a chastening place to think about race. A separate racial identity did not seem to have been the solution for Anglo-Indians, but then what was?' He got to know the characters:

> Several of the men had retired from the railways. Mr Jim King's proudest possession was a photo of the locomotive that had hauled King George V to the Delhi durbar, driven by his father. And if you asked these men how they were, they would reply 'Oh, pulling along, pulling along' as if they themselves were engines.
>
> The women wore frocks and (in the cool season) cardigans and socks. They were kind and lively: 'Have some more plum cake,' said Mrs Rosario. 'Try my guava jelly,' said Mrs Tip-Top. Photographs were passed round: Conrad in Romford, Tyrone in Ontario, brown men in white countries trying to adjust.[2]

While I photographed Judy Tip-Top sitting under a lime tree next to her jars of salted lime pickle, two neighbours gathered at her garden table: Harold Menezes, who, despite his name, looked and sounded thin and threadbare Irish; and Christopher Da Costa, who, despite his name, looked Indian. Christopher told me that by now, although surnames differed, all the McCluskie-ites were members of two

families, the Tip-Tops and the Menezes. They had married in rather
than married out and what choice had they? 'When we still had the
club we used to say: "If the Tip-Tops and the Menezes are here we
shan't want any more seats. Everyone's present."' He added: 'We are
not only the last but the very last.' It was money that determined
whether you stayed or left, Christopher said, and that was why these
days everything was down at heel. Those with money had cleared
out, and they included Harold Menezes's elderly brother, who had
just inherited enough money to buy a house in Dehra Dun. Harold
nodded at this and looked sad.

It was Christopher who did most of the talking. Younger and
more energetic than the others, he had just returned from working
in Saudi Arabia. Later he introduced me to his lively wife, whom I
called Mrs Dale, as she was the granddaughter of a British soldier of
that name, and his three teenage children. The two girls were on their
way to rivalling Victoria Jones. He was an enthusiastic supporter of
Joseph Galstaun MLA, who was applying his considerable power to
getting things done: water stand pipes, electricity generators, a police
outpost, a medical dispensary and, above all, improvements to the
one road lifeline – all the necessities to lift McCluskiegunge out of
its genteel poverty. Galstaun said there was not enough community
spirit any more: 'I say to them "Unless you get yourselves together,
no one will come and help you. You've got to help yourselves."'
Christopher agreed with that.

Sitting round the garden table, everyone perked up when we
talked about Christmas:

Judy:	We love everything to do with Christmas.
Harold:	In the old days we would start to get ready a month before.
Judy:	I remember my mother 24 night: everything ready, cookies, cakes, even the dinner so she would not have to cook on Christmas day.
Christopher:	Then we had a New Year's ball. It was a one-week programme. We all went for a group walk on Boxing Day and took picnics.

Judy: As children we would watch the grown-ups with their
               fancy dress costumes. We did foxtrots and waltzes and later
               on the jive. The last dance we had was seven years ago.

I asked them if they still went to church on Christmas Day? Of
course they did, said Judy, but since the 1970s the services were
conducted in Hindi. She agreed with the sense of this, for nearly
20,000 Indians now live in McCluskiegunge and a sizeable number
are Christians. Nevertheless, that day of changeover must have been
a watershed. These days the McCluskie-ites sit in pews on one side
of the church and the Indians sit on the floor on the other. After the
Christmas service, continued Judy, the A-Is meet for a drink and play
'Housey-Housey'.

Christmas is the biggest event in the A-I calendar. I read in Melvyn
Brown's *The Anglo-Indian Archive* (he advertises it as 'The A-I Book
for the Millenium') an article written by Arundhati Roy on cooking:

> Culinary preparations for the *Burra Din* [an Urdu word meaning
> Great Day] begin months in advance with the bottling of *Kala Jamun*
> [Indian blackberry] wine. Huge quantities of Christmas cake batter
> are handed over to the *Rotiwallah* a few weeks before the Great Day
> to be baked in half-pound boxes. These are then handed round the
> family. The Calcutta Christmas cake is made with preserved *karam-
> cha, petha* [crystallised pumpkin], green cardamom, cinnamon and
> lots of rum.

The same article gives the menu for a typical A-I Sunday lunch:

> *Dal* soup [lentils with a hearty beef stock and spices]
> *Kofta* or beef curry with yellow rice [rice with turmeric], a salad and
> tasty pickles.
> Bread and Butter pudding, or Roly Poly or marmalade trifle.

'Chutney Mary', incidentally, is another slightly disparaging term
applied to dark Anglo-Indian women who powder themselves to try
and appear white; a 'pickled John' is the male equivalent.

I asked the McCluskie-ites if they felt superior to their Indian
neighbours:

Judy: We used to, but you can't say that anymore, just differ-
                ent. We used to wear frocks and jeans but people make
                fun of you now. It's more acceptable to wear a *sari* in
                public anyway [Pause]. Mind you, Indian behaviour is
                so different, completely different. I had a man came
                here to stay at the hostel and he was spitting out from
                my doorstep. Spitting *paan* [the green leaf of the betel
                vine with flavouring added; a popular taste like chew-
                ing tobacco].

Christopher: Some have no table manners. They go [imitates loud
                chewing], which is disgusting.

Harold: I feel embarrassed sometimes when I'm with them.

It occurred to me that feeling superior is a form of defence for the
Anglo-Indian. If you don't keep up appearances, you let the side
down and disappear into the mass, for better or worse. That is why
they disapprove of Kitty (a contemporary of Judy), as I became aware.
She speaks Hindi and has 'gone jungli', they said.

The bodyguard was looking restless although the midday scene
was tranquillity itself. I asked about the *naxas*, and old Captain
Mendonca growled from his chair. Judy said they did not let the bandits bother them, although she had been shot at once, and they never
went out in the evening. Herbert was more put off by the noise of
drums coming from the woods at night, and Christopher wondered
what they had left to steal anyway? I wanted to ask one more question, the journalist's cliché: 'what about the future?'

Christopher: Actually, I think we'll be wiped out in ten years. Anybody
                with money will leave. It's a pity. It could be second
                heaven. There's no pollution, green everywhere. *Chhota
                England*, mini-England, this place used to be. But as time
                goes by we can't keep up these appearances anymore. So
                mini-England fades away.

| *Harold*: | I'll pass my life here now. But old is gold. I want the old days back. |
| *Judy*: | Oh yes! Oh Yes! |

We took Christopher with us in the car to find Kitty. Down the dusty main street, the bodyguard slowing to show us with pride a plaque on one of Galstaun's installations, slowing again at the near empty station to see if Kitty was on the fruit stall and then up the hill behind to find her house. The track ended, so we walked the last half mile up and over scrubland, past, among the trees, the deserted houses, where, Kitty later told us with an instant recall, the Stewarts, the Palmers, the McInnes, the Smythes used to live. Finally, almost completely obscured by a mango orchard, we came to Woodlands, the Texiera bungalow. From the front it was more of a hut. Behind the wooden, paint-peeling veranda were two windows with wire mesh set either side of an open door in the cement-covered wall. I noticed holes in the asbestos roof were stuffed with rags. Silence.

Christopher called out 'Kitty', and then, coming out of the outside privvy and with the presence of mind to wash her hands under a new Galstaun standpipe, came a thin, wiry woman, prematurely aged, her face deeply lined and burned by the sun. She wore a faded red *sari* under a knitted pullover with holes in. Not surprisingly she looked alarmed. We shook hands, which seemed to give her confidence and made me feel, absurdly, as if I was the explorer Stanley coming across a female Dr Livingstone. She explained that she was just out of bed after five days with amoebic dysentery and I remembered Galstaun saying there were absolutely no medical facilities of any kind in McCluskiegunge. Our meeting, dramatic for me though it was, did not compare for effect with Ian Jack's first meeting with her mother twenty-eight years previously: 'Kitty's mother, Marjorie, took me into the parlour, where goats were nuzzling some old wicker chairs and the floor was strewn with leaves. A Winchester shotgun lay upright in one corner. "Mine," said Mrs Texiera. "You need it in these parts."'

We went inside. The living room was also Kitty's bedroom, scarcely decorated or furnished except for a simple wood-framed bed, a chair and the family pictures. Pride of place went to the two pictures with cracked glass and wooden frames: a photo of Kitty's mother as a young woman and the bearded old Welsh patriarch, Kitty's great grandfather. Then there was a tinted photograph of a couple in smart European clothes holding a baby – the woman in bobbed hair and a neat white blouse, the man in a blazer and white flannels: Mr and Mrs Texiera and baby Kitty. The pictures would have been more at home in Woodlands, Tunbridge Wells, instead of a hut in an Indian wilderness lived in by a wild, semi-ragged outcast. 'My daughter', Marjorie had told Ian Jack, 'is a perfect little tribal'.

'Perfect' seemed more appropriate than 'tribal', for two daughters dressed smartly in *salwar kameez* then emerged from the back room carrying tea and biscuits. They looked Indian but said 'Hello' and introduced themselves as Sylvia and Yvonne. Kitty called out for their sister: 'Linda, come on out. Don't be shy. You are so-o-o jungli. She's a lazy girl who stays in bed until eight o'clock.' Kitty had a shrill but refined voice and an English vocabulary that belonged to an earlier era. She apologised for her 'jumbly' clothes and said that without electricity a TV would be 'a white elephant'. The hut was clean, without sign or smell of goat. Sitting on the bed with the girls standing we were a sedate group. We drank tea and looked at the photo album with pictures of Marjorie and her two sisters, Muriel and Katherine, and their father, a rather brutal-looking man with khaki shorts and a red face who had been, apparently, the personal assistant to the governor of Assam.

Kitty's main possession is her memory, and her main quality is a fighting spirit. She reached down for a trunk under the bed and got out sheaves of yellowing papers. These were the evidence in a court case that had dragged on for years but, exceptionally for India, had resulted in a victory for the humble plaintiff. At stake were 9 acres of good land round Woodlands on which Kitty now grows thirty mango trees. 'We won the case at the Patna High Court but [until this last successful action] no ejectment [*sic*] order came forth from the Ranchi Bench,' she said, her voice rising with disgust. Mangoes are now her source of income, for she sells them door-to-door. 'Kitty was round here the other day,' Judy Tip-Top had told me, 'selling her mangoes.' She also depends on the philanthropy of others. She got the three girls and their absent brother through the Don Bosco Academy thanks mainly to Galstaun, so consequently they can all read and write in English and Hindi. Now her son is in Kolkata and sends back money. Her remaining task is to get her daughters away from McCluskiegunge, and she would not mind 'one bit' if they married Indians.

Ian Jack wrote of Marjorie: 'The undertow of every sentence said; my birthplace is an accident, the world to which I properly belong lies elsewhere.' Her daughter would never say this. She is proud of her ancestry but has long made her peace with this little patch of India. She has followed the Frank Anthony plea: 'Let us cling tenaciously to our language and way of life but always remember that we are Indians.' The future of Kitty's daughters lies firmly in India, and if that means the end of the Anglo-Indian Texieras, then it's a price worth paying.

When Ian Jack said goodbye to Marjorie, who died in 1988, they walked together through the trees and shook hands. She said: 'It's been so nice to talk to my own kind for a change.' Kitty would not say this. She accepted with composure the small amount of money (for me) that I gave her and hid it in the folds of her *sari*. I extended my hand but saw in her face that this was not what she wanted. We embraced and I kissed her cheeks – in manner still members of the same tribe.

On the way out Christopher took me to the Christian burial ground. As in the church, Indian graves were on the left and Anglos on the right. As usual in Indian cemeteries there were many small children's graves, testimony to the lack of medical services. One tomb caught my eye. It said 'In Memory of Dorothy Thipthorpe'. Of course! How could I not have realised? 'Tip-Top' was an assumed name. Perhaps it had begun as a nickname; another of those dated words of which the Anglo-Indians are so proud. 'Tip-top' as in 'my guava jam, or my loco, is in tiptop condition'.

Since my visit to those parts, Joseph Gaulston, MLA departed this life on 18 June 2010.

Chapter Six

TULLY-SAHIB

Listening to BBC Radio 4 at six o'clock on a Sunday morning, I drift in and out of consciousness with the voice of (Sir) Mark Tully. It is a benign and reassuring voice, the words enunciated clearly, as they were in the BBC of the 1960s. It is what Indians call a *pukka* voice, from the Hindi *pakka* for 'ripe and mature' but used to mean 'proper'. 'India', for example, comes across as 'Injyar'. 'That religious chap', as Tully is called by those too half-asleep to remember his name, is presenting his anthology of readings and music on religious themes called *Something Understood*; except that his programme is more than an anthology, for it is his own spiritual quest, and that is why we follow him. Indeed, we have done since 1996, when the programme first began.

Trying to put a face to the voice, as one does listening to the radio, I recall my recent meeting with Tully in a London pub. Over from his home in New Delhi for the summer, he shuffled in slowly because of arthritic ankles, his hair above his dome-like forehead now receding and grey, his eyebrows beneath unkempt and bushy; but his smile was as welcoming as ever. It occurs to me listening to *Something Understood* that Tully is now in the third stage of the Hindu life. This is the stage of *vanaprastha*, the reclusive's stage, when a man who has retired from career and household becomes free to contemplate the meaning of coming death and rebirth. Drifting off again, I try to concentrate by remembering my previous encounters with *Tully-Sahib*, as he is known in India.

In 1994 he stood at the podium of the Radio Academy attacking 'Birtism' at the BBC. (Lord) John Birt was the then Director General, who saw his mission to overturn traditional practices with revolutionary modernisation. Tully said 'an iron structure has been set in place ... to make sure that producers do not have freedom, that they conform to what has come to be known as Birtism ... The Corporation is a prisoner of the latest management speak.' It was defiant, and we cheered, but it was a vulnerable performance. Tully was taking on the bureaucratic machine of the BBC from his outsider's position on another continent. More than that, as the Foreign Correspondent in India who had been born during the Raj, the BBC *wallah* who attracted a huge Indian following amounting to a personality cult and the rumbustious character with an indiscreet private life, Tully was out of his time. In the new age of political correctness, his face did not fit. It was easy to caricature Tully as an old-fashioned amateur and Birt did just that, mocking him as 'an old soldier sniping at us with his musket'.

I remembered a happier occasion four years earlier. I was producing a BBC TV series *Living Islam: What it means to be a Muslim in Today's World* with a Pakistani Muslim presenter, and we wished to film in India. The Indian government press office was endlessly evasive over permits, whether because of the subject, Islam, or the presenter, Akbar Ahmed, we never knew. As the Chief of Bureau, BBC Delhi, Tully went into battle. Direct and determined, he put the press office to shame with his enthusiastic beliefs in both free speech and a multi-faith India. Our permits in hand, we met him in Delhi. A tall, distinctive figure with wavy black hair and a ready laugh, he strode rather than walked towards us. The BBC office was above his flat, and he ran both staff and household with a patriarchal air. Wearing *kurta* pyjamas and attended by his long-standing servant, Ram Chander, Tully exuded an obvious affection for India. An Indian cheroot and an Indian beer were never far from his lips. He could have been the better sort of district officer, an enlightened Edwardian in some ways; but his views on the Raj were increasingly critical. This was Tully in the midst of the second stage of life, called in the Hindu religion *garhasthya*, the householder stage of life when a man has responsibilities to his family and community.

Tully had been suddenly launched to stardom, on his way to becoming the most famous Englishman in India, twenty years earlier in 1972. I was then working at the BBC with his sister-in-law, who knew Mark's background as a BBC administrator and former ordinand of the Church of England. She could scarcely believe that Tully was becoming a household word in India, almost another Anglo-Indian phrase meaning 'an English man on the radio who speaks the truth about our country'. The Third Indo-Pakistan War had just ended, and East Pakistan was about to become Bangladesh. Mark Tully had just returned to India from London as the new BBC Chief of Bureau. Such was the mistrust of All India Radio and Radio Pakistan that many Indians listened to the BBC, and the voice they heard on the English-speaking World Service was Mark Tully's, as were the scripts that were read out in his name on the vernacular language services. Illiterate peasants in remote villages of Bangladesh who had no idea how to tune a radio or what the BBC was, nevertheless had a mark etched on their transistor radios showing them where they could hear the BBC Bengali Service. It was said that whole bazaars went quiet when the local language services of the BBC were broadcast. 'Are you Mark Tully?' any white journalist was asked. Initially it was a relief in Pakistan to say 'no', for Tully was considered to be in the Indian government's pocket. Subsequently, a British journalist in Lahore (Pakistan) was told: 'You, the BBC, were right. Our own radio and newspapers were wrong and misled us.'

The reputation of the BBC and the voice of Mark Tully were making him a household name and his fame continued for a quarter of a century. His return to India coincided with the mass use of the transistor radio, so that, when he left the BBC in 1994, the BBC Hindi, Bengali and Urdu language services together had a total listenership of 30 million. His resignation coincided with the rise of television satellite transmissions into India, so that the age of *Tully-Sahib* was also the great age of BBC radio. He said: 'I'm only a bloody journalist,' but *Tully-Sahib* was a lot more than that. To simple

Indians he was almost an object of veneration, like the Dalai Lama or Mother Teresa, in his case the physical embodiment of Truth.

Mark Tully was born in Calcutta in 1935, his father a senior *box-wallah* working for an Anglo-Indian investment company. He had the usual Raj childhood, during which he was taught that Indians were inferior – an awful prejudice that angers him to this day:

> Of course my father accepted without question the convention that the British in India must remain above India and not become part of it. He employed Nanny Oxborrow from England to make sure we kept our distance to avoid social contamination. To 'go native' was still a meaningful phrase then and a pejorative one. Nanny did no work herself; there were children's maids and Jaffa, the nursery boy, to do that. Her responsibility was to see that we did not get too close to these Indian servants. When, for example, we went for our morning pony ride, Nanny would come too – walking alongside and slowing our progress – in case we were tempted to talk to the groom, or syce, in his own language. Once I got a sharp slap from her when she found our driver teaching me to count up to ten in Hindustani.[1]

Nevertheless, despite Nanny as chaperone, Mark found that the real India was getting under his skin:

> I would go out for my morning walk with Nanny and see people performing their morning offices quite openly; a guy washing his bottom or cleaning his teeth with bits of twig. It's very difficult to have halfway-house feelings about India. It either grabs you completely or turns you off. I suppose it grabbed me more deeply than I realised.

What he could not reconcile at this early age was the contrast between the reassurance of Christianity, as he experienced it, and the violent idolatry of Hinduism:

> There was a lovely little chapel where we were all baptised called the Oxford Mission. I was very fond of it and went every Sunday. Father

> Douglas told us all about the Ten Commandments so I knew idolatry
> was a terrible thing. I felt quite sick and horrified at the Hindu pro-
> cessions where the gods and goddesses were taken out of the temples
> and drowned in the river. I was disgusted.

Listeners to *Something Understood* will know that the ubiquity of the
religious experience in India now strengthens his belief.

Mark Tully was taught that the British Raj was a good thing. In
fact, British school textbooks in India had a final chapter entitled
'Blessings of the British Raj'. As James Morris, the author of the
peerless trilogy on the British Empire (*Heaven's Command*, *Pax
Britannica* and *Farewell the Trumpets*) wrote elsewhere: '70 years ago
every conscientious Calcutta schoolboy, looking around him at the
electric tramways and the General Post Office, or the High Court
built to the pattern of Ypres Town Hall, could enumerate them pat:
law and order, public health, irrigation works, schools, roads, bridges,
railways and telegraphs.'[2] And the young Tully believed it: 'I once
thought colonial rule was excellent, that the only thing wrong with
empire was that it went on too long and that India ought to build on
what we left behind.'

After the war and an idyllic infant school in Darjeeling, young
Tully was sent Home to England to prevent Indianisation. It was
a common assumption in the Raj that belonging to a superior
civilisation required a British private education. It was a common
experience that this proved miserable, and so it was with Mark,
'locked up behind the high walls of a traditional prep school'.
Marlborough College proved little better, but he did enjoy the freedom of Cambridge University, where he studied theology under
the future Archbishop of Canterbury Ronald Runcie. After a dreary
time as a personnel administrator in the BBC, Tully realised that
the pull of India was too strong to resist. In 1965 he returned as an
Assistant Representative in the BBC Delhi Office:

> I arrived at my hotel, walked out onto the balcony and immediately
> smelled the gardeners cooking their curries – the same smell that
> came from the servants' quarters of my parents' house. The whole of

my childhood in Calcutta flashed back to me. I had been searching for
my roots in all the wrong places.

And Tully has been there ever since. India is not just under his skin
but in his heart: 'I was a confused young man when I returned to
India. Whatever I have achieved – and it's not much – it is because of
it. I owe everything to India and if you asked me if I care more for
India or England, I'd say India every time.'

Strictly speaking, the broadcasting legacy of the Raj is the state-
owned All India Radio. The clever title (AIR) was the brainchild of
former BBC producer Lionel Fielden, who went to India in the 1930s
to set up a national broadcasting network. However, AIR never bene-
fited from the BBC ethos of a public-service broadcaster independent
of government and, it has to be said, under the Raj it was censored
too. It was 'his master's voice' and took no part in the Independence
Movement. Prime Minister Jawaharlal Nehru wanted a 'semi-autonomous' AIR when India became independent, but the temptation for
government control was too strong and remains so. For many years
after Independence there was an interchange of personnel and broadcast scripts between AIR and BBC Delhi, so to that extent they grew
together. Nevertheless, the distinctive image of the BBC in India over
all other broadcasters, domestic and foreign, is its longstanding reputation for credibility, impartiality and prompt, uncensored news. This, in
an indirect way I concede, is a legacy of the Raj.

The BBC World Service has been on the air to India, Pakistan and
Sri Lanka since 1932, when King George V made a Christmas broadcast on what was then the Empire Service. The first of the BBC
Indian-language services, the Hindustani Service, began in the last
years of Empire and the grimmest days of the war. In 1940 the import
of wireless sets into India was 30 per cent up on the previous year. 'If
ever there was a time', wrote Zulfiqar Bokhari of AIR, 'for the BBC
to make an effort to win over the hearts of the Indians, it is now.
The days of iron are gone, these are the days of ether.' So the new
BBC service was opened with Bokhari as its Programme Organiser
in London. And it is still winning the hearts of Indians. Listener-
correspondent panels were set up as early as 1943, the beginnings of

audience research, and, from the first, reports came into London that 'frank' and honest broadcasting was what Indians wanted.[3]

No voice on the BBC Hindustani Service was more effective than that of the anti-imperialist George Orwell. He broadcast a weekly news digest in English and made no secret of his wish for an independent India. Nevertheless, he took the consistent view that, however much he disliked the British Empire, it was benign compared to the evils of Nazi Germany and Fascist Japan, and, if they won the war, then the chances of an independent India would be non-existent. He was keenly aware of the power of propaganda and knew that his audiences were also listening to Subhas Chandra Bose, the Indian freedom-fighter who had thrown in his lot with the Fascists and was broadcasting from Radio Azad Hind in Berlin and Rangoon. Once again it was the openness of the BBC inviting an anti-imperialist to broadcast to India that enhanced its reputation.

In these early days the Indian audiences were mostly the edu-cated elite who could afford the wirelesses of the time and after 200 years of colonialism their cultural tastes were extraordinarily British. Before the BBC representative Derek Holroyde arrived in Delhi in 1954, he was briefed: 'Remember, Holroyde, they all have Third Programme minds.' In the same way, the British Council represent-ative in Bombay in the 1960s, Lyon Roussel, found that 'the best British ambassador was William Shakespeare'. Holroyde reported that, when the poet Dylan Thomas died in 1953, the appreciations in several Indian newspapers were more knowledgeable and authorita-tive than in the British press. The cultural menu of the BBC language services (for the Urdu and Bengali services began with Partition in 1947) contributed to this one-sided exchange. For one BBC critic, writing in 1947, it was too much: 'Some plays are not suited to our purpose: Noel Coward's *Private Lives*, for example. I don't think our listeners in India are interested in the matrimonial and conju-gal complications of the upper-middle classes of this country. And I need hardly say that the music-hall type of programme makes no appeal whatsoever to any Indian.'

The early post-war BBC reps like Holroyde and his predeces-sor, William Ash, were determined to redress the balance. Their own lifestyle did not go down well with the *pukka sahibs*, who still occupied the High Commission, for Ash slept on a rush mat and Peggy Holroyde dressed in Indian *saris*. 'We were called India freaks,' remembered Ash, 'but I countered this by quoting back one of my Indian friends who said, "the trouble with the British was that they had ruled at the top but knew nothing of Indian society at the bottom".' They insisted that the BBC should take broadcast 'feeds' of some of the programmes from AIR that reflected the prominence it now gave to Indian culture; the Republic Day parades, for example, when musicians performed from all over India. When Holyrode left in 1958, his BBC boss gave him a pompous, double-edged, valediction: 'It is arguable whether you have been a good representative of the BBC in India; but it is certain that you have been a good representative of India in the BBC.'

In some ways, however, the BBC Office was still run along traditional lines. Holyrode's successor, Peter Albany, remembered:

> When I first went there it was still almost Victorian. The *peons* [from the Portuguese *peao* for 'foot', therefore 'footmen', or in modern parlance 'messenger'] all had those wonderful fan-shaped turbans, and every time I went in or out of the office they jumped to attention. I put a stop to that. There were no longer shouts of 'Boy' down the passageway. The BBC was still run very much on Raj lines, a legacy from the old colonial days.

This was still the age when Indians were not welcome on the BBC domestic services, because they spoke English with an Indian accent. They were very often regarded as either unintelligible or funny because of the comic impersonations of the *Goon Show* mimic Peter Sellers. The BBC Correspondent at this time was Donald Milner, whose sensitive but questioning reports about India did much to inform listeners to, for example, the long-running weekly BBC programme *From our own Correspondent*. He broadcast a rebuke: 'There are many things that are funny in India, but that is not one of them. It is a matter of tuning one's ear or of getting used to a different accentuation of voice.'

The beginning of Tully's career in broadcasting was not promising. When he arrived in 1965, the BBC Delhi Office had a largely administrative function. It was in India to serve visiting correspondents, to exchange transcripts with All India Radio and to maintain diplomatic relations with the Indian government. This was a wasted opportunity, and, encouraged by Mark Dodd (Peter Albany's successor), Mark began to write and broadcast his own scripts on non-news outlets like the Home Service *From our own Correspondent*. Then Mark Dodd fell ill, and he was left to his own devices. By the time he returned to England in 1969 he was on his way to making the BBC Delhi Office a broadcasting service in its own right, providing radio reports for British and Indian audiences.

The next year, however, it was TV that caused a mighty row between the BBC and the Indian government. In Britain colour film and the new television channel BBC 2 were bringing India into viewers' homes as never seen before. TV film presenters like James Cameron and Malcolm Muggeridge were falling in love with India but airing their personal, trenchant, opinions about it, and the Director General of the BBC, Sir Hugh Green, was supportive of their right to do so. Perhaps a row was inevitable. In 1970 hostile Indian politicians, as seen from Britain, clashed with arrogant broadcasters, as seen from India. The clash became known as the Louis Malle Affair. Although Mark Tully was back in Britain at the time, it led directly to his return to India as the first Chief of Bureau with overall responsibility for reporting and servicing BBC programmes.

Louis Malle was then a French documentary film-maker whose series of films about Indian life was first shown on French television and then repeated in five episodes on the BBC in 1970. Many Indians in Britain viewed it favourably, but a vociferous minority saw the reality it depicted as denigrating Indian life. Certainly the episode on Calcutta, then overwhelmed by refugees from East Pakistan, did not spare the perception that Calcutta was what Kipling called 'the city of dreadful night'. The writer Simon Winchester was there at this time and wrote a vivid, poetic description that in my memory corresponded with the film: 'The hot stench of the slow-decaying poor, the mobs flowing ceaselessly over the scalding bridge, the treacle of the Hooghly swamps below, the bent and broken limbs and the rotting rubbish piles and the screeching horns and the rickshaw bells and the infuriating calm of the cuddling cows …'[4]

The protest was more than the common complaint that all the press and broadcasters want to show are the negative sides of a third-world country. Questions were asked in the Indian Parliament and elsewhere that could only be asked of a former colonial ruler. Why did the BBC not censor the films, as the British government had censored AIR, its own broadcaster in India? Why did the BBC behave in an unfriendly way to a member of the family, however extended the family? Should not a broadcaster work for the good of the people? The BBC was bemused. An official said: 'Such general opinions as Louis Malle offered were mild, almost reticent, compared to the assertive generalisations one expects from a Cameron or a Muggeridge commentary.' The response must have seemed almost hysterical, like one of those sudden upsurges of violence that break through the tolerance of day-to-day life in India.

The truth was that the Louis Malle series was 'the straw that broke the camel's back'. The Government of India had compiled a dossier going back ten years complaining of BBC distortions and innuendos. The BBC correspondent Ronald Robson did not help by his brusque, 'rajist', rejection of criticism. Reading the account of the episode by S.K. Singh, the Director of External Publicity of the Indian government at that time,[5] I get the impression that Robson's accredition was removed with some relish; and the BBC Office was closed down too. The Indian High Commissioner in London took a step back and provided the right perspective: 'We are having a revolution in India … This is a new chapter in our history and we are having a new technology and a forceful society. Let the storm die down a little.' And it soon did.

When Mark Tully returned to India in 1972, he took over a bureau, no longer an office, on a new site in Jorbagh, New Delhi, which had a studio attached. He ran the operation, so that in theory at least he was in control of what was going on, and he had day-to-day contacts with the Indian government. In fact such was the parsimony of the BBC that he did not even possess a VHS machine to watch the TV films made by his colleagues about which he had been consulted. He and his assistant, Prakash Mirchandani, now ran a slimmed-down operation responsible both for news reporting and for representing the BBC. It was a busy time. He had to cover a vast area as a reporter, not just India and Pakistan but Afghanistan, Nepal, Bangladesh and Sri Lanka too. His aim was to provide a fast and reliable news service that for anyone who knew India in those days, with its phones that did not work, permissions that were endlessly delayed and transport that was rarely efficient was an ambitious mission statement. Nevertheless, his love affair with India was so clear that critics at home said he had 'gone native'. This, he said, amused him and was evidence of a 'colonial hang-up'. He pointed out: 'No one says Alistair Cooke has "gone native" just because he has chosen to live in America.' But a catastrophic row with the Indian government was about to stretch his sympathies to the limit.

In 1971 Mrs Indira Gandhi had won another general election, with a large majority. After a short war with Pakistan her victorious army handed her East Pakistan on a plate in December 1971. With electoral and military victory in the same year, and with her decision to establish the new independent state of Bangladesh appearing as a magnanimous gesture, her prestige was at its height. She had the Congress Party, the country and the subcontinent at her feet. But, as Tully wrote: 'She forgot the famous maxim "All power corrupts, and absolute power corrupts absolutely."' Indira Gandhi's upbringing had been insecure, despite her self-reliance, and so she found the habit of Indians to deify their rulers too hard to resist. She concentrated power increasingly on her own family. Now began the 'dynastic democracy' of the Nehrus.

In particular she indulged her younger son, Sanjay, whom Tully found 'a brash and self-confident young man with a deep-seated scorn for ideas and a passion for action'. Over the next few years he tried to kickstart India's politicians into action by, for example, forcible clearance of the Delhi slums and, allegedly, forcible male sterilisation in order to control population growth. But it was his attempt to manufacture the first wholly Indian car, the *Maruti* or 'Son of the Wind God', that brought charges of corruption. It also caused Tully to become a marked man in the Nehru family. Under Indian socialism and state planning, a licence was required to invest in industry, and this led to 'crony capitalism' in which bribery was common. When Sanjay was given a licence based on little more than an unfinished apprenticeship with Rolls Royce in his youth, there was uproar in Congress. In fact, the 'Son of the Wind God' did not get off the starting line and eventually the half-finished car was sold to the Japanese firm Suzuki. Mrs Gandhi was embarrassed, so that, when Tully broadcast that *Maruti* meant *ma roti* or 'the mother is crying', the joke hit home.

In 1974 opposition to Mrs Gandhi's autocratic rule led to a new mass movement called the 'JP', after its leader Jayaprakash Narayan, which advocated non-violent civil disobedience to bring down the government. The Prime Minister countered by asserting her authority, first by smashing a railway workers' strike and secondly by ordering Indian scientists to explode a nuclear device to demonstrate India's super-power status. Then the High Court in her hometown of Allahabad accused the Prime Minister of electoral corruption. The opposition called for her to resign, and in this unstable political climate she called a State of Emergency, egged on by Sanjay. In June 1975 the President announced 'India is Indira, and Indira is India', and with these words India moved from democracy to dictatorship. Opposition leaders were arrested and imprisoned. Tully himself had a narrow escape. The rumour spread to the Prime Minister's office that he had announced on the BBC that some members of the government had also been placed under house arrest for disapproving of the Emergency. The Information Minister recalled:

The day the Emergency came in I was sitting at home when Mohammed Yunus [a close friend of Mrs Gandhi] telephoned me and said: 'The BBC has said that senior members of the Government are under house arrest. You send for Mark Tully, pull down his trousers, give him a few lashes and send him to jail.' Immediately after I put down the phone I sent for the monitoring report of the BBC and the BBC had not said this. That evening I drew the Prime Minister's attention to this.[6]

It is a sign of the authority of the BBC, says Tully, that Indian politicians sometimes claim to have heard a report on the BBC because that gives credibility to a rumour they wish to plant. In 1975 it was a sign of the iniquity of a dictatorship that the government tried to plant the rumour that he was a spy, apparently because he was learning Hindi! Worse was to come. Sanjay Gandhi demanded to see AIR's news bulletins before they were broadcast, and very soon the foreign press and broadcasting media were censored too. Initially, journalists were required to submit their copy for censorship, then to sign a document saying they 'complied with the Government guidelines' and would not reveal what had been censored. This was an ugly time. Prakash Mirchandani remembers that all Indians who worked for foreign media organisations were expected to 'act as spies' and alert the government about 'biased' reporting. Mark Tully remembers his indignation at the prospect of signing the censorship agreement 'because we were being asked to tell lies. Further, we were not allowed to say that anything was censored and yet we were expected to report on it.' The BBC saved Tully the dire repercussion of refusing to sign by pulling him out of India. 'I have thought about this time and time again,' he says. 'At the time I thought this was absolutely the right decision and I still do.' Yet he was deeply unhappy. He languished outside India until Indira Gandhi surprisingly called, and subsequently lost, a general election in February 1977.

Did the BBC's decision to stop broadcasting from its Delhi office have overtones of colonialism? Mirchandani thinks so.

> Putting on my Indian nationalist's hat for a second, the BBC quite cheerfully accepts censorship in other parts of the world. There was a feeling here that the BBC was trying to exert its colonial past; that it had a special relationship with India, which was a colonial relationship. There's no doubt that some of the BBC's managers came from the colonial service and thought that this upstart country had to be taught a lesson. It was a dreadful mistake.[7]

Twenty years later Tully accepted part of this verdict: 'Our attitude towards being in China is very different from being in India. At the same time India has to accept that it is a democracy and should set itself a higher standard than China.' Nor did he explicitly reject the notion of a colonial hangover, but typically he saw it from an Indian perspective:

> I have always said that Indians who talk about Western colonial domi-nance through the BBC, or even more extreme things like the BBC attempting to undermine India, show a great disrespect for their own country. India is far more stable and advanced than many other nations. The concept that we can overthrow it or destabilise it is abso-lute nonsense. As for the idea that the freedom of the press is a western ideological position that should not apply to a third world country, I don't see that myself. The press is a vital element in a democracy. It is not the only vital institution. Democracy consists of institutions that have a mutually balancing and controlling role – the judiciary, the bureaucracy, the parliament, the press. India really is a free and demo-cratic country and it could not be so without a free press. [He was not including India's radio and television in this judgement.] It is not a position that we have imposed on them.[8]

The State of Emergency increased the importance of the BBC World Service in India, because AIR was so mistrusted. Tully returned in triumph to cover the 1977 election and witness the fall of the gov-ernment that had caused his exile. His relations with Indira Gandhi remained difficult after her return to power in 1980. Soon after Sanjay was killed in an air crash, and her elder son, Rajiv, entered politics in his place. Tully said in 1984: 'He is the one that I could talk to. He actually wants to know what is happening. Mrs Gandhi has become an oriental monarch who surrounds herself with syco-phants.' She was assassinated by a Sikh dissident soon afterwards, and Indians saw the revealing photo of Rajiv, in the depth of the Indian countryside, listening to the news on the BBC World Service radio because AIR had not yet been given permission to broadcast it.

BBC radio was extraordinarily popular at this time. This charming story related by Kailash Budhwar, then Head of the BBC Hindi and Tamil Sections, could only have happened in India:

One of our Hindi broadcasters was travelling in India on a night train on which the main dynamo had been vandalised so there were no lights in the compartment. The train stopped and the poor man opened his mouth for the first time to ask where the train was. It was just his voice as it was dark all around. He could not see the other passengers. They could not see him. Before he could complete his sentence, a voice suddenly interrupted. 'Are you not the one who answers Listeners' Letters on the BBC?' My colleague tells me that within a twinkling of an eye he was surrounded by a compartment of admirers eager to find out all about the Hindi broadcasts on the BBC.[9]

Mark Tully is the least egotistical of broadcasters. He frequently says it is the story that matters not the messenger who brings it. His reticence was sorely tried when BBC World TV began in India in 1991 and quickly replaced Doordarshan (AIR's TV counterpart) as the main source of news for the English-speaking elite. Now he was seen as well as heard. 'Perhaps there is some BBC training manual which teaches you to answer the question "You are Mark Tully, aren't you?" I just stutter some inanity.' It is not just modesty. The rumour-mongering in India, added to the volatility of Indian crowds, has resulted over the years in Tully's home being besieged (1984), his life being threatened (on several occasions), and him being taken hostage (1991). He said on the last occasion: 'Sometimes, when violence flares, I am afraid that intellect could be overcome by fear and emotion, that chaos might envelop it all and the country crack up.'

He attributed some of the blame for this volatility to the Indian government's control and misuse of its broadcasting. In the Nehru Memorial Lecture he gave in 1991 he said that, nearly half a century after Nehru had asked for 'a semi-autonomous broadcasting corporation', India 'had got nowhere near that'. In his customarily forthright way, he stated the implications for Indian democracy: 'This misuse has been a major contributor to the growing feeling among Indian voters that politicians do not respect them, a feeling which is a serious threat to Indian democracy. The basic weakness of the government's radio and television strategy is that it assumes the electorate cannot see through the game, and Indians do not like being taken for fools.'[10] It was little consolation to him that India's loss was the BBC's gain.

In 1993 Tully ceased to be Chief of the BBC Delhi Bureau, and, in one of those bureaucratic job redesignations intended to disguise corporation disapproval, he became a 'South Asia Correspondent'. His opposition to the ruling BBC regime and its dislike of his personality cult (ironic in an organisation that increasingly celebrates celebrities) led him to resign the following year. Since then the proliferation in India of satellite and cable TV – from without, like CNN and Star TV; from within, like ZEE TV and Sahara – has forced Doordarshan to move more with the times. But Tully remains very critical.

I visited Mark Tully at his home in the Nizamuddin area of Delhi in October 2006. A large plaque outside the house – MARK TULLY – identified what is a landmark for Indians and visitors alike. He shambled to the door wearing a crumpled shirt and sagging trousers that, said a journalist once, 'fit him like a sack'. We moved to a divan in front of a large coffee table displaying some of his prized objects. One, I learned afterwards, was a *paan dan* or box for betel nut and another was a set of oval brass plaques unscrewed from Indian trains: 'BURN & CO: carriage & wagon builders: HOWRAH'. On the walls were Indian prints, above us Aladdin-style lamps and at Mark's feet his Labrador dog.

I turned on the tape recorder. Without preamble Mark leant forward and said as if in the confessional:

> Let me first tell you something that is on the BBC website about me that I must try and get rid of. The BBC says that on my twenty-first birthday I drank twenty-one pints of beer. That is not true. I placed twenty-one shillings, that's a guinea, on the counter of Morley's Wine Bar in Delhi and told the barman to make sure a group of us spent it on beer.

Bold, combative Tully is as insecure as the rest of us, but few of us are so candid. Even so, I was surprised how sensitive he is a decade

after his row with the BBC, so I looked him up on the BBC website. He was right; for a publicity blurb it is remarkably indiscreet.
Afterwards it struck me, as it has other journalists, that Tully is something of a Graham Greene character; an expatriate, seeking for his
faith with the insecurity of someone leading a double life. In his case
this is literally true, because he has a wife in the UK and a partner in
Delhi with whom he shares his home – a well-known *ménage à trois*
that still causes him embarrassment. Honesty and self-publicity do
not often go together, but that is what makes Tully the journalist so
likeable – and vulnerable.

I had come to discuss with Mark the legacy of the British Raj. He
is no longer the uncritical admirer he was in his childhood. What he
wanted to focus on, what he frequently complains about in his writing, is what Indians call the *neta-babu raj*. He introduced the concept
to a British audience in his book *From Raj to Rajiv* published in 1988:

> There is no better commentator on modern India than the *Times
> of India* cartoonist, R.K. Laxman. He has three regular charac-
> ters: a politician, an apparently sycophantic bureaucrat and an old
> man watching their antics with bemused amusement. According to
> Laxman, the old man represents 'the man who stands in the queue,
> the man who shares all the miseries of India, the victim of the politi-
> cians and the bureaucrats'. [11]

The *netas* are the politicians and the *babus* are the bureaucrats. In his
later book *India in Slow Motion* (2002), Mark described their unholy
alliance: the *netas* want to exercise total control over the *babus* at all
levels, and the *babus*, who are overstaffed and underpaid, have surrendered their autonomy. In other words, the independence of the civil
service has been over-ridden by the power of politicians who use it
to their advantage. There is almost no aspect of life, says Tully, that has
not been corrupted by the *neta-babu raj*:

> The civil service and the politicians, instead of keeping an eye on
> each other, join hands to share the spoils of office, and so corruption
> is an inevitable by-product of the *raj*. Politicians don't trouble to hide

the links between office and money. They talk openly about 'lucrative ministries'. The railways, for instance, are still a department of government. As a result, according to M.N. Prasad, a former Chairman of the Railway Board, 'Indian railway has the dubious distinction of being the only major railway system in the world where major decisions on investment policy and organisation are taken by politicians according to their whims and fancies'. And time and time again what the press calls 'the loaves and fishes of office' are blatantly used to persuade legislators in state assemblies to allow the *neta* to get their way.[12]

The other by-product of the *neta-babu raj* is bureaucracy. Exacerbated by the Soviet-style economic planning that lasted from Nehru's time to the threatened national bankruptcy of 1991 – the era known as the 'licence raj' – form-filling is a way of life, red tape a constant hindrance along the way. Mark gives the example of a senior *babu* who proudly announced that a procedure had been simplified so that only five instead of fifteen forms were required, but when asked how many signatures were still needed replied, with a sheepish smile, 'fifteen'. A friend of mine recently applied for an Indian driving licence and, among other absurd bureaucratic requirements, had to sign his signature twenty-two times. Anyone who reads Indian newspapers is aware of political corruption, and anyone who buys a ticket for a train journey experiences red tape – the by-products of the *neta-babu raj*. But why, I wanted to ask Mark, is this the legacy of the British – what he calls in *India in Slow Motion* 'the problem of an unreformed colonial administrative system'?

In the first place, said Mark, the Indians inherited the system; the Indian Civil Service (ICS) became the Indian Administrative Service (IAS), and for many years the same bureaucrats were behind the same desks. In the second place, the old paternalistic attitude persisted; the British Raj was known alternatively as the *Mai Bap Sarkar* or Mother and Father Government, a government that claimed to do everything for its subjects, just as parents do for children, and this paternalism has now become an interfering officialdom. But, said Mark, it was more than that:

The whole ethos of the British Raj was keeping law and order and control. The Indians inherited not only the system but also the ethos. The police, for example, go round behaving like paramilitaries, and the idea of serving the public is nowhere. Moreover, the ICS was not geared for politics. You see, under the British there was no separation of powers, because there was not a political/legislative body for the administration to be responsible to. They were the rulers. Now it is similar in a different way. The police, for example, are entirely responsible to the politicians, whereas they should be kept in check by a judiciary. You saw that in the Gujarat riots. If the police could have turned to the judiciary, they would have had that independent body against political interference. There's still no separation of power.

We joked about the reputation of the British Raj for form filling and red tape. In his book *The Ruling Caste* David Gilmour refers to the policy of 'tranquil procrastination' among the ICS a hundred years ago. 'Round and round', noted the Viceroy Lord Curzon, 'like the diurnal revolution of the earth went the file, solemn, slow and sure.'[13] Mark remembers a prayer still hanging in the house of an elderly member of the IAS:

> Oh Lord grant that this day we come to no decisions,
> Neither run into any kind of responsibility,
> But that all our doings may be ordered to establish
> New and quite unwarranted departments.
> O Thou who seest all things below
> Grant Thy servants may go slow,
> That they may study to comply
> With regulations till they die.[14]

'The British had a feeling', said Mark, 'that if you wrote everything down you could explain a system just as it should work. If you were going to control Indians, everything had to be buttoned up. Then you could throw the rule book at the ticket inspector, so to speak.' The lower levels of the ICS were 'grossly overstaffed' too, and each member contributed a bit to the inefficiency. 'Under the Raj there wasn't much cost-cutting or attempt at work efficiency and there was quite a bit of corruption in the lower levels. The clerks might have been corrupt, the police station might have been corrupt, the traffic police were most certainly corrupt.' It is true, Mark went on, that at the top level of the ICS there was a cadre that was 'almost incorruptible', partly because of good pay and partly because of the ethos that dishonesty meant disgrace. After Independence both these guarantees gradually disappeared: 'Now once that happens, the machinery stopping corruption at a lower level breaks down.'

The basic trouble is, Mark went on, warming to his theme like the good teacher he could have been, too many of the Indian elite after Independence were too admiring of the Raj. In a previous book, *No Full Stops in India* (1991), he stated his belief that India should establish its own identity and grow away from the notion that there was no worthwhile civilisation before the British. Nirad Chaudhuri wrote in *The Autobiography of an Unknown Indian*: 'All that was good and living within us was shaped and quickened by British rule.' Tully has no time for this hyperbole. He believes that the Raj survived only because it created an Indian elite who shared the British conviction that their culture was inherently superior. After Independence this elite, 'who themselves were stranded, neither in India nor in the West', damaged India by embracing Western ideas to the country's disadvantage. Nehru's enthusiasm for 1940s British-style socialism was a prime example. In 1990 the descendants of that elite were still influential in India, so that the British still maintained a 'cultural hegemony' over the subcontinent.

I did not ask Mark whether this admiration for British ways persists in the very different economic circumstances of today – admiration for the BBC World Service excepted! He certainly believes that the status of the English language as the language of the elite has undermined Indian culture and confidence. 'The best way to destroy a people's culture and identity is to undermine its religion and its language. We, the British, did that as India's rulers and we continue to do that.' Instead I asked him to evaluate the legacy of the Raj in a broader sense. He did not hold back:

You must look at the Raj in a balanced way. Of course, there were positive things and there were very negative things. The most negative thing is that India got the industrial revolution through the Raj and the Raj had its own priorities. Even the railway network was based on the Raj's defence and commercial priorities.

My question is this: India, having an ancient culture and a culture where maths and sciences were always understood; India, having always been a crossroads of the world, who is to say that the seeds of the industrial revolution wouldn't have been blown here by the trade winds anyway? And who is to say that parts of India would not have used the industrial revolution according to their own priorities? After all, Japan was never colonised and it became a big industrial power. I'm not saying that this would have spread all over India. My guess is that India would have developed more like Europe. The revolution would have come to the west coast and resource centres would have built up there. The east and centre, as in Europe, have the raw materials like coal and ore. Some regions would have developed faster than others. Of course, there were hinterlands under the British too.

The late afternoon was fading to twilight. In the words of the missionary hymn sung by my grandmother in Ceylon a hundred years ago, 'now the day is over, night is drawing nigh'. The dusk shielded Mark's study from the world outside, but close by was the shrine to the *sufi* saint Hazrat Nizam-ud-din. I had filmed the pilgrims of many faiths there for the TV series *Discovering Islam* and I remembered the intense devotion, the smell of incense mingled with sweat on that hot night, the chanting of the *quawali* singers. It was time to talk about religion. Mark's voice, always quiet away from a microphone, seemed to gather intensity, as if this was the subject he really wanted to discuss. I felt like a sixth-former visiting his head of religious studies and exchanging confidences over a glass of sherry:

Somewhere in me there's always been religion. Not long ago I was very ill with measles and I could have died. I realised in my heart of hearts that I was religious and life didn't make much sense without God. That got me thinking and I started to believe two or three things. In the first place I believe very strongly, absolutely, that you need a religious practice, you need to belong to a religious tradition. I learned from Gandhi, and I'm very happy in this, that the religion you grew up in is probably the one most natural to you. This realisation gives me a deep love of the Church of England.[15]

I thought I heard the harsh sound of a peacock in his garden interrupt his discourse. He added as a sort of aside: 'I am emotionally more of a Gandhi man than a Nehru man. I am religious and conservative, and India has strengthened my belief in religion in general. I wish there had been more of Gandhi in Nehru.' He returned to the sermon:

In the second place, pluralism works in India because of the basic Hindu-Buddhist understanding that there is no perfect understanding. There is no need to be certain. In fact it's dangerous. Therefore I don't worry about the virgin birth or even the resurrection, though I'm utterly convinced something extraordinary happened. That's the importance of learning from other religions. You realise there are other ways to God. Gandhi said 'religions are different roads converging to the same goal'. He kept his feet on the Hindu road, and in fact the Gita says 'better is one's own law though imperfectly carried out than the law of another carried out perfectly'. So I am a Christian, but this respect of other faiths and uncertainty of mine sits more happily than how I began, which was to believe in the Nicene Creed and that kind of thing.

Mark Tully believes in the Hindu idea of 'karma' or destiny. It was his destiny to be born in India, to be educated in Britain and then to return to India for the rest of his life:

There's a hell of a lot to do with luck and fate and that leads towards this sense of place. Since 1965 I have lived all my life in India, and if I had not been influenced by India it would have been a futile life. My place now is in India and I've got a huge sense of gratitude. I would be very happy to be buried in India – buried according to the rites of the Church of England.

As I left I asked one final question that had been nagging me. Why had he not become an Indian citizen? This is another dual loyalty Sir Mark Tully worries over: 'I've thought about it many, many times. There's the problem of travel and this hyper-excitement in the UK about anybody with a brown skin. Then, you see, I have this emotional tie to Britain …' His voice trailed off.

I left the house and headed for the taxi and rickshaw rank, where drivers were expecting another lucrative fare from a visitor to *Tully-Sahib*.

Chapter Seven

SELLING OFF
THE RAJ

During the last days of the Raj in 1947 the British in India
packed up to go home:

> ICS men squared off their paperwork and handed their files to Indian
> colleagues. Precious possessions, such as the horses and hounds of the
> Peshawar hunt, were destroyed rather than left to fate. Advertisements
> appeared in *The Times of India* placed, for example, by the Montpellier
> Hotel in Budleigh Salterton asking speculatively 'Are you leaving for
> England?' Troops mustered their equipment, loaded it onto trains and
> lorries and began a familiar but final journey down from the hills and
> across the plains to embarkation at Bombay.[1]

At 8.30 am on the Appointed Day, 15 August, the Union Jack was
hauled down across the subcontinent, from frontier fort to governor's palace, from law court to town hall. The last of about 200 flags
that had flown over the ruined Lucknow Residency night and day
since the Mutiny was not only hauled down but its base filled with
concrete to prevent further use, a bitter symbol of the end of empire:

> Shot thro' the staff or the halyard, but ever we raised thee anew,
> And ever upon the topmost roof our banner of England blew.[2]

The last British Army regiment to leave was the Somerset Light Infantry. On 28 February 1948 the First Battalion marched to the Apollo Bunder on the Bombay harbour front and formed up by the Gateway of India, that prodigious triumphal arch marking the spot where the King Emperor, George V, had landed in 1911. An Indian regiment was waiting. The bands played 'God Save the King' and the Indian anthem *Vande Mataram* ('Hail to the Mother(land)'). A Sikh officer presented his English counterpart with a silver model of the Gateway inscribed: 'To commemorate the comradeship of the soldiers of the British and Indian Armies, 1754–1947.' While the bands struck up 'Auld Lang Syne', the King's and Somerset's Colours were trooped through the Gateway itself to a waiting transport ship. The curtain had come down on the Raj.

Yet the Raj had not quite left this particular stage. For immediately behind the Gateway was the Royal Bombay Yacht Club (RBYC), its verandas and lawns packed on this occasion with British spectators watching what was for some simply a historical drama but for others a bitter tragedy. It flourishes today, its name intact, as a perfectly preserved memento of the Raj.

In fact only a few months before the farewell trumpets sounded, the RBYC had lost its lease and it was in the process of moving across the Apollo Bunder to rehouse in its Residential Chambers. And there it stays today. It occupies a confused-looking building that combines English neo-Gothic with half-timbered Tudor architecture. This demonstrates, in the words of the official history, 'the disintegration of stylistic cohesion that characterised turn-of-the-century architecture in Bombay'. One reason for the non-renewal of its lease was its refusal to admit Indian members. Too late, the Secretary of the RBYC sent an ingratiating note to the Port of Bombay Trustees:

> It is not generally known that there is nothing in the Constitution of the Club that in any way prevents Indian Gentlemen from becoming members of the Club. To remove this misapprehension my committee are perfectly prepared to accept a definite covenant in the renewal of the lease that no discrimination whatsoever on racial grounds shall be shown.[3]

The Trustees were obviously unimpressed. In fact, Indians were not admitted either as members or even as guests until 1953, when at the decisive meeting a disgruntled British member was heard to say 'one might as well pack up and go home'. He was a few years too late.

In 1946 the centenary of the RBYC was celebrated in style. If some members felt the anniversary was also a wake, there was no mention of it in the President's address:

> Gentlemen [he announced], I have recently read in a home paper that the year 1946 has been a vintage year. It has been a year whose claret, so to speak, has been as good as its champagne. This, I think, is a tribute that might aptly be applied to those men of moral and physical energy and intellectual vigour who founded this Club on 3 March 1846.[4]

For its first hundred years the RBYC had prided itself on its exclusivity, not to say snobbery. It was a club neither for Indians, unless they were maharajas, nor for those vulgar enough to be engaged in trade. *Boxwallahs* were refused membership even if their name was Sir Thomas Lipton, the tea magnate, who was a friend of King Edward VII. The King threatened to resign as President of the Royal Yacht Squadron unless 'Tommy Lipton' was accepted, and he duly was; but the exception proved the rule for some years yet.

The appeasement of Edward VII must have saved the RBYC worse embarrassment, because its flag was, and is, the Blue Ensign with the Star of India surmounted by the Imperial Crown. In fact the Imperial Crown lasted longer than the exclusivity of its former British subjects in Bombay. It was not until 1977 that the Crown was removed from the railings outside the club as a 'Pre-Independence Symbol' (so said the Commissioner of Police) and the Blue Ensign flew on Public Days until 1996, when it was replaced by the flag of India.

The first years after Independence were depressing times for the diehards of the RBYC. Following eviction came prohibition. In March 1948 the Bombay Excise Department wrote: 'I have the honour to inform you that from 1 April you will not be permitted to sell or serve liquor or to allow the drinking of liquor.' The Christmas

Party that year must have been a gloomy occasion, though members tried their best. P.Y. Scarlett Esq. 'performed the duties of Father
Christmas' and Mrs A.J.C. Hoskyns-Abrahall allowed her daughter
Amanda to be Fairy at the Children's Party. The nadir was reached
in June 1950 when the General Committee was opened with a
pathetic announcement: 'Gentlemen, this meeting makes history for
our Club, being the first and we hope the last meeting at which we
cannot have a *chhota peg.*'[5] The RBYC remained a dry club until
1961, when a liquor licence was granted for the Dolphin Bar. At
about the same time the first Indian took his seat on the General
Committee, but no doubt the timing was coincidence. Good times
returned to stay.

I entered the club past the reception desk manned by *tindals*
(Anglo-Indian word from Tamil, meaning 'senior boat crew') and
stopped at the RBYC notice board. Why are Indian club rules so
officious, particularly when they refer to dress codes? The answer
normally given with a polite smile is because 'we inherited them
from the British':

- Chappals. Open sandals without straps are not permitted.
- T-shirts are permitted only if they have sleeves and support
  no logos except brand names.
- Shorts are permitted in the lounge only up to 8 p.m.
- Ladies are expected to dress appropriately as per the occasion.

Past the foyer stretched a gloomy, Gothic arched corridor lined with
honours boards, showcases, a gentleman's weighing machine and a
ship's bell. No wonder, I thought, the publication *Elite Clubs of India*
says that the RBYC is 'steeped in the musty colonial atmosphere of a
Paul Scott novel'. (The author of the *Raj Quartet* and *Staying On* has
become a cliché for anything vaguely *fin de Raj.*) Yet no amount of
mustiness could detract from the model of the elegant, graceful *Water
Queen*, the 74-foot loa with two lateen sails built by the Bombay
shipyard for Sir Henry Morland in 1856. It lay in its showcase outside
the lounge as a reproach to its land-lubberish surroundings. In the
lounge, under a portrait of the Queen, I met Lieutenant-Colonel

Graham Tullet OBE. Remarkably, considering that the 1,200-strong membership of the club is now entirely Indian except for three Britons, he was elected President as recently as 2004. He told me that his job was to give 'credence' to the history of the RBYC.

Wearing what looked like a Lillywhites T-shirt with light cavalry twill slacks, he reminded me of a military version of Prince Charles, particularly the cultured, self-deprecating voice and smile: landed gentry coping in the modern world. In his youth, Tullet admitted, he had been a bit of a bounder and freebooter. He became a professional soldier with the Worcestershire Regiment in the 1960s ('the vein slicers', they called themselves in the Indian Mutiny) but was attached to the Protectorate Levies during the unsuccessful defence of Aden in the mid-1960s. Then it was 'intelligence work' in Oman, for which he studied Arabic at the Middle East Command Arabic School in Beirut, before rejoining the Regiment. His time back was short, because 'I was a naughty boy and told to push off'. So in the 1970s he joined the Abu Dhabi Defence Force under Sheik Za'id (later the first President of the United Arab Emirates) and raised his own levied company – 'probably the last Englishman to do so' – the *Sariyathalaniya* (No. 8 Company). As there were not enough young Bedouin around, he recruited from India. 'There's rather a funny story about this actually,' said Tullet lowering his voice:

> I was standing with Sheik Za'id on a sand dune when my wet sweeper came past wearing my No. 1 dress hat, as he was carrying my night soil on his head. 'Who's that and what is he doing?' asked Sheik Za'id. I told him. 'Oh, I know his father. Why is he doing that?' I said, 'You don't expect me to do it, do you?' 'Major Tullet,' he ordered, 'go over to India and get any young man who can carry a rifle and will do any job like that. I want them in my army.'

And that was how Tullet's recruitment company began in Mumbai. Now, over thirty years later, he supplies labour for construction works in the Middle East and West Africa. 'Don't laugh, I'm also building some gold mines round Timbuctoo,' he added.

A hundred and fifty years ago Tullet would have made a dashing cavalry officer in one of those freebooting regiments like Hodson's Horse. In fact he played the part in the Indian film of the Mutiny *Junoon*. To his chagrin he was only given a 15.2 hand polo pony to ride: 'Normally I'm nothing unless I'm on a horse at least 17 hands, but that was one better than Mark Tully, who wasn't trusted with more than a sabre.' It is Tullet's boast that several times during the hunting season in Britain he drinks at the RBYC until closing time on a Friday, then picks up a bag from his bearer at home and catches the 1 a.m. KLM flight to Amsterdam. One short-haul flight to Bristol and a good breakfast at his Somerset house and he is riding to hounds at eleven the next morning. Whether that qualifies him as a second phase stayer-on I do not know!

Tullet told me about a preposterous character, an Irish chartered accountant who had died in Mumbai in 2005, who had insisted he should be addressed as Callaghan of India. His claim to title was that in 1965 Prime Minister Lal Shastri had joked with him that he knew India so well he should adopt the title; so he had, and kept it for forty years.

> He wore a three-piece tweed suit and brogues whatever the weather. Set himself up as the Honorary Irish Consul. I invited him to dinner once. He demolished two bottles of claret and kicked my bearer out of the way when he escorted him out. He stood in the monsoon rain bellowing and ordering cars to stop. Next morning, at eight o'clock, a handwritten thank-you letter arrived.

Such boorish behaviour was all too common in the days of the Raj and must have continued afterwards when Indian deference was still customary. Perhaps it still is, because 'Rajist behaviour' is one of those coded terms implying criticism, as in 'trying to get your way in India by assuming British superiority'. One expat I met said Callaghan had been 'barking'.

Tullet was worried about the Remembrance Sunday parade and service he was in the midst of organising, as he does every year; hence his OBE. It takes place down the Colaba causeway at the Afghan church built in 1847 to commemorate the disastrous First Afghan War and the bloody Sind campaign a few years later. 'The Rajput Army supply the pipes and drums but the bandsmen can't read music and their memories are going a bit. They've got to get "Flowers of the Forest" right as we enter the church – makes all the difference.' He is very proud of the British Indian Army's record in the Second World War: 'It was the largest volunteer army the world has ever seen – 189,000 volunteers in 1939 and 2.5 million in 1945 – and it won more awards for gallantry, 3,600, than any other allied army; thirty-two of them were VCs. Two holders live here in Mumbai and I give them maintenance grants every month.'

Over 300 ex-servicemen with their families will attend the service, and he is not worried that only about a third will be even nominal Christians: 'I'll cut Christ out of all the prayers, you don't notice really, but God's OK.' Many distinguished old soldiers will be there: Brigadier Mehta, who served with the Royal Indian Artillery in Burma; Admiral Gandhi, who was Mountbatten's last ADC; and General de Souza: 'He fought his way up through Italy with the Mahratta Light Infantry and won the MC. I'll get him to give the address and Frank will read one of the lessons.' Tullet suddenly looked preoccupied: 'It's an important occasion for us and a lot for one man to set up.' I left him ringing a small bell on his drinks table, known in the Club as a *koi hai*, and went to check in. I hoped I might come across Major Frank Courtney OBE, MC, who is the longest-serving *koi hai* of the RBYC.

My 'chamber' was the size of a squash court with wood-panelled walls and a view through the Gothic-shaped window towards the Gateway of India, so close I could feel the buzz as beggars and hawkers plied their trade and boys dived into the sea swell. Behind the Gateway ferries crossed the shimmering water to Elephanta Island. Turning round into the dim recess of the squash court I found a door that led to a huge bath and geyser on a pedestal under a fan. Exploring further, I realised I had entered a time warp. Almost all the decoration and most of the furniture in the club, from the dining room, through to the breakfast room and lounge to a mysterious empty room called the 'Anchorage' dated from the Raj period.

Most of the table chairs in the breakfast room, for example, were
Bombay blackwood based on Victorian design and quite possibly
antique; the tables were heavy Victorian mahogany. In the dining
room the furniture style was art deco, popular in Bombay in the
1920s and 1930s. The walls were covered with photos: of club presidents and commodores; of regatta days, where the men wore yachting
caps or solar *topis* above striped blazers and ties; of Edwardian outings
to Sapper bungalow on Hog Island; of the Regatta Dinner in the
old ballroom. One showed the Regatta Dinner of 1930, when His
Excellency Sir Frederick Sykes and Lady Sykes, owners of the yacht
Minnick, were guests of honour – the table a long 'U' with guests in
the dress uniform of the club, and turbaned waiters with cummer-
bunds stood behind every chair. Some Regatta Dinner menus were
signed and framed; 1923, H.L. Wilson, J.S. Campbell, M.A. Moran,
Hilda Barlow. By now the time warp was affecting my imagination
and, not for the first time, the words of the historian G.M. Trevelyan
came to mind: 'Once on this earth, on this familiar spot of ground,
walked other men and women, as actual as we are today, thinking
their own thoughts, swayed by their own passions, but now all gone,
one generation vanishing into another, gone as utterly as we ourselves shall shortly be gone, like ghosts at cockcrow.' Trevelyan found
this 'quasi-miraculous', but for me, stuck in the time warp, it was a
morbid thought.

Many of the alcoves were filled with large, tarnished silver cups:
the RBYC Challenge Cup, the Barry Coningshaw Cup, the Tolani
Trophy, above all the Lysistrata Cup, presented 'to the Members
of the RBYC by Mr J. Gordon Bennett with a view to encourage yachting in Bombay waters, 1911'. The name 'Gordon Bennett'
struck a bell with me, or rather sounded an expletive, because that
is how it is used these days – 'Gordon Bennett!!' as in 'we're out of
gin!!' or 'Gordon Bennett!!' as in 'I don't believe it!' Does it come
from 'gor blimey' or 'God in Heaven'? Graham Tullet did not know,
but he told me about its progenitor:

He was the son of an American–Scottish newspaper proprietor, a
prankster, and during his engagement party he urinated in the grand

piano and that was the end of that [Oh, Gordon Bennett!!]. So he set sail in the steam yacht the *Lysistrata* and got to Bombay, where he applied to join the club. He was rejected, but he still donated two cups with slightly different names, and its twin was sold at Sotheby's New York about eight years ago for $100,000. This one weighs 18 kilos of silver. He still could not join the club, but he did buy *The Times of India*.

That evening I met Major Frank Courtney in the Dolphin Bar, sitting alone but watched solicitously by a waiter. At ninety-one he is the oldest member of the club; frail and a bit rheumy, with spectacles and walking stick to hand, but mind as sharp as ever. He was once a keen yachtsman, and he still dressed the part with a naval T-shirt over light blue slacks. Frank was born in Dulwich in 1916. He told me that he had been stationed in India with the Royal Fusiliers from 1935 and then he fought in Syria and Egypt with the 4th Indian Division, winning the MC and Bar. 'You got those for surviving' he said. Then he had returned to India:

Don't think that in 1947 the Bombay Brits played 'Auld Lang Sync' and all went home. It wasn't like that at all. Many of us young men were coming out, businessmen, lawyers, bankers, hoping to get good jobs with a cheap cost of living and steer clear of this new socialist Britain. The 1950s were good times over here. It wasn't until the 1960s that Indian companies became more self-confident and wondered why they were employing British staff who demanded air-conditioning, a car and British education for their children when Indians cost a lot less money.

In fact it was not until Major Courtney's Presidency of the RBYC in 1967–75 that Indian members outnumbered the British for the first time.

So Frank stayed. He found a job producing radio and TV commercials for Ceylon Radio, for much of that country's post-war imports came from the Bombay area. His beautiful Armenian wife, Catherine, opened a boutique in the majestic Taj Hotel just round the corner from the RBYC. She called it *Pompadours* and, being a formidable lady, she soon acquired the prefix 'Madam' in her title. Rumour has it that she was not short of admirers, including a maharaja and an Australian jockey, who contributed to the Courtney lifestyle. Frank joined the Yacht Club and remembered the tense meeting that voted to admit Indian members in 1953:

> I wasn't there but it was a bit bloody. High time of course. Our time had been up years ago. Of course Indians had to manage themselves. I am pro Raj mind you. I miss the order and lack of corruption in public life under the British – many people with memories will tell you that. Now I don't get any deference and I don't want any.

That is true, but Major Courtney is still a figure of the Raj. He refuses to learn Hindi or call Bombay 'Mumbai'. A keen flier of the Royal Ensign, he revived the UK Citizens Association and the League for Ex-Servicemen. Colonel Tullet has taken this over.

Frank has a house near Southampton and his daughter lives in Monaco, but he does not intend to leave. One major reason for this, frequently given by elderly stayers-on, is that Indians make good carers. His own bearer has been with him for years, and, said Frank, he could 'nowhere near' afford the same quality service in England. (Major Courtney never did leave, for he died in Mumbai on 30 January 2008.)

The next day, a Friday, I came across Graham Tullet at lunch in the bar before he was leaving for his weekend house in Goa. I asked him why the RBYC resembled a Raj museum?

> Quite deliberate and quite recent! It dates from my Presidency but it wasn't my idea. We just thought we'd display all these old photos that tell the Club's history. You see we've all grown up over the last fifty years and now we simply regard the past as our heritage. In fact the club has benefited from years of neglect. No one ever thought of modernising it in some stupid way, as often happens, so this pictorial theme, so to speak, fitted in very well with the overall look of the place. Mind you, we've only been here since 1947.

Both Graham and Frank were at the General Committee meeting
about ten years ago when the discussion was held about keeping
the title Royal Bombay Yacht Club. In fact it was they, the only two
British at the meeting, who raised the 'royal' issue. Was it any longer
appropriate?

> I was asked to write to Buckingham Palace asking if the club was enti-
> tled to call itself 'Royal'? I got a letter back saying that Her Majesty
> was most happy for us to continue using the title bestowed by her
> great-great-grandmother if that was what we wanted to do. All the
> Indian members loved this answer, so we kept our title. As for 'Bombay'
> or 'Mumbai', why should we change? We were formed during the
> Bombay Presidency, like the Bombay High Court, and that hasn't
> changed its name, so why should we? We've had no pressure really. One
> of our members insists on writing his cheques to 'The Royal Mumbai
> Yacht Club' and the bank honours them; but that's just a gesture.

I was interested in the motive behind this maintenance, even resuscitation, of the look of the past. Was there any kind of nostalgia,
historical identification or political statement behind it? 'Good Lord
no! Members like the idea that the past of the club used to be a bit
posh. Very few know much about the history and I doubt today if
they have views on the Raj. That's where I come in, as I give credence to the past; but don't read much more into it.'

The RBYC regards the past as a decorative theme; like pubs and
hotels nowadays, it is part of the heritage industry. The difference is
that, unlike, say, the Imperial Hotel in New Delhi, the past belongs
to the club. It is not artificial, nor kitsch, nor over the top. In fact the
RBYC has moved with the times. The current *Lonely Planet Travel
Guide* may say that 'the clock seems to have stopped in the late nineteenth century', but the club now has air-conditioning throughout,
a computer room and colour TV in all chambers. Yet it knowingly
markets the past as an added attraction, and just occasionally it
encourages its members to live it too.

The occasion was the 150th, the 'Sesquicentennial' Celebration,
in 1996. The club was given permission to hold the celebration on

the lawn in front of its former Waterfront Building, where, in former
times and over the other side of the harbour wall, country craft with
lateen sails such as the Malabar Coast *kotiah* and the Gujarati *dhow*
used to bob up and down at anchor next to Seabirds, Pixies and the
stately yachts. In keeping with this backdrop, Major Courtney made
his entrance wearing the full dress uniform of the club, namely:

> An evening dress coat of blue cloth with buff facing, three gilt buttons
> on each front and two at waist behind, two small gilt buttons on each
> cuff.
> Buttons: gilt mounted. The Anchor and Cable. Officers (including
> Flag Officers) shall be distinguished by the addition of 3 gilt buttons
> horizontally on the cuffs. 5½ up and 1¾ inches apart.
> Dress Waistcoat: single-breasted white Marcella three small gilt buttons.
> Trousers: plain blue evening dress material.
> Tie: White bow necktie.[6]

Not to be outdone, Lieutenant-Colonel Tullet carried with him
the famous hammered-silver Claret Cup, which contained 'at least'
three bottles of claret. It was certainly the right occasion to show
off the family silver. Circulating round the guests was a 'superbly
clad' (boasted Graham) elderly club servant bearing the ornate silver
Angaar Container for the use of gentlemen cigar smokers. The
General Committee was not worried about ostentation, but it was
concerned about sponsorship. Presumably on the assumption that
the Raj has a commercial value that can on occasions demean the
heritage, the minutes read: '150th celebration. In keeping with the
tradition of the club, sponsorship for such an occasion would not be
correct.'

Elsewhere in Mumbai the Raj does have a definite commercial
value. The old Chor bazaar – the 'thieves' market – where anything
old and British is on sale, from antiques through reproductions to
junk, is not what it was; but more respectable antique businesses
are booming. And the buyers are now Indian. Close to the RBYC
on Wellington Circle (now Mukherji Chowk) is Phillips Antiques,
founded in 1860, and situated as it announces 'in the centre of the

city's heritage precinct'. Phillips is more Bond Street than Portobello Road. Its showroom has a high ceiling supported by black Corinthian columns; between them, octagonal glass-fronted cabinets display tribal art, but British silver and porcelain too, lacquer work-boxes and cut glass. On the walls are reproduction maps and pictures of, for example, East India Company uniforms.

The owner, Farooq Issa, told me he specialises in 'twilight of the Raj'. There were two reasons for this. Lately the Indian government has prohibited the sale abroad of Indian 'antiques', defined as items more than 100 years old. In any event, the expensive, quality, antiques have disappeared off the market since the heady days of the late 1960s and 1970s, when, following Prime Minister Indira Gandhi's removal of their privileges and privy purses (subsidies) in 1967, the maharajas auctioned off their possessions. In fact, said Farooq, much of the maharajas' antiques had been sold to European buyers by private treaty so as to avoid publicity and had never reached the market. Frank Courtney told me an amusing story that illustrated this. In the 1970s he had known the owner of a horsebreeding stud in the UK who had flown over mares in foal ('two for the price of one') and sold them to maharajas in return for their vintage Rolls Royces. These had been driven back home by the 'gap-year' students of those years.

Phillips Antiques sell mainly twentieth-century Raj remains. There are ready buyers for camping (sold as 'campaign') equipment such as folding tables and chairs, camp beds and canteens of picnic cutlery. Art-deco furniture sells well too, and there is a lot of it available, as the adjacent Bombay – that is, the Oval and Marine Drive area – dates from that period. Such is the demand for old photos of, say, tiger hunts or royal visits that Phillips has run out of originals and sells reproductions. I looked through a portfolio. Here was Lord Hardinge and party in the Kashmir, 1916; George V landing in Bombay in 1911; Maharaja Ganga Singh on an elephant with his Rolls Royce coupé in the foreground, 1939. Reproduction maps are popular too. I bought a coloured lithograph by W. Lloyd from his series *Scenes of India Life, c. 1890*. It shows two army lieutenants with rucksacks in a high, cool, Kashmir valley. The caption reads: 'To think, we could be in Cawnpore now!'

What caught my eye was a portfolio of advertising posters, again copies, dating from the 1920s and 1930s. A young Indian couple was puzzling over them. We looked at a stern Hindu lady wearing a red sari and sitting in a lotus leaf with her toddler on her knee, naked except for a small lotus as a 'fig leaf'. Underneath it said: 'PEARS SOAP, PURE AS THE LOTUS. Learn without sorrow, the eternal truth that youth is Godlike and beauty is youth'. I told them that every year in the UK the company had selected a bubbly-looking blonde toddler as 'Miss Pears' and put her on a poster. Perhaps this was the Indian equivalent? More puzzling was the advertisement for 'Valet auto-strop safety razor'. 'The razor still exists,' said the Indian couple with reassurance, 'but why is it being marketed like this?' The poster showed a maharaja in his *howdah* and down one side of the elephant was a gold cloth emblazoned with the name of the product. 'Ah, I see,' said the young man, 'it's saying maharajas use Valet auto-strop to shave their whiskers, so it's an exclusive product.' We were mystified, however, by the poster advertising 'THE PERFECT COMBINATION; SHELL MOTOR OIL AND MEXPHALTE, THE PERFECT ROAD SURFACE.' It showed an idyllic rural scene. A tarmac road devoid of any traffic, whether animal, pedestrian, or vehicular, wound from the entrance to a palace that looked like a mini Gateway to India, past a picturesque cottage and groomed shrubbery, to a Shell petrol pump. Standing by it was a smiling, uniformed and turbaned Indian about to fill the tank of a sports coupé driven by a young Brit wearing an immaculate white jacket and black bow tie. The scene looked completely unreal. Then it struck me that this was the adman's equivalent of a motor tour through an English village, minus only the village green and pub, transposed to what he thought was an Indian setting. It dated from the 1930s, when the middle classes were buying baby Austins and touring round the countryside. As A.J.P. Taylor put it, 'the car was the great formative influence of the new England'. But this was the old India and the adman's concept was clearly phoney. I explained this to the Indian couple. 'Ah,' said the young man again, 'you had a writer called Rudyard Kipling, who went on about snake charmers and the Indian rope-trick. At least they aren't in the picture.'

Opposite Phillips and next to the art deco Regal Cinema is Framroz Sorabji Khan & Co., Jewellers and Art Dealers. The owner's son, Hoshang, was anxious to tell me that they dealt in 'collectibles' more than antiques, because these were less than 100 years old. As a matter of fact I did point out several East India Company silver rupees with Queen Victoria's head, but Hoshang pretended to ignore them, quite unnecessarily, because they are sold all over India. It is a Chor bazaar sort of place, the familiar bric-à-brac curiosity shop with old postcards, small items of silver and jewellery and cheap art-deco ornaments. There were two notable collections. One was of enamel billboards advertising, for example, Brylcreem, Horlicks, Badshahi Depilatory Powder and Standard Lights Kerosene Lamps. They were stacked at the back of the shop accumulating rust, but at *c.* 10,000 rupees each (£120) not at all a bargain. The other was what Hoshang called 'breweryana'. Dating from the prohibition period and increasingly popular were 'distillery items': a jug marked 'Encore Whisky' ('probably extinct now'), a Bulldog lager glass, Dewars Whisky and Carslberg Lager trays and assorted ashtrays. Hoshang said his buyers found breweryana 'glamorous'. One of his favourite items was a British Lion jelly mould.

Sitting behind the counter under a painting of his Parsee ancestors was old Framroz himself, in much the same chair as he must have occupied seventy years before. He recalled the last British leaving for embarkation, 'the Union Jacks, the bands and marching troops', and he remembered with great respect a few British collectors of ancient Sanskrit manuscripts and Persian Art:

> They have all gone now and who has replaced them? Some British collectors who came here had a genuine love of art and they would tighten their belts until they could afford to buy. Today's buyers are Indians, a new class of industrialists, who don't recognise fine art. They think the bigger an item is the more expensive it must be. They have no class with a capital C – no breeding. Only a few people like us care about the Raj now. Many things like the discipline and the cleanliness have gone. Look at the bribery and corruption! Spitting! Men cough on your face! Children steal flowers! But the trouble with some

British was that they were too British. They held back Indians, who
had to stagnate at lower levels, and they did not want Indians to com-
pete with them. That's why they had to go.

The antiques dealer I most wanted to see was Farrokh Toddywalla of
Ardeshir Dady Street, the metal forging area some miles away, where
anchor chains and defunct machinery lie rusting outside and the air
is rent with the noises of welding and cutting – a rough place where
taxis do not go. I remembered feeling apprehensive on my first visit
about fifteen years ago, as I climbed the five flights of steep stairs in
Toddywalla House, that the coin and medal dealer might have appropriated one of the forges for his own purposes! I soon found this
suspicion was misplaced. In his office, old Toddywalla was in negotiation with a London buyer, the latest Spink's catalogue between them
– an unlikely encounter in a Mumbai backstreet. Threadbare and dif-
fident he may be, but Farrokh Toddywalla and his son Malcolm are
familiar figures at Coinex and Baldwin Auctions in London.

On this occasion I found the office equipped with computers
and a smart secretary, perhaps a granddaughter, checking prices
from a World Coins catalogue. Malcolm offered me a sparse assort-
ment of British India coins, but when I complained, as a former
customer, he opened a safe and pulled out a plastic wallet of at least
fifty gold mohurs. Treasure! One of the earliest East India Company
coins with an English inscription, the mohur shows on the reverse
a magnificent lion under a palm tree and on the obverse WILLIAM
IIII KING. No wonder a race in Bombay's first sailing regatta, in
1830, was for a sweepstake of one gold mohur. The two-mohur gold
coin is the equivalent to a collector of a Tudor gold sovereign, historically fascinating, aesthetically marvellous and in good condition
quite rare. It is the prize of a collection and can easily reach £3,000
at auction. Malcom invited me to take a pick of his one-mohur
coins, with a starting price of 70,000 rupees or £830 each, expensive by any standards. On his desk was a large notice prohibiting the
sale of antiques.

What I had really come to see were the Toddywalla medals. I still
remember my excitement that first visit when scores of them almost

cascaded out of the safe when he unlocked the door, unidentified and in most cases unwrapped. I chose two and that began my collection of Queen Victoria medals for army campaigns in India. The British government first awarded medals in the 1840s for officers and men alike in the British Army and Navy who had served in the Napoleonic Wars and were still alive. (The exception was the Battle of Waterloo, when a government medal was awarded at the time.) These medals extended to soldiers, both British and Indian, who fought in the East India Company army. Then individual imperial campaigns attracted their own medals. The custom became for a short while a mania, so that obscure border campaigns in India still merited a campaign medal – Ghuznee 1839, Jellalabad 1841–2, Gwalior 1843, Scinde 1843 – so many were awarded that even the fictitious Captain Flashman (the anti-hero of George MacDonald Fraser's novels) complained that they were given away with the rations. It is the design engraved on the silver reverse that is always so stirring, at least for those of us brought up on *Our Empire Story* and *Fights for the Flag*. For example, from the official citation: 'Major-General Sir Walter Gilbert, on horseback, receiving the surrender of the Sikhs' (Punjab Campaign Medal 1848–9); 'A standard helmeted figure of Britannia holding a wreath in her outstretched right hand and over her left arm is the Union shield. Behind is the British Lion and above the word "INDIA"' (Indian Mutiny Medal, 1857–8); 'A scene of troops on the march with an elephant carrying a gun in the centre. Around the top is the word "AFGHANISTAN"' (Second Afghan War, 1878–80).

Each medal has the name of the recipient engraved round the rim, so it is easy from India Office or Public Record Office records to trace his service career, provided he was British. It is not possible with Native Infantry – that is, the Indian soldiers from the fighting races of Sikhs, Gurkhas, Pathans, Punjabis and Mahrattas who signed up with the East India Company Army before its disbandment in 1858. From my medal collection a favourite character is Ensign Phillip Moss Walmisley, 16 Grenadiers, Bengal Native Infantry, who was awarded the Gwalior Star. He exhibited distinct Flashman characteristics, the difference being that Walmisley was dishonourably dismissed in 1849, whereas Flashman would have been promoted. Walmisley signed up in London in 1843 to escape responsibility for a wife and child and volunteered for India. Six years later he was court-marshalled for 'highly unbecoming conduct and abuse of authority':

> When commanding a detachment of his regiment returning from Patna to Calcutta by vessel on the river Ganges, being in a state of intoxication, he landed a large portion of his detachment from his vessel and marched them into Patna with fixed bayonets, with the view of rescuing from the police station two persons in confinement who had accompanied him into town earlier in the evening and been arrested for disturbance. Lieutenant Walmisley then proceeded to Calcutta in direct disobedience of orders.

Malcolm Toddywalla apologised for his lack of interesting medals: huge market in the UK; couldn't get rid of them quickly enough. This may well be true, as prices are rising fast. For example, a Defence of Lucknow bar on an Indian Mutiny Medal of 1857, which was awarded to the original defenders of the Residency and General Havelock's troops who fought their way in but could not get out again, may change hands for at least £10,000. But the Toddywallas took my email with the promise of offers to come.

All three dealers I met knew of Farida Hoosenally. They spoke of her with some awe, as if she was the queen of the antiques furniture business. Her daughter in New York said I must ask Farida to show me round her warehouse: 'It's like Xanadu in *Citizen Kane*, it's incredible!' (Xanadu was the baroque palace in Orson Welles's film about the newspaper magnate Randolph Hurst, who lived imprisoned by his possessions stacked in the vast recesses of his palace.) I was shown a taster when I visited the Hoosenally home. Straight away I encountered a circular Regency table with eight Chippendale chairs; next to it an elegant bureau-cabinet from the same period, rosewood inlaid with ivory that had belonged to a viceroy. At the end of the room were early Christian antiques from Portuguese Goa, including a sizeable Madonna carved from a single ivory tusk. These were placed on a Chinese camphor chest of drawers heavily carved with sea scenes. Next door was a magnificent East India Company four-poster bed made of Burmese teak, recognisable by the motif of two lions rampant on the headboard. The company motto 'they grow in harmony' was missing (presumably referring to spices rather than conjugal activities), but its spirit was there.

Farida gave me a crash course on British India furniture, which I later supplemented by a visit to the Victoria and Albert Museum. When the Portuguese arrived in the sixteenth century, they found that Western-style furniture did not exist in Indian interiors. People ate, read, socialised and slept on the floor. Being accustomed to elevated furniture, the European colonisers commissioned from native carpenters their familiar Western-style tables, chairs and beds, but they chose native ornamentation. Some of the hand-made furniture from centres of craft excellence were very sophisticated pieces worked with intricate patterns and inlaid with precious materials. What have always appealed to collectors are familiar forms of furniture made out of prized materials and embellished with exotic decoration. India has these in abundance.

This was the age of harmony, I reminded myself, when 'going native' was not the pejorative term it later became. Europeans of both sexes wore Indian cottons, including turbans, smoked the hookah pipe, chewed betel nut and watched the *nautch* (dancing) girls. Many European men kept *bibis* (mistresses), and some married them without incurring disapproval. The furniture of the period reflected this orientalism. Much of the decoration was as exotic to the craftsmen as it was to the buyers, for it was designed to appeal to European concepts of the East rather than to traditional tastes.

India, of course, is at the crossroads of trade between Europe and the Far East, and the fascination of Euro-Indian antique furniture is that it reflects this. Not only do you see the different styles of, say, eighteenth-century Portuguese, Dutch, French and British furniture but also the different styles and materials of the many cultures that made up the Indian subcontinent. In the Victoria and Albert Museum, for example, are Dutch chairs from the Coromandel Coast made from ebony and richly carved with motifs from Hindu mythology and Christian imagery; from Murshidabad, the former capital of

Bengal, an ivory oval table embossed with ivory gilt and clearly of British Regency design that was presented to Warren Hastings; from Bombay, a portable writing desk carved from sandalwood, the exterior with geometric parquetry of ivory and ebony (known as *sadeli*) and a silver lock from Britain.

From a cultural point of view, the stupidity of the British began in 1803 when Lord Arthur Wellesley, the Governor General of the East India Company, captured Delhi and proclaimed the British *de facto* rulers of the Mughal Empire. Thus began British sovereignty and ideas of the master race. The Indian became 'the poor Hindoo' in need of conversion to Christianity to save him from his wretched moral state. With superiority came the need for prestige, and the symbols of prestige were European. It now became extremely bad taste to appear in anything of Indian manufacture or even ornaments, however beautiful. In the colonial marketplace, in European shops like Taylor and Co. in Calcutta, European furniture was accorded a cachet and Indian furniture a stigma, growing as the century progressed. The new pejorative word was 'country':

> 'Country' is a peculiar adjective in Anglo-Indianism that at once diminished the value of anything. It is a sneer and a condemnation. 'Country goods' are a synonym for inferiority. On the other hand, anything 'English' or 'imported' at once acquires a special value, and an imported dog, iron bedstead, carpet or article of furniture stamps the owner as a man of taste and means, and sheds dignity over him.[7]

In the East India Company the English language was enforced and Indian wives were banned. It was a reign of cultural terror. It was said that 'no collector's wife will wear an article of Indian manufacture even to save her soul from perdition'.[8] Perdition came in the form of the Mutiny, but the stigma against things Indian continued.

And so to Farida Hoosenally's *godown* (warehouse) somewhere in the endless conurbation of Mumbai. Covering three floors, piled high to the ceilings, crammed into every space and gathering dust were the household and office furnishings of the British in India over a century ago. Most of it was Victoriana: heavy mahogany tables,

Bombay blackwood chairs, partners' desks from solicitors' offices, wooden filing cabinets from railway stations, swivel chairs and folding deckchairs, many mahogany or teak bedframes and some with the East India Company lions. It reminded me less of *Citizen Kane* than of a converted airfield I know in Lincolnshire – a parking place by the A1 where furniture vans en route to the Continent, loaded with Victoriana gutted from the once grand northern mansions built by the rich of the industrial revolution, are temporarily emptied so that their contents are available for the wholesale trade. It was hard to see this furniture as proof of British superiority.

The closer we picked our way to Farida's office, the nearer we were to the 'top end' of the trade. Here was the orientalist furniture, some of it exquisite. In her office was a Thomas Chippendale (1749–1822) display cabinet with its original glass, probably shipped out from England, though Indian craftsmen worked to his designs from the *Gentleman and Cabinet Maker's Directory*; its eight shelves and back were painstakingly carved with the motif of the iris flower – 'that's the Chinese influence. He was very influenced by it,' said Farida. Then there was a library case made of ebony from south India. Down the sides were three-dimensional carvings of animals, the British lion at the top, elephants and monkeys underneath. 'It was a melting pot, you see, and that's why European galleries like it. It's not a typical Chippendale, or a typical Hepplewhite, because one style borrows from the other; it's a blend.'

Outside her office, squatting on one of the few vacant areas of floor, were Farida's restorers. They had just stuffed horsehair into an elegant Regency *chaise longue*. Now the hunt is on for porcupine quills and ivory bangles or even billiard balls to restore inlaid workboxes, for buying elephant tusks is illegal. They seemed overwhelmed by their work or just intimidated by the piles of furniture stacked precariously above them. Farida was serenely indifferent to the ban on exporting antiques: 'It's Indian antiques that can't leave the country. I would never export Mughal art, for example, but this is quite different. This is colonial furniture, never part of our tradition. In fact the Delhi Law Courts are being modernised at the moment so they are selling their Victorian furniture. No one objects to that.'

She does not advertise, does not want a showroom:

> I want buyers to come here, and they do, so they can see my furniture
> is genuine. Most of them are Indians these days, though the Germans
> are my best foreign buyers, and the trade is absolutely booming. The
> good stuff is harder and harder to get [she waits for tip-offs from her
> contacts and then catches the first plane in order to view], but once
> you get it you know it will increase in value; the craftsmanship and
> quality of materials are so high.

My last visit in Mumbai was to meet stayer-on Eric Foy Nissen,
who lives in the top flat of an apartment block on Malabar Hill.
Here the air was cleaner and cooler, for down below the tempera-
ture was a humid 35° centigrade, although it was November. His
flat looked as if he was either coming or going; packing cases everywhere loaded with books, cluttered tables containing medicines
and magazines, a pile of fold-up cane chairs. Pinned on the walls
was an intriguing set of pictures that seemed even at first glance to
tell a story. One was a painting of a Victorian sailing steamship. Then
there was a photo – very sepia and tattered – of an attractive young
European woman *c.* 1870s with long brown hair and a slim waist.
Next to it was a group photo taken some time later that showed a
princely bodyguard, posed formally with uniforms of much braid
and plumes, and among the bearded brown faces were two white
men, one much older than the other. Finally there was a recent
photo of a grave in an overgrown Indian landscape with a bungalow
in the background.

Foy Nissen got up to meet me. He is a bachelor of seventy-five,
of Anglo-Indian-Danish descent, who looks out on the world from
behind round glasses with a bookish, bemused expression. He has
never left India, apart from schooling in England, and is, therefore,
another of the small band of stayers-on who remembers the Raj era.
He worked in Bombay for the British Council between 1960 and
1986 and that is why I had come to see him.

Foy had other ideas. He straightaway produced a press cutting
from *The Times* of London dated 24 December 2003. It showed him

standing under a Hindu statue next to a little girl, obviously a picture prop, who looked even more bemused than Foy. Next to the photo was a headline: 'The dying man, the maharaja and a cache of price-less jewels.' Foy was shy about the article. He said it was inaccurate, it was sensationalist, it embarrassed him; but not only did he want to talk about it, he was clearly obsessed with it. Scarcely believing my luck, I turned on the tape recorder. Foy began a detailed and much-told story, but, like a tribal elder who contains in his head the oral history of his tribe, he seemed weighed down by the responsibility of his memory. He had to get the facts exactly right. Several times he repeated himself verbatim, other times he corrected himself and worked over the grounds of memory again. He did not deny the description in *The Times* of the treasure at the heart of the story:

> Impossibly gorgeous diamond rings set in solid gold, diamond ear-rings studded with emeralds, ruby and pearl necklaces that would have graced the neck of maharanis. The centrepiece is a woman's cres-cent shaped pendant, fashioned from a pair of lion's claws, adorned with turquoises and clad in beaten gold depicting the Tree of Life.
>
> 'These pieces are impossible to replicate today. They are, quite liter-ally, priceless,' says Mr Nissen.

The Nissens were originally Danish, and the start of Foy's story is reminiscent of Hans Christian Andersen. Until the 1970s his parents lived in a beautiful art deco bungalow in Bombay, where they looked after his grandmother. Under her bed was a box that no one was allowed to open. Then developers tried to persuade them to leave, and, when they refused, the developers set fire to the *godown* next door. This began a stressful period during which the grandmother died and Foy's father was diagnosed with terminal cancer. Fearing the worst, he told Foy's mother to give her son the box. It wasn't until Foy's father had died and the bungalow was sold that Foy remembered the box. He opened it. Inside, among photographs and a family history, was a will in the name of Georg Christian Nissen signed in 1888 to his son, Foy's grandfather. It said that he passed to him, the first-born male heir or his successor, the family treasure of priceless jewels that was deposited for safekeeping in a bank near his solicitor's office in Kingston upon Thames.

The story then becomes a small footnote to the history of the Raj in Gujarat. This is what Foy discovered. In 1857 his great-grandfather left the poor village of Simmerbølle on the Danish island of Langeland to seek his fortune. In Liverpool he was press-ganged into the crew of a merchant sailing steamer bound for Valparaiso in Chile and then across the Pacific to, eventually, Bombay (the picture on the wall was of the actual ship). By now Georg had served his time, so he stepped ashore a free man and eventually, using his head for heights acquired climbing the ship's rigging, joined a gang of railway bridge build-ers pioneering a new line into Gujerat. He stopped at Baroda (now Vadodara), lived with the British railway foreman and his wife, and, charmed by their description of the wife's sister, persuaded her, Sarah Davis (the sepia photo), to come out from Britain. They married and had three children, including a son named Ferdinand. Georg became a mercenary soldier, a lieutenant in the private army of the Gaekwar of Baroda, one of the Mahratta warrior princes. He served him well. He built up the army, was promoted to colonel, and was eventually joined in the Gaekwar's bodyguard by his son Ferdinand, as shown in the photo. In 1869, at a magnificent ball in the Makapura Palace, he was rewarded for his loyalty to the Gaekwar crown. The maharaja showered Georg and Sarah with jewels for services rendered.

A condition of Georg's insurance company, Pelican Insurance of Kingston upon Thames, was that the jewellery should be kept in an English bank, so Georg went over to Surrey and arranged this through a solicitor. He returned to Baroda and not long after he was sent to the remote district of Dhari, near Amreli in Gujerat, to subdue a band of *dacoits* (bandits). It was here that Sarah died. Only a few years ago Foy discovered her gravestone with its inscription in Danish (the final photo). Georg died in 1897, but his son Ferdinand (Foy's grandfather) became the commander of the Gaekwar's army, and he fought in the First World War.

So in the late 1970s Foy Nissen began the hunt for his inherit-ance. Why neither his grandfather nor his father claimed it he does not know. To his surprise he found that the solicitor's practice in

Kingston upon Thames was extant, but it was extremely slow replying to his enquiries. Then, sitting at his desk in the British Council and indulging in his lunchtime hobby of reading *The Times* Law Report, Foy read the summary of a civil case that seemed to show him the next step. It concerned a British woman who at the start of the Second World War had deposited her jewellery with her local bank and then emigrated to Canada. Almost half a century later she came back to claim her jewellery, only to find that the bank had sold it, assuming that she had died in the interim. She sued. The judge awarded her generous compensation and delivered a severe reprimand to the bank. Foy sent this Law Report to the solicitors in Kingston upon Thames. Now things began to happen. They replied that the local bank had been taken over by the National Westminster, which was responsible therefore for the Nissen jewellery. He wrote to it. The bank replied that in the 1960s it had tried to locate his family, eventually by asking the Indian High Commission to instigate a search of all Nissens still living in India. This had taken several years and came up with nothing. So the NatWest had contacted the nearest relative it could find, an old spinster living in Hjering in the Danish province of Jutland, and sent her the treasure. The arrival of a treasure chest of antique Indian jewellery had caused quite a stir and was reported in the local paper. The article said that the old lady, without any claim or aspiration to fortune, intended to hand over the unwanted treasure to the Hjering Court.

Anticipating further procrastination or prevarication, Foy Nissen contacted the court. Very quickly, to his relief, he received a 'human' letter from the clerk. She confirmed that her court still had the jewellery; indeed, from time to time she tried on the necklace and admired its beauty. She congratulated him. She enclosed an inventory written up by his great-grandfather Georg, so that Foy for the first time realised the extraordinary nature of his inheritance.

Foy Nissen went over to Denmark. Roughly a century after his great-grandfather made out his will, Foy set eyes for the first time on his priceless inheritance. I asked him the journalist's cliché 'how did it feel?', but he did not tell me. Perhaps he felt such a question indelicate, but more likely he was already concentrating on what was to

him the crucial next stage of the story; exactly how he proved he was
the rightful heir. This became all the more pressing because he had
begun to receive letters that revealed a wider family than he had ever
known. Eventually, his claim was proved, and, as he was a bachelor
with little use for the jewellery, he told me that he gave much of it to
his new-found relatives.

He kept the Tree of Life, exotically, sensually Indian: the crescent-
shaped pendant, fashioned from a pair of lion's claws, adorned with
turquoises and clad in beaten gold. Not a relic of the Raj but a treasure from a richer, more ancient culture. Where it was, how much it
was worth and what he intended to do with it, I forbore to ask.

Chapter Eight

THE LAST
STAYERS-ON

In All Souls church, Kanpur (Cawnpore in British times), a monument of fourteen tablets stands behind the altar and on them are
carved over 1,000 names. There is a grim, not to say grisly, inscription: 'Our bones are scattered at the grave's mouth as when one
cutteth and cleaveth wood upon the earth, but mine eyes are unto
thee O God, the Lord.' The monument commemorates the worst
atrocity in the history of British India, the slaughter of almost the
entire British and Anglo-Indian population of Cawnpore in the
Indian Mutiny between 6 June and 15 July 1857. The names of the
dead were collated by Jonah Shepherd, one of a handful of survivors,
and the clerestory windows of All Souls bear the names of all the
officers who perished bar one, Major Edwin Wiggins, who was considered a coward.

All Souls itself is a memorial church, because it was built on the
site of the Entrenchment, in 1857 a scrub of open ground with two
small barracks surrounded solely by a 1-metre-high mud wall. Old
General Hugh Wheeler chose the site for the British community
of Cawnpore, about 700 civilians and 300 soldiers, to make their
last stand against the mutineers. He made a disastrous mistake, for
about 350 persons perished during the constant bombardment of the
Entrenchment between 6 and 25 June. During the day one cannon
ball on average every two minutes ploughed into the defenders, who

were huddled in ditches under the blazing sun. Jonah Shepherd, an Anglo-Indian, was the only one to escape. Today the outline of the defensive positions may just be seen, and the well where many were shot risking their lives to obtain water remains intact.

The survivors of the Entrenchment believed that the rebel leader Nana Sahib had given them safe passage down the Ganges River about 2 kilometres away. They were mistaken. When they boarded the boats at Satichaura Ghat on 27 June, the mutineers opened fire and slaughtered a further 300 people. A pretty Anglo-Indian teenager, Amy Horne, cowering in the bottom of her boat watching the carnage, 'was sure the hour was not distant when we [she and her little sister] should have to stand before His dread presence'. She was saved by a *sowar* (rebel cavalryman), who abducted her. She eventually escaped but lived the rest of her life in ignominy among the British in Calcutta for choosing dishonour rather than death. Nana Sahib went down in British history as 'the perfidious Nana'. One boat managed to pull away from the ghat and from it four British soldiers escaped to tell the tale. The rest were recaptured and returned to Cawnpore, where they were shot, as were all the men who had survived the earlier massacres. A memorial in the Entrenchment commemorates some of them: 'these are they that came out of great tribulations'. Satichaura Ghat today remains much as it was, but the monument commemorating the massacre there has disappeared.

The remaining 180 or so women and children were imprisoned by Nana Sahib in the infamous Bibigarh, so called because at one time an Englishman had housed his Indian mistress there. They were slaughtered in the third massacre on 15 July. The next morning their bodies were thrown down a nearby well, some still alive, and this time there were no survivors. An advance party of Highland soldiers from the relieving army of General Havelock arrived soon after sunrise on 17 July and viewed 'with wet eyes and quivering lips' the terrible scene. One found a chilling note in a girl's handwriting on the floor of the Bibigarh that summarised the Cawnpore Massacres:

Entered the barracks May 21st
First shot fired June 6th

Aunt Lilly died June 17th
Uncle Willy died June 18th
Left barracks June 27th
George died June 27th
Alice died July 9th
Mama died July 12th

Caroline Lindsay herself and her sister Frances must have been killed three days later.

It was the deaths of women and children – the Angels of Albion – that so consumed the British with guilt and vengeance. The catchphrase 'Remember Cawnpore!' became a self-admonishment as well as a threat. Queen Victoria declared a Day of Humiliation on 7 October 1857, when, preached the vicar of All Souls, London, 'a wail came across the ocean from the well of Cawnpore'. It was widely, and wrongly, believed that British women had been attacked sexually, so that rape became a sort of imperial anxiety, as exemplified in the great novels of British India, *A Passage to India* and *The Raj Quartet*. Soon a Memorial Garden was landscaped around the scene of the worst massacre at the Bibigarh and a white marble memorial screen placed round the well itself. Count Carlo Marochetti designed the centrepiece, a marble angel holding palm fronds in her crossed arms, which was placed over the well. A contemporary guidebook tells us: 'Her arms are folded, denoting resignation; she holds in her hands the martyr's palm.' Marochetti's angel became the most hallowed shrine in British India, visited more frequently than the Taj Mahal. 'The Ladies' Monument [as it was called] is approached by visitors from many lands with sad thoughts and respectful steps' says an old guidebook.

For several years the guide to the Ladies' Monument was Private Murphy of the 84th Regiment, one of the four survivors from the boat that got away from Satichaura Ghat. The two young officers who swam away, Lieutenants Henry Delafosse and Mowbray Thomson, both became generals and have separate monuments in All Souls church. Thomson lived until 1917 and said he owed his life to Holborn Baths, where he learnt to swim as a lad. The fourth soldier,

Private Sullivan of the 1st Madras Fusiliers, died soon after from cholera. That left one other, mysterious, survivor. Fifty or so years after the massacres a missionary doctor and Catholic priest were called to a Muslim house in the Cawnpore bazaar. There an old lady received the last rites and confessed that she was General Wheeler's Anglo-Indian daughter, Ulrica, who had also been abducted at the ghat. Her sowar had been kind to her, and until her deathbed she was too ashamed to come out of hiding.

On Independence Day 1947 Marochetti's Angel was damaged by overenthusiastic young Indians and so removed to the grounds of All Souls church, where it stands today. Subsequently the mound on which it had stood was flattened so as not to attract attention. In 1952 the new Indian district magistrate of Cawnpore ordered a statue of Tatya Topi, the rebel leader during the First War of Independence (as Indians called the mutiny), to be erected on top of the well to replace Marochetti's angel. He claimed he did not know what lay underneath. After protest, Tatya Topi was removed and placed some distance away. Now Indians play cricket in the area oblivious to what happened 150 years ago. The nearby Hanging Tree, from which the mutineers were strung by the British after they had recaptured the city, has recently fallen down and been removed.

Many other memorials in Kanpur to the British dead of 1857 have disappeared altogether. There used to be several graves near the Ladies' Monument. Just outside the pathetic Entrenchment was a second well down which the survivors threw the bodies of their comrades at dead of night. It, too, remains, but monuments next to it have been removed. The Government Harness Factory and the Experimental Farm that once had graves nearby have passed from view altogether. Some graves remain in the churchyard of Christ Church, which used to be in the Civil Lines.

Of course, Cawnpore had several peacetime cemeteries where the British were buried, from their arrival in the town in the late eighteenth century until their departure in the 1960s. First came Kacheri Cemetery (1781–1865), which contains over 700 graves, nearly 300 of them with inscribed headstones according to an inventory of them collated in 1985. It is one of the very few British cemeteries to be maintained by the Archaeological Survey of India. Then came Mirpur Old Cantonment Cemetery, abandoned in 1969 and now built over. The New Cantonment Cemetery (1818–1943), now closed, must have been a vast place, because between only 1883 and 1898 some 550 British dead were buried there in seventeen plots; all their names and epitaphs are preserved on file. Concurrent with it were Hiraman Ka Purwa Cemetery (1796–1918) and Subadar Ka Talao Cemetery (1910–17), both abandoned in the 1960s. Finally, there is the New Cemetery, which includes forty-eight graves from the First World War. It is not a war cemetery run by the Commonwealth War Graves Commission, of which there are many in India dating mostly from the Second World War, but a civilian cemetery that belonged to a past, foreign government – the British. In other words, today it is the responsibility of no one, unless the local Indian Christian community cares for it. This applies to hundreds of old British cemeteries throughout India, the repositories of so much history. After Independence the British High Commission classified them as 'open', 'closed' and, later, after deconsecration, 'abandoned'. The Indian government issued a decree that 'abandoned' cemeteries were to be protected until they 'reverted to nature', but that decree has little effect.

That we know so much about the cemeteries and memorials of Kanpur is due to Theon Wilkinson and his sister Zoe, who were born in Cawnpore in 1924 and 1922. Zoe became the historian of British Cawnpore. It is from her book *Traders and Nabobs 1765–1857* (volume 2 is called *Boxwallahs 1857–1901*) that I took the story of Ulrica Wheeler and it was she who wrote *A Guide to Kacheri Cemetery*. Zoe also recorded that her cousin had lived in a garden cottage near the Ladies' Monument and used to observe her dogs behaving oddly. They became agitated when they looked in the direction of the marble screen, as if dreadful things were happening behind. On one occasion, she said, she saw the ghosts of 'two blond boys running this way and that around the mouth of the well as if desperately trying to find somewhere to escape'. Ghost stories about the Mutiny are common, which shows, if nothing else, how indelibly the events were stamped on the collective memory of British India.

Theon, too, was influenced by the memorials of Cawnpore, for
he is the founder of a remarkable organisation called the British
Association for Cemeteries in South Asia (BACSA). He began it
in 1976 and he is still the inspirer, the *mai-bap* (father figure), of the
organisation. His working assumption, which, of course, cannot be
proved, is that up to 2 million Britons left their bones in the lands
of the former East India Company. BACSA's mission is to preserve
a few of the historically important cemeteries, turn the abandoned
ones in cities to 'social uses' and collate all sources of information
for historical and genealogical purposes. BACSA's files are neatly
arranged in the India Records Office of the British Library, and six
of them cover the cemeteries and memorials of Cawnpore – a stack
of photos, maps, pro-forma surveys and memoirs collated and added
to by BACSA members over the last thirty years. It will be the final
record of the last stayers-on. (BACSA will be Theon's final testament too, for he died on 26 November 2007, when the first edition
of this book was with the publisher.)

Theon Wilkinson MBE worked in a cubby-hole behind the
reception desk of the Asia and African Studies Reading Room of
the British Library, which contains the former India Office records.
Here BACSA, supported now by a small staff, maintains its papers
and online services. For some time Theon carefully and helpfully
supplied me with flagged-up pieces of paper about BACSA, as he
must have done to hundreds of researchers over the years who were
anxious to trace a relative's grave in south Asia. Owlish is the word
that comes to mind about Theon, as he looks at you over his half
glasses someway down his nose under a thatch of whitening hair;
a wise and kind old owl, retiring about himself but unstoppable
about BACSA. He could be a retired professor, though he spent his
careers in the colonial service in Kenya and as a senior member of
the Institute of Personnel Management; first African chiefs and then
trade union officials. Like others with a lifelong fondness for India,
his home is full of memorabilia. Here is an original Charles D'Oyley
watercolour from the early nineteenth century showing two 'grif-
fins' (newcomers to the East India Company Army) at mess; there
a portrait of an Anglo-Indian descendant of a survivor of the Black

Hole of Calcutta painted on the lid of a wooden sherry cask; upstairs two pictures, side by side, of Nana Sahib on mica, one painted by an Indian showing him as hero, the other by a British artist showing him as 'perfidious'.

Theon spent the first six years of his life in Cawnpore. He remembers his parents' large, old white house on the bank of the Ganges, with its high rooms, flat roof and Greek columns supporting the veranda and imposing porch, but his main memory is of the gardens, where he would play with the children of the staff. Then there were large servants quarters. These housed a veritable community of different faiths and castes who were bound to the Wilkinsons in a sort of feudal relationship in which the *burra sahib* was part responsible for health and welfare in return for services given. In some cases this had pertained through generations. Theon flew kites with the son of his father's bearer, who in turn was the grandson of the original family bearer, a connection of at least sixty years. When Theon married Rosemarie, whose family had been in India for three generations, his bearer came to the wedding in England.

Theon's father was the Director of the Elgin Mill and eventually the Managing Director of its owners, the agency Begg Sutherland. This was the biggest managing agency in Cawnpore, having under its control cotton mills, an electric power station and sugar plantations in Bihar. One hundred years ago Cawnpore was the supply base for the British Army in India and in the Empire too. The Elgin Mill, founded in 1864, turned out khaki for the troops and police, everything from tents to army uniforms and blankets. Down the road was Cooper Allen, where leather was fashioned into army boots and saddlery. Cawnpore was and is today an unlovely town, where the judder of the looms and the stench from the tanneries are part of daily life. Zoe Yalland (her married name) said that she grew up in 'a filthy, overcrowded, smoke-belching city'. She had one particularly vivid memory:

> When I was a small girl in Cawnpore, I woke every morning to hear the hooters of the Elgin Mills calling the men of the first shift to work. As the sound drowned away with a downward note, suddenly

running out of puff, the hooters sounded from Muir, New Victoria,
the Lalimli, Cooper Allen – all the great mills of Cawnpore vying
with one another to call their men to work. When they called, the
men set out from overcrowded lanes in the bazaar, from modest brick
and concrete quarters in mill estates and outlying villages some ten
miles away. They converged in thousands towards the mill gates, their
heads in winter wrapped against the chill air, some carrying bags of
food or a black umbrella.[1]

No wonder Cawnpore was called the Manchester of the East.

The British arrived in numbers only from 1770. The first to march
across the sun-baked, flat brown plain beside the sluggish Ganges was
a detachment of soldiers, who had taken probably six or seven weari-
some weeks to march from Calcutta up the Great Trunk Road. Then
followed the merchants, who preferred to come by boat from Calcutta,
a two-month journey over 800 river miles. At the time of the Mutiny,
Cawnpore was established as a communication centre and the largest
military cantonment in north India. The railway had almost reached
town. When it did soon after the Mutiny, the reviving prosperity of
the town was assured, and its second life as an industrial city began.

The heyday of Cawnpore came with the climax of empire. Less
than half a century after the town had been laid waste and the British
community wiped out, it rose again as a mighty industrial centre.
The South African War meant boom time for army supplies. For
every 100,000 pairs of boots, 60,000 were made in Cawnpore. Tents
made in Cawnpore covered the South African veldt. It was the first
city in India to boast electricity and trams. When Queen Victoria
died in 1901, all work stopped – and then recommenced to build a
huge statue in Queens Park.

Fifty years later, after Independence, the statue was removed by crane
during the night and replaced by a statue of Gandhi. When that happened, the Managing Director of the British India Corporation (BIC),
which had taken over Begg Sutherlands, John Christie, suggested as
a joke that Queen Victoria should be reassembled in the middle of
the Ganges River. She would be submerged during the monsoon but
emerge from the river when the water was low as a goddess of fertility.

His sense of humour would have been sacrilege in 1901, when the Chamber of Commerce expressed 'deep grief and heartfelt sorrow at the death of their never-to-be-forgotten Sovereign'.

Theon left Cawnpore for education at Home in 1930 but returned nine years later on the last steamer through the Suez Canal, the SS *Strathnaver*, to be with his parents during the war. He remembers soon after his return watching *Gone with the Wind* at a Cawnpore cinema. The Europeans sat in armchairs on the balcony with the rest of the audience below. 'This was the time to meet the different groups of Brits, because the mill folk, many from Lancashire and Yorkshire, lived separately from the railway community, who were separate from the army and so on. They had their own clubs too.' He was sent to St Paul's School in Darjeeling, and then he became a junior officer in the 3rd Gurkha Rifles, the Queen Alexandra's Own, and was sent off to Italy just before the end of the war.

When he returned to Cawnpore with the rank of captain, he was aware of a new, more aggressive mood in a town that has always been troubled by riots. 'There were crowds shouting things at you like "Quit India". I would wave back and shout: "Yes, I'm going!"' Partition was a terrible time, temporarily relieved by the euphoria of Independence. Such was the tension that the police were forced to impose a twenty-three-hour curfew for several consecutive days, a form of punishment when most houses had no lavatory nor running water. Senior Superintendent George Boon left a graphic account for *Chowkidar*, the BACSA magazine, in a special edition that asked the question 'Where were you in August 1947?'

Late one stifling night, the atmosphere was supercharged. One could feel it. I was on the roof of the *Kotwali*, the central police station, and I could sense the evil silence hanging over the city. And then the people seemed unable to contain themselves any longer and swept out into the streets, defying the curfew order, looting and burning down the other side's houses. Every time a shot was fired an eerie wail of terror arose from the city to reach me on the roof. I have never heard anything like it before or since; the crescendo of sound was positively frightening.

My good friend Krishan Chand, the District Magistrate, was with
me. We sent out orders to the armed motor patrols to shoot to kill
anyone attacking, looting or starting fires. There came a sudden crash
of controlled gunfire. And immediately all was quiet and still; there
was not a sound from the whole city. I have no doubt that we saved
Cawnpore that night from veritable carnage.

Theon had left Cawnpore a few months before. In 1946 he had
been given 'accelerated release' from the army to go up to Worcester
College, Oxford University. His parents followed Home shortly
afterwards. Zoe, however, remained in Cawnpore until 1959, starting
a school and marrying the Deputy Managing Director of BIC. So
Theon kept in touch with India, but he did not return until 1972,
when the idea for BACSA became a gleam in his eye.

The last years of the British in Cawnpore make a sorry story.
Despite its resurgence as the Manchester of the East, the infamous massacres cast an unwelcome shadow over the town. The
guidebooks have always conditioned the visitors' mood, though
the language has softened with the years. *Murray's* in 1882 said
dolefully: 'There are no buildings worth visiting, the sole interest
attaching to the place being from the frightful massacres which
took place here.' *India through the Stereoscope* (an American publication of 1907) dripped with sanctimonious misery: 'If I were asked
to name the saddest and most pathetic spot in the entire world,
I would say that over which over the pure and brooding angel
stands.' *Murray's* of 1962 gave a brief warning: 'Mournful associations for those of British birth' and *Lonely Planet* of 2006 was
only slightly less sad: 'Poignant reminders of the brutal tragedy of
1857.' With this information to hand, who could blame tourists for
giving it a miss?

More conspicuous, however, particularly for those who have
managed to close their minds to the events of 1857, is the industrial
decline. Elgin Mill and others remain, but the tall red-brick chim-
neys and the factories where the looms juddered back and forth
seem little more than crumbling industrial archaeology rising above
polluted and congested streets.

The 1950s house magazine of the British India Company has tales to tell. Undoubtedly the war and Independence loosened up relations within Begg Sutherland. Before the war, when Theon's mother organised social occasions, the wives of Indian staff would have their own tea party behind a screen on the lawn, 'not exactly in purdah but away from prying eyes, which was how their husbands wanted it'. Now the screens were removed and club dances, amateur dramatics and so on appear in the magazine as fully integrated occasions. But there are lengthening paragraphs headed 'Departures'. These culminate in the 1959 edition with an article headed 'End of a Chapter'. The Managing Director of the BIC Group, John Christie, is resigning and the magazine is closing down too. His valedictory speech asks to be read between the lines: 'The BIC has tremendous reserves of strength but anything I now say would have to be prefaced by too many "ifs". I cannot pretend that everything in the garden has been lovely, but I have made many friends I shall always value.'

With him went his Deputy, Ron Powell, who was married to Zoe Wilkinson. A photograph shows the Christies, garlanded with flowers, being seen off from Kanpur station, an iconic tableau of these last British years. Under the article, in italics, is printed a prayer that in the circumstances seems to be a coded message as well as catching the melancholia of Cawnpore: 'I expect to pass through this world but once. Any good, therefore, that I can do now, or any kindness that I can show to any fellow-creature let me do it now. Let me not defer or neglect it, for I shall not pass this way again.'

In fact, the recently mighty BIC was in receivership. John Christie, a former ICS officer whose very appearance spoke rectitude and probity, had spent the previous eighteen months trying to protect it from its new Chairman, a charming, clever but crooked Marwari businessman called Haridas Mundhra. It was a confrontation of opposites.

The previous Chairman, Sir Robert Menzies, had longed to go Home and spent much of his time in England. Carelessly, he had sold his shares to Mundhra, who then acquired a majority shareholding by, in Christie's words, 'duplicating, nay multiplying share

certificates of various companies he controlled and using the worth-
less paper as security for large overdrafts with a number of banks. He
would move the deposits round, not leaving them long enough in
one place for the fraud to be detected. It was a simple confidence
trick.' Having become Chairman, Mundhra tried to use the BIC for
his own advantage. He attempted to plunder the mills, appoint his
own friends to jobs and get rid of Christie and Powell. The climax
came when Christie, who realised that his movements and his house
were being watched by Mundhra's men, made a clandestine visit to
the BIC strongroom at dead of night, removed a batch of forged
share certificates for court evidence and took them round to the
local Bank of India manager, whom he got out of bed in the early
hours of the morning and swore to secrecy. After a long series of
trials, in which the determined Christie spent thirty hours in the
witness box, sometimes catching the eye of his adversary, who would
wave to him cheerfully from the back of the court, Mundhra was
sent to prison for forgery and cheating. Eventually the government
replaced the Receiver with a nominated Indian Board. 'The transfer
of industrial power in Kanpur [wrote Christie in his autobiography
Morning Drum] was less than an edifying experience. It was time for
our drums to beat retreat. We boarded a P&O ship in Bombay. I did
not throw my *topi* over the stern: I had no *topi* to throw. It was the
symbol of a vanished age.'[2]

Six years later, in 1964, the travel writer Eric Newby and his
wife, Wanda, spent Christmas in Kanpur while sailing *Slowly down
the Ganges* (his book on his voyage). Like other tourists, they visited
Kacheri cemetery:

> With its crumbling temples, obelisks, truncated pyramids and col-
> umns symbolically broken it was like the ruins of ancient Rome in
> microcosm. But the small boys playing cricket among the tombs,
> saying 'Ullo, Ullo, 'ow are you' and 'Very well thank you', the nim and
> banyan trees whose leaves dappled their cricket pitch with shadows
> and the anaemic-looking cows nuzzling the outer wall left one in no
> doubt that this was a long way from the Imperial City.[3]

The Newbys became increasingly depressed in Kanpur; by its ugliness, its history and the knowledge that they would spend Christmas on their own. One afternoon:

> in a desperate attempt to exorcise suicidal feelings we walked mile after mile, in the ghastly atmosphere of Sunday-afternoon Aldershot: through deserted military lines; past old, pre-Mutiny bungalows with white-columned porches and tiled roofs and contemporary ones not yet finished, whose owners picnicked proudly outside them in tents; past what had once been the Church of Scotland, which was now the US Baptist Church where some elderly, sad-looking Anglo-Indians were clustered on the porch. Eventually we arrived at the Memorial Church.

It obviously did not lift their spirits, as they found the church 'the colour of pink salmon' and Marochetti's angel 'sickly-looking'. They sensed that the British community, now in its last days, was avoiding them. The remnants had withdrawn into their lines, whether from suspicion, defensiveness or depression they did not know. On Christmas Day the Newbys returned to All Souls:

> The congregation consisted of about twenty of the British colony and a number of Anglo-Indians who made brave efforts to look their best; but although we sang lustily and smiled benignly when we thought anyone was looking in our direction, it was no passport to the British colony and although, as the bank official had told Wanda previously when he had cashed her cheque, everyone knew who we were and where we had come from, we walked out of the church without anyone saying a word to us.
>
> 'If they behaved like this with the Indians then they deserved to be massacred,' Wanda said. It was an unseasonable thought, but it was difficult not to agree with it.

Theon Wilkinson returned to India in 1972 to show his son where three generations of his family had spent a good part of their lives. Naturally enough in the circumstances, they visited British cemet-

eries, as many tourists do, but the reasons for so doing surely go
beyond the search for family or general history. What exactly is the
appeal of these melancholy places?

In the first place, you cannot mistake the British cemetery. It is
now the most ubiquitous British architecture in India. The famous
early cemeteries like South Park Street in Calcutta or Kacheri in
Kanpur appear as grotesque cities of the dead, a dense mass of stone
pyramids, obelisks, urns and pavilions visible over a wall from the
street outside, so completely separate from modern India. Then there
are the instantly identifiable Christian cemeteries that date from
the Victorian period. If they are maintained by the local Christian
community, then visible through a red-brick Gothic porch are the
familiar vertical or horizontal white slabs marked with a cross or
angel and laid out in rows. If they are abandoned, given up to nature
and vandals, then visible through a broken wall or across barbed
wire is a wasteland of monumental masonry, stone slabs poking
out from encroaching undergrowth, tombs broken into by vandals.
Sometimes the grave top has been removed altogether for its flat
surface, useful for a fashionable coffee table or for grinding curry
powder perhaps.

British burial grounds are not quite the same as cemeteries,
because they are defined as unconsecrated plots of land, though to
the secular mind this surely makes little difference. More important
is that the monuments therein often tell of violent death and hasty
burial away from home. This adds to the drama of seeking them out
and then spotting them, sometimes in an incongruous location, like
the tomb in Delhi vegetable market to Lieutenant Alfred Harrison
of the Gordon Highlanders, who was killed in the skirmish of Badli-
ki-Serai in 1857. Sometimes you find them at the side of the road,
and these may be 'marching cemeteries', where the casualties of heat
stroke were buried when the column halted for the night, or 'cholera
cemeteries', where a unit buried its dead and carried on marching
from camp to camp until there were no more cases. Frequently an
isolated gravestone shows where a traveller died, a 'griffin' perhaps
journeying up country having just landed at Calcutta – always a vulnerable time for catching disease – or where British fugitives died

in flight or were killed by their pursuers; markers of a wayside death with power to stir the passer-by:

> What is the world? what asketh men to have?
> Now with his love, now in his colde grave
> Allone, with-outen any companye

(Chaucer)

In 2006, BACSA investigator Sandy Lall rediscovered the graves of two infants, Elliot Markillan and Laetitia Domina, whose sad deaths in 1857 linger in the mind. They had been in hiding with their father, the Collector of Fatehgarh, at a farm nearby, enduring the extremes of heat and the fear of discovery and death at the hands of the mutineers. After three months they died and were quietly buried. Later, reported the villagers of Khasaura in the Hardoi District of Uttar Pradesh, the British had erected a monument over the spot, with iron railings, a low wall and a gate. But after 1947 it had been vandalised and eventually disappeared altogether, the iron stolen and the stone removed to sharpen agricultural implements:

> I walked along a footpath, with a *talab* or water tank on the right, and towards a neem tree fifty yards ahead. Near the tree is a small raised triangular bit of earth. There was no trace whatsoever of a *pukka* tomb, but a local man dug down a few inches and revealed part of a large stone slab. We poured water on it and revealed a reddish sandstone. Only a very small portion was visible and I could see no inscription, it could have been face down or part of the plinth. I was satisfied, however, that this was the memorial to the unfortunate mites caught up in the 'Devil's Wind of '57'.[4]

It is not unknown in the files of BACSA for a complete cemetery to come to light. About five years ago someone stumbled upon an eighteenth-century British cemetery south of Calcutta that was not marked in any records. The name of the location had been Kedgeree in British days but is now Khajuri.

Wherever the British trod they left graves of their dead. Once again Kipling catches the spirit of imperial adventure:

    The ports ye shall not enter
    The roads ye shall not tread
    Go make them with your living
    And mark them with your dead.

BACSA lists over 850 'cemeteries' in India, Pakistan, Bangladesh and Sri Lanka. I have chosen three for illustration from different points of the compass: three cemeteries – one that contained the grave of the gentle missionary scholar, another that simply reveals a continuity of quiet worship going back 300 years, and a third dedicated to the final resting place of an ostentatious merchant – that say so much about the British in India.

At remote Sibsagar in Assam there was a cemetery, now abandoned, containing but two graves: Dr Ward, a missionary who translated the Bible into Assamese and died in 1873, and his first convert, Levi Nidhi, who died the same year. Dr Ward had an epitaph:

                His Earnest Labours
            Sweet Hymns and Translations
                Of Portions of Scriptures
            Perpetually Fragrant Memory
                CHRIST ALL IN ALL

The cemetery has now vanished from sight, but BACSA has removed the two memorials to Dibrugarh cemetery nearby, a rescue of last resort but sometimes necessary.

Then at the other end of India is the cemetery of St John's church at Tellicherry in Kerala. The East India Company built a fort here in 1708 but long since deserted. The old church remains and is worshipped in by a small group of local Christians who maintain the graves that date from 1759 until 1919: 'Sacred to the memory of Robert Richmond who departed this life on 6 March 1860 aged —'. The rest is illegible.

One of the earliest British cemeteries is on the west coast of India at Surat, where the British first landed (1608) and built a factory. A huge 15-metre-high tomb here commemorates in language from the age of merchant adventurers the factory manager, Christopher Oxinden. The epitaph appears to be addressed to his East India Company 'masters' more than to the Almighty:

> Here he brought to a termination his undertakings and his life. He was able to enter in his accounts only days, not years, for death suddenly called him to a reckoning. Do you ask, O my masters, what profit you have gained, or what loss you have suffered? You have lost a servant, we a companion, he his life; but on the other side of the page he may write 'Death to me is a gain'.

Melancholy, of course, is a pleasurable sensation not to be underestimated. There are far worse places to go on a baking, claustrophobic, day in India than a British cemetery. Gazing at the graves, I, for one, feel a sense of identity, a rising of a collective memory. Although I never had forebears in India, the first time I went I felt I had been there before. And so the questions, out of some sense of wanting to share the history of the dead: what were they doing there so far away from home? were they happy or unhappy? I assume, based on the suddenness and sadness of many deaths, that the answer is usually unhappy – but that is not the prerogative of British India. Above all, why did so many die so young? The 'woefully short' lives of the British buried in Kacheri cemetery depressed Eric and Wanda Newby:

> Sophie, second wife of Wm Vincent Esq of Nudjuffughur,
> who departed this life on the 9th February, 1845,
> aged 36 years, 1 month and 19 days
> and of their four children
> Marie-Helene, Eugene, Marie-Lise and Maria,
> who departed this life respectively, on the 14th June, 1841,
> the 19th January, 1844, the 7th June 1844, and the 4th February, 1845.

Since the Newby visit this tomb has disappeared.

The chief killer was the water-borne disease of cholera, and it remained so way into the twentieth century because doctors persisted in thinking it was not water-borne but airborne. Death was incredibly sudden: 'We have known two instances of dining with a gentleman [i.e. at midday] and being invited to his burial before supper time,' wrote a resident of Madras in 1805. There is a monument in Agra dated in the 1890s that tells of 146 men of the Yorks and Lancs Regiment who died from cholera within two days of the appearance of the disease. Other killers were typhoid, dysentery, smallpox, plague, malaria, heat-stroke and rabies.

The first goal of the 'griffin' was to survive two monsoons ('two mussouns are the age of man' was the almost biblical saying), because in some places the annual mortality rate was 50 per cent. In the healthier areas like Madras, Europeans were considered 'salted' or acclimatised after five years, and if they lived until they were fifty then, according to London insurance companies, their life chances were greater than at Home. Nevertheless, I wonder that any life insurance company was prepared to do business in India. Among the soldiery in the nineteenth century the chances of returning home were seven to one against. Excluding infant and child mortality, the average age of death was well under thirty for men and twenty-five for women. Even in the late nineteenth century, in Kipling's time, death was so commonplace that the deceased was soon forgotten:

> Ay, lay him 'neath the Simla pine –
> A fortnight fully to be missed,
> Behold, we lose our fourth at whist,
> A chair is vacant when we dine.

So why did they come? Fear of death does not seem to have put people off. They were lured by the opportunity for fame or fortune. Merchants wished to emulate the nabobs of the East India Company who came home and bought huge estates. Robert Clive made £234,000 out of his victory at Plassey in 1757 and bought 10 square miles of rural Shropshire for only £70,000 and a house in Berkeley

Square for the even cheaper £10,000. Young soldiers wanted to
follow in the footsteps of the sun-baked veterans who yarned about
faraway frontier wars and showed off their campaign medals:

> Doth he curse Oriental romancing,
> And wish he had toiled all his day,
> At the Bar, or the Banks, or financing,
> And got damned in a common-place way?

The title of this poem is 'The Land of Regrets' by the old India hand
Alfred Lyall (1835–1911), and it became the exile's lament. The truth
is that nostalgia for Britain was a constant feature of British life in
India, a mild illness perhaps but a very prevalent one. Lyall himself
confessed to a sort of rage that he had 'left the pleasant lands which
should be his habitation by birthright'. He became particularly
homesick in the summer, when letters from Home were 'redolent
of flowers, hay and innumerable babies'. It does not take much reading between the lines of epitaphs to sense the homesickness rising
from the graves. Returning home was not the answer. Exile became
a permanent state. Retired to Chipping Norton, the old India hand
now replaced nostalgia for pubs and Cotswold meadows by a yearning for 'the smell of wood smoke in the early dawn and the ride
before breakfast'. Kipling felt this nostalgia after leaving India aged
only twenty-three:

> It's Oh to see the morn ablaze
> Above the mango-tope,
> When homeward through the dewy cane
> The little jackals lope,
> And half Bengal heaves into view
> New-washed – with sunlight soap.

Theon Wilkinson returned to the disappearing cemeteries in 1974
and 1975, increasingly concerned that more should be done to
preserve the memory of those who had endowed the British heritage in India. He saw himself rather like an archaeologist surveying

Roman Britain with the mission of rescuing evidence of that era. He found out that until 1947 the military cemeteries had been maintained by the Military Engineering Services (MES) and the civilian cemeteries by the Public Works Department (PWD). The new Government of India had inherited all these cemetery lands but passed them back to the new British High Commission for upkeep. To this end an Act of Parliament in 1948 had voted a sum of money to be administered by Provincial Cemetery Boards in India (now defunct). They had deemed it sensible to distinguish 'open' cemeteries from 'closed' ones. When the latter could not be maintained by the Christian community, they were deconsecrated and defined as 'abandoned'. An exception was made of a few cemeteries and monuments of particular historical significance, such as the Lucknow Residency and Kacheri cemetery in Kanpur. These were on a list compiled by the early TV archaeologist Sir Mortimer Wheeler and placed in the care of the Archaeological Survey of India, which agreed to 'protect' them.

Whatever the state of British cemeteries and burial grounds in India, there is a long history of written records, and they now underpin the BACSA filing system. The most extensive record is the Provincial Series of *Lists of Inscriptions of Tombs and Monuments* that was compiled by the ICS between 1896 and 1935 as an ongoing exercise. The two most contrasting volumes were written by Julian Cotton (Madras) and Miles Irving (the Punjab, Kashmir, Afghanistan and the North-West Frontier Province). As it happens, their grandchildren are members of BACSA.

Julian Cotton's opening quotation is another haunting verse of Alfred Lyall:

> Hath he come now, in season, to know thee,
> Hath he seen, what a stranger forgets,
> All the graveyards of exiles below thee,
> O Land of Regrets?

Madras was the first European presidency and its territory covered much of southern India. Cotton tells us that the oldest Christian tomb in India is the 'Cochin slab' of a Portuguese merchant dated 1524. Incidentally, the inscription on the tomb of the first Englishman known to have died in India, John Mildenhall, who was buried at Ajmere in 1614, was originally written in Portuguese. Cotton points out that the Armenian cemeteries in Madras dating from 1666 are the best evidence of the history of that virtually extinct community (he wrote in 1910), and the cemetery in Tranquebar is the sole evidence of the extinct Danish community. It was the Dutch, he continues, who were the most ostentatious adherents to the *culte des morts*. They exported their *metselaars* or stonemasons to India to carve elaborate bas-relief such as the piper playing on a recorder and dressed in a long-flapped coat over the tomb of Matthys Pfeiffer in Parangipettai near Pondicherry. A Dutch sculptor carves the hope that his words will endure to the 'laaste opstaanding'; and presumably many of them have. As for the British cemeteries, Cotton writes that 'the history of old Madras is written upon its tombstones' – a settled history since 1639 with greater life expectancy than most other places because of the healthier climate.

Irving's volume covers the wild frontiers of British India and is therefore very different; death on the onward march of *Pax Britannica*. His introductory verse sets the mood of maudlin patriotism:

Never the lotus closes, never the wildfowl wake,
But a soul goes out on the East Wind that died for England's sake –
Man or woman or suckling, mother or bride or maid –
Because on the bones of the English the English flag is stayed.

He writes that 'we may follow by the tombstones of the dead the advance of the British flag'. So we do, from the capture of Delhi (earliest tomb inscription that of Sergeant Walker 1808) and then the Gurkha war to the First Afghan campaign, the two Sikh wars in the Punjab, the Indian Mutiny and then the Second Afghan campaign. The inscriptions honour death in battle, deplore death by 'the hand of the assassin' and lament Sir Henry Durand, who died in Tonk when his elephant tried to squeeze through too low a gateway. A tomb in Peshawar commemorates George Hayward, who

was immortalised by Henry Newbolt's high Victorian melodrama
He Fell Among Thieves. Captured by bandits Hayward is given until
dawn to live:

> He flung his empty revolver down the slope,
> He climb'd alone to the Eastward edge of the trees;
> All night long in a dream untroubled of hope
> He brooded, clasping his knees.
>
> . . . . .
>
> And now it was dawn. He rose strong on his feet,
> And strode to his ruin'd camp below the wood.
> He drank the breath of the morning cool and sweet:
> His murderers round him stood.
>
>
> Light on the Laspur hills was broadening fast,
> The blood-red snow-peaks chill'd to a dazzling white.
> He turn'd, and saw the golden circle at last,
> Cut by the Eastern height.
>
>
> 'O glorious Life, Who dwellest in earth and sun,
> I have lived, I praise and adore Thee.'
> A sword swept.
> Over the pass the voices one by one
> Faded, and the hill slept.

Finally, recorded by Irving, are the inscribed tombs from the *jihadist*
frontier wars at the end of the century. Here, in Waziristan and Swat
and Buner, expeditionary forces engaged with the Taliban of their
day, the so-called 'Hindustani fanatics'. 'So from Delhi to Kabul and
from Gilgit to Rajanpur', Irving concludes, 'we have sown the bones
of our bravest and what the harvest will be we still know not' – an
epitaph that could be written today in the midst of another Afghan
war against Hindustani fanatics.

In fact the British began publishing records of their cemeteries
as early as 1803. It was *The Bengal Obituary*, however, that made the
subject popular. This unique *memento mori* was published in Calcutta

in 1848 and reprinted due to popular demand three years later. Theon Wilkinson calls it 'that great lexicon of death in the east' and BACSA has reprinted it too. *The Bengal Obituary* is exactly what it says it is:

A record to perpetuate the memory of
DEPARTED WORTH
such as have pre-eminently distinguished themselves in the History
of British India since the formation of the European Settlement
to the present time
1848
A compilation of tablets and memorial inscriptions from
various parts of the
Bengal and Agra Presidencies.

Within this compilation of obituary notices, epitaphs and biographical notes about the 'departed worth' we see what the British of the time valued – a belief in British progress, a tough self-reliance and Christian virtue. 'These were their achievements,' it is saying; 'let us remember them and think about our own deaths.'

Today it is of interest because of the social history it reveals, not least about the attitudes of the age towards women. Pride of place must be taken by the famous 'Begum' (Hindi for 'lady of high rank') Johnson, whose tomb may still be seen in St John's churchyard in Calcutta. Between the ages of thirteen and nineteen she married four times and had six children, three of whom survived infancy. She lived until she was eighty-seven, the oldest British resident in Bengal, 'universally beloved, respected and revered'. She was given a state funeral with a bodyguard to accompany her mortal remains to St John's. Not surprisingly she must have been a garrulous old lady, which is hinted at by her very human epitaph: 'she abounded in anecdote, possessing easy affability of communication, her conversation was always interesting, without any tendency to fatigue the hearer.'

This makes a pleasant change from the many protestations of piety about worthy women. Mrs Hill, for instance, 'was converted to God at the age of fourteen' and died hearing the Heavenly Choir: 'am I

dreaming or is it music I hear?' The assumption that the wife's role
was subordinate to her husband's could not be more clearly expressed
than in this epitaph to the daughter of Captain P. Crawford, who
was buried in Shergati cemetery in Bihar: 'she became the wife of
G.J. Morris Esq., once Judge of this District, to whose happiness she
was permitted by God to contribute for nearly thirteen years. He
resigned her to the Lord on 26th December 1831, in her 31st year.' A
wife's duty was to her husband and her function to rear a Christian
family, yet her ideal virtues were often expressed in more elevated
epitaph: 'Her form was elegant, her deportment noble. Possessed
of every virtue, every grace that could adorn her sex, she was religious without superstition, prudent without meanness, generous
without prodigality, the sweet companion and the steady friend'
(Mrs Woodhouse, Cuddalore, 1777). The reality was often grim, so
the sweet, sentimental language about this child-bride on a tomb
in Azamgarh, in the United Provinces, may have been a comfort:
'Sacred to the Memory of Mrs Sarah Ammaun and her stillborn son
who departed this life on 29th June 1820.'

> Just fifteen years she was a maid
> And scarce eleven months a wife
> Four days and nights in labour laid
> Brought forth and then gave up her life.
>
> Ah! loveliest of beauties
> Whither art though flown?
> Thy soul which knew no guile
> Is sure to heaven gone
> Leaving this friend and thy kindred
> Thy sad exit to mourn.

For sheer pathos I prefer the plainer language of later years: 'she had
no fault, but that she left me' (a colonel in the Murree Hills, of his
wife). Or this inscription by a *bibi* (native woman) at Chunar on the
Ganges: 'Lucy, his woman, erected this tomb in memory of them'
(Private Snape and infant son, died in 1808).

Theon held the first meeting of his new society in London on 13 October 1976. Six months later BACSA was registered as a charity, and so was born what Theon describes as 'the liveliest society in Britain for the deadliest subject'. It struck a chord, largely among the generation that had lived and worked in the subcontinent over the period of Independence in the 1940s and 1950s, both British and Indian. Its members come from the British and Indian armies (the first chairman was Major-General 'Moti' Dyer), politicians and ambassadors (the late Rt Hon. Peter Rees and Lord Gore-Booth), ex-members of the ICS and IAS, planters, businessmen and church people. It was and is inclusive and representative of the once stratified society of the subcontinent. Theon began to lobby governments for support and he wrote *Two Monsoons* to publicise the cause, from which I have gathered much of this material.[5] He said he felt 'rather like the paddler of a small canoe following a distant star through unknown waters and being unexpectedly escorted by vessels of all sizes going in the same direction'.

The first of BACSA's aims is to bring together as much information as possible – photos, surveys, accounts of visits – about as many cemeteries as possible in all the lands once administered by the East India Company and the British Government of India, from Muscat to Macao. At first the information was stored at the India Office Library and Records then in Blackfriars Road, London; now it is in the African and Asian Department of the British Library. Much of the work done by Theon and his volunteers collates existing material and then adds to it in a systematic way. Cross-references are made to other reference books like the Provincial Series 1896–1935 and to other institutions like the National Army Museum and the Society of Genealogists. *The Ecclesiastical Records of European Christians in India 1700–1947* (births, marriages and deaths) are nearby in the British Library for those keen to trace a forebear on the subcontinent. One by one the larger town cemeteries have been researched and monographs published; in the case of larger towns like Calcutta, Cawnpore and Quetta, monographs have become booklets. Between 1979 and 2004 BACSA members carried out surveys in almost 100 towns on the Indian subcontinent.

Probably the most indefatigable, even obsessive, cemetery researcher in the history of BACSA is Sue Farrington, who collects inscriptions as others do old coins or stamps; or, as she puts it: 'people remember routes and towns by the pubs and hotels they have visited; I use the cemeteries in Pakistan.' In 1981, when working at the British High Commission in Islamabad, she gave herself the daunting task of recording all the surviving gravestone inscriptions in Pakistan. It took her fifteen years. She had as references Miles Irving's volume in the Provincial Series compiled seventy years before and a list of 184 sites that had been handed over by the British government in 1947. By the time she had finished she had expanded this list to more than 350 locations, including battle monuments, regimental memorials and about eighty churches. Many were the adventures and hardships experienced by this middle-aged lady from Somerset as she trekked the dangerous border lands of the North-West Frontier searching for signs of the British dead. Strange was the knowledge she accumulated along the way:

> It may sound a gloomy way to spend your time, but, had I not been studying the cemeteries, I would never have known about *peshqabzs* [a Persian-style dagger], and the Frontier Corps, battle monuments and the Heatstroke Express, the Faqir of Ipi [a desert prophet worshipped by the Pathans, who admired the Fascists in the 1930s] and the Quetta Earthquake, mule trains and gricing [train spotting] ...[6]

She found, not surprisingly, that many headstones had been stolen, covered by leaves or mud or washed away entirely. Others were illegible or never had inscriptions because there was no one to carve them. Entire cemeteries had been abandoned long before 1947, and some individual graves had not been maintained by the PWD or MES. It was a daunting task that required luck too. One morning in Lahore, at least half a mile from her destination, she was approached by a young man on a motorbike who offered help. 'I'm looking for Kapurthala House, please.' They got talking and, 'rather sheepishly', she told him she was looking for the tomb of a young girl who had died in 1827. 'Oh, that is no longer in the grounds of

Kapurthala House. A building has been built in the garden, but I know exactly where to find the grave': proof indeed that a tomb is also a memorial.

Sue Farrington finished her task just before BACSA's 20th anniversary:

> I am pretty confident that 99.9 per cent of all surviving inscriptions have now been recorded, and these number between 16,000 and 17,000. It would be pure guesswork, but if I had to put a figure on it, I would estimate that this probably represents about 50–60 per cent of actual burials.
>
> Archaeologists struggle to interpret life from fragments they unearth generations later – I was in a unique position to capture an unrepeatable period of British history before it too disappeared.

Theon estimates that BACSA members may have added possibly 100,000 tomb details to the total previously recorded. Ironically, Sue first came across BACSA when she was searching for her great-great-great-uncle's tomb at Half Way House on the old road from Dehra Dun to Mussoorie. She found it, but by the time she had finished her epic research it had disappeared in a road-widening scheme. Only her photo of it remains in the BACSA files.

The main aim of BACSA is to provide as full a record as possible of the cemetery, even if it is doomed to disappear. Sometimes, however, BACSA raises an appeal to donate money for specific repair purposes, but only if the local will is there to carry out the work. I found a good example in the file on the cemetery of St John, at Tellicherry in Kerala, mentioned earlier. In the file are assorted photos, a map and two pro-forma reports. The first, on a visit in 1989, says: 'the graveyard is completely overgrown and neglected. Many gravestones are invisible under a carpet of creeper.' The writer doubts whether it is worth BACSA remedying this, because the Revd Joseph is 'charming but thoroughly ineffectual'. Obviously someone at BACSA had faith, because a small grant of 350 rupees was made and the next report, in 1991, says: 'a substantial effort has been made. Two thirds of the graveyard is now free of jungle.'

After repair comes maintenance. BACSA encourages the employment of a *chowkidar* or watchman not by paying him but by helping
him grow produce in a cemetery garden that can be sold for his
livelihood – an English solution that, says Theon, seems to work:

> In St Sepulchre's Cemetery in Pune, for example, there's a big rose
> garden, and the roses are sold for a profit. In part of South Park Street
> Cemetery in Calcutta we let off a corner of the land to a man who
> grows potted plants that he then hires out for parties so you can liven
> proceedings with chrysanthemums and palm trees and so on. Now
> there's more money around in India than there used to be, we're
> trying to encourage endowments whereby the capital stays where it
> is but the income is used for a twice-yearly spring clean, for example.
> This will perpetuate the upkeep of the cemeteries, which is what we
> try and do.

From time to time a major project is undertaken. The first of these
was the renovation of South Park Street Cemetery in Calcutta. It was
known as 'The Great Cemetery', presumably because of the size of
its monuments, but according to historians of funerary architecture
its importance is less for its ostentation than for its seminal influence on graveyards in the UK. The necropolis or city of the dead in
South Park Street, Calcutta, was begun in 1767 at a time in the eighteenth century when there were no public cemeteries in England,
when city churchyards were squalid and vandalised and the dead
were buried 'under Ailes and under Pews in churches with Tawdry
Monuments of Marble stuck up against Walls and Pillars'. South Park
Street cemetery was necessitated by the need for quick burial away
from the city centre, and it was inspired by the beautiful Mughal
tombs often built in a garden setting. The monumental style is an
exotic blend from different cultures and continents, an extraordinary
Elysium built with geometric shapes set in stone – squares, rectan-
gles, circles, polygons, pyramids and domes.

The trouble with this Elysium was human disease, the virulence
of the 'sick season' in Calcutta. Already by 1812 the necropolis of
South Park was so packed that a garden setting had become a city

centre. Whether the result is like walking through the streets of a town 'as old as Herculaneum or Pompei', as Kipling thought, or like visiting 'a salvage yard of outsize masonry' (according to Joe Roberts in *A Celebration of Calcutta*) depends on a point of view. For the architectural historian, 'the size and richness were not equalled in Europe until the great necropolis of Pere Lachaise [in Paris] and its successors were laid out after 1804 ... So it was that the first great Classical cemeteries of modern times were realised in British India and not in France.'[7]

By 1978 South Park Street cemetery had become less an over-crowded Elysium than an overcrowded and squalid Calcutta. The cemetery was in a state of dilapidation, the home of vagrants and feral dogs, and unless it was rescued the only answer was to pull it down altogether. BACSA set up a sister organisation, the Association for the Preservation of Historical Cemeteries in India (APHCI) and contributed £5,000. After clearing, landscaping, planting and repairing, the necropolis rose again, not to life but once more to a glorious afterlife. Now it is maintained and publicised as a major tourist attraction of British Kolkata.

The very first name of BACSA was the 'Indo-British Association' and in some ways this is still the more appropriate. BACSA is far more than an association to befriend cemeteries. It is a coming-together of those interested in preserving the memory of the Raj and East India Company. That it is such a thriving organisation is due not only to Theon but to Dr Rosie Llewellyn Jones, the Editor of its magazine, *Chowkidar*. Rosie used to live in Lucknow and writes about its glittering history with authority and a fluency in Urdu. Now she lives with a retired Indian general in south London and has edited the annual two editions of the BACSA magazine since the beginning in 1977.

Members were asked 'what should it be called?' Answers displayed British humour – 'Grave News', 'Among the Tombs'. Then Rosie had an inspiration:

> I recalled the old habit of India's watchmen, who would patrol the urban streets, crying out the hours and guarding the sleeping town.

Chowkidar, of course, the watchman. BACSA was to patrol the Asian cemeteries, report back where something was wrong and provide the means to put it right. It was also to 'cry out the hours', thus opening people's eyes and ears to the urgent needs of the cemeteries.

Over 1,500 copies are distributed, mostly to members of BACSA in the UK, but also to South Asia, Australia, the United States (the libraries of Congress and Yale subscribe) and Europe. In fact *Chowkidar* is the recruiting sergeant for BACSA, which now, says Rosie, has 1,574 members, of whom 300 or so live abroad. She is particularly proud of the Indian membership:

Well, we've got Ruskin Bond, the author. We're very fond of Ruskin. He's done a lot on the Mussoorie cemetery and he acts as an unofficial guide. Also in Mussoorie we've got Hugh Gantser, who is an author and travel writer. He's done a lot. He took me round the Camel's Back cemetery. We've got Admiral Dawson in Bangalore. He's very useful. In Kolkota we've got Cedric Spanus, the Secretary of APHCI, and he's reasonably influential … The people who have played no part at all are the government representatives in India like the High Commission.

Theon is quick to add that BACSA is a conservation movement irrespective of religion or race: 'We have an orthodox Brahmin at Sibpur and a Muslim benefactor at Dhaka for instance.'

Apart from *Chowkidar*, BACSA publishes its own books written by members. Of the thirty published so far, some are autobiographies such as *Morning Drum* by John Christie and *Merchant Prince* by Owain Jenkins, from both of which I have quoted. Others are biographies and some of these are scholarly studies. At a time when university presses are retreating into restricted areas, BACSA is filling a need at a fraction of the cost. Rosie has also commissioned fiction from established writers who are members of BACSA such as Gillian Tindall, Ruskin Bond and Lee Langley. All their books, *The Great Eastern Adventure, Of Tigers, Tombstones and a Coffin* and *The Sugar Palace*, have since been republished elsewhere or broadcast.

Not surprisingly, the annual meetings of BACSA attended by 130 members or so are lively occasions followed by a talkative lunch. Then there are outings; to the British Empire and Commonwealth Museum in Bristol, until it closed, or to the private British in India Museum in Colne, Lancashire, which houses in an old mill the collection of a BACSA member. Noting down memorial inscriptions must be an acquired enthusiasm, because BACSA members also record tomb inscriptions with British India connections in UK cemeteries. Well over 2,000 are on file.

Is all this simply recording the Raj or attempting some kind of resuscitation? Is it simply tracing family roots or indulging in imperial nostalgia? It does not matter, of course. It is all proof that, whatever may be the fashion of political correctness, many of us are proud of our nation's history on the subcontinent. As Lord Radcliffe, who mapped out the controversial borders that partitioned British India, said in 1947:

> In all recorded history up to the present, no people has ever so mixed its dust with the dust of the wide world … We have been such wanderers that the mud of every country is on our shoes. Eccentric, tiresome, interfering, if you like, but surely too, adventurous, ingenious, courageous and enduring. And yes, for better or worse – very remarkable.

'Earth's proud empires pass away' leaving behind the remains of those who built them until they too are covered by the everchanging landscape. Meanwhile it is Theon's hope that these last remains become Indianised, so that in the end they are part of a common history:

> In the long run, I want the local Indians to be sufficiently interested in the history of the place that they regard the British remains as we regard the Roman remains in this country. The British built the roads, they built the canals, just like the Romans, and if the local people can regard them as part of their heritage and not our heritage, then that is really my aim.

Postscript

THE INDIAN
MUTINY OF 2007

It was September, and the cemetery of St John's church in Meerut, just north-east of Delhi, was overgrown with creeper and wet grass. With Dr Rosie Llewellyn-Jones of BACSA, I was leading a twenty-strong tour party visiting sites of the Indian Mutiny of 150 years previously. Dripping with sweat in the post-monsoon heat and preceded by *malis* cutting our way, we found the path to the back of the cemetery. Here lay the graves of the British dead who had been killed by Indians that first night of the 'Great Uprising' of 1857:

To the Memory Of
CHARLES JOHN DAWSON
Veterinary Surgeon, Bengal Cavalry
and
ELIZA HIS WIFE
Both Murdered at Meerut
10 May 1857

We looked round the old garrison church, built in 1821 in the classical style, and noted how little it showed the scars of that dread Sunday night, for the 'devil's wind' (as Indian contemporaries called the events of 1857–8) stormed on to Delhi, leaving Meerut in British hands. We obtained permission to visit the army cantonment, and there still was the bungalow of Lieutenant-Colonel George Carmichael-Smyth of the 3rd Light Cavalry, who ordered his men to bite the notorious cartridge and, after they had been cruelly punished for refusing to do so, ignored 'with contempt' the warnings of mutiny. We lunched well with a local historian, Dr Amit Pathak, who spoke to us about the beginnings of 'The First War of Independence', and afterwards we visited his new diorama, which shows the Indian version of events. Then came the first sign of trouble.

Outside we were virtually *gheraod* by press and photographers, out for a story and insistent. Why had we come? Why did we call their War of Independence 'a mutiny'? The prime target was Sir Mark Havelock-Allan, the great-greatgrandson of General Sir Henry Havelock, who 'relieved Lucknow' and in his time was almost as famous as Nelson and Wellington, as his statue in Trafalgar Square attests. He answered with confidence: to find out more of the Indian perspective on the 'great uprising' of 150 years ago; to commemorate the dead of both sides; to visit the graves of ancestors. The press mood was excitable but intrusive if you are not used to this sort of reception. As far as we knew we were fairly reported.

Two days later we attended a low-key commemorative service in St James church, Delhi. Fr Ian Weathrall told us in his address how the Revd Jennings had held a final service in the church on the eve of the Mutiny, but he tactfully refrained from telling us that the Revd Jennings's hostile views towards Muslims and Hindus had helped to cause it. We were not aware that afternoon that, according to *The Times of India* that day, 'an unpleasant note was struck' at Meerut the day before. It was to prove as seminal an incident in 2007 terms as the cartridge incident of 150 years before. The day after our visit (19 September) a party of old soldiers from The Rifles Regiment took along to St John's church a plaque that said: 'To commemorate the 150th anniversary of the bravery and distinguished service of the first battalion of the 60th, The King's Royal Rifle Corps, at Meerut and Delhi between 10th May and 20th September 1857. Presented by their successor regiment, The Rifles'. They had asked permission in advance from the Bishop of Agra to present their plaque but had received no reply. They had emailed the priest of St John's, Fr Peter

Baldev, with details of their visit, and he had replied, welcoming them but not their plaque to his church. They took it nevertheless, and Dr Amit Pathak, the historian, with whom they did not speak, told the press he found it 'inappropriate and objectionable'.

The spark of protest was ignited. From then on in the press 'commemoration' became 'celebration'. The perception in most of our 'historians' group that the 'great uprising' had brought shame on both sides that had harmed Indo-British relations for at least a generation was perverted by the press, so that we were in India to boast of our 'victory'. It was no use protesting that our group and The Rifles were different, particularly as some of the time we were travelling together.

And so, like the Uprising of old, the protest spread and increased in ferocity. It seemed to miss out Delhi, but in Agra our hotel was invaded by a mob shouting *Angrez Hatao* ('English Out!') and *Mangal Pande ki jai* ('Long live Mangal Pande', the first Indian martyr in the War of Independence). Conspicuous in the crowd was a bearded politician from the BJP (the Hindu nationalist party), whose photo I saw later on election posters around the town. I recall one of our party trying ineffectually to close the doors to a hotel corridor down which two of our elderly 'memsahibs' walked with slow dignity, ignoring the mayhem behind them. In Gwalior we were pursued everywhere outside the hotel by press and photographers, despite police protection by now, and the following morning a howling mob with banners and more slogans physically attempted to hold back our bus from leaving. Behind us, in Meerut, graves were being desecrated; ahead, in Lucknow, the local BJP was full of threats.

The eight-hour train journey to Lucknow was tense. Forty or so mostly elderly Brits – that is, our 'historians' party together with The Rifles party – were confined to a carriage under armed police guard (well, the police carried wooden staves called *lathis*). The advice of the UK High Commission in Delhi was careful – 'as long as you think the police will protect you, then continue but keep a low profile. As soon as you think otherwise then go home.'

Mobile phones told us that Lucknow was once again going to become the set piece of the 'mutiny'. On the one side, the Archaeological Survey of India welcomed us to the ruined

Residency, that shrine of the original uprising where a few thousand European and Indian men, women and children withstood a six-month siege between June and November 1857, losing about a thousand of their number; provided we held no commemoration. Both the State Governor and the District Magistrate welcomed us to the town. On the other side, the BJP leader, Lalji Tandon, was calling our visit an insult to the martyrs of the 'freedom struggle' and threatening to block our entrance to the Residency. He was abetted by a leading Shia cleric, Maulana Kalbe Jawwad, who said our visit was a 'humiliation'. His message was, how dare the British celebrate *Vijay Diwas* ('Anniversary of Victory'), meaning Havelock's first relief of Lucknow in September 1857, whereas to them it was *Shaurya Diwas* ('Anniversary of Sacrifice'), commemorating the Indians killed by the British during Havelock's advance. With less of an eye to history and more to press coverage, Anil Tiwari, a member of the World Hindu Council in Lucknow, said simply that we should be 'hanged from a tree and [our] bodies put on the first flight out of India'. This last threat was requoted in the UK *Daily Mail* on 26 September under the headline 'Death threats and a terrifying hotel siege'. Friends and family feared a rerun of history.

At 9 p.m. on 24 September, just as Team India was winning the Twenty/ Twenty cricket final (what would have happened had it lost?), our train stopped at Charbagh station, Lucknow. Anti-riot police were thick on the ground wearing flak jackets and crash helmets and carrying *lathis*. Their vehicles nearby had tear-gas mortars on the roofs. We were shepherded to our coaches in one long file, our baggage following. Jeers and insults came from a small but obviously well-orchestrated mob, and then there was a sudden 'whooshing' sound as empty plastic bottles and pats of dried dung (so it turned out) were thrown at us. Bringing up the rear, I saw in front of me a former ambassador shielding from the projectiles another of our party, an elderly lady who had difficulty walking. I was filled with disgust. Twenty minutes later we were in the Taj Residency hotel, safe but about to submit to our own residency siege.

Although our local travel guides assured us that sightseeing was possible provided we were secretive – that meant visiting the Residency at 5 a.m. – it became clear that they were wrong. A BJP crowd was in wait outside, harassing unsuspecting visitors to the Residency and daubing paint on the cemetery graves. We were stuck. That evening the Nawab of Avadh visited the hotel bringing with him a *nautch* (dancing) girl and musicians. Sir Henry Lawrence, a descendant of the Chief Commissioner who was killed defending the Residency in 1857, played Irish marches on his mandolin and taught two younger members of our party how to juggle. It was surreal. Very early the next morning Sir Mark Havelock-Allan made a furtive visit to the Alambagh, near where his great-great-grandfather is buried.

Police intelligence warned us to expect more trouble ahead in the 'badlands' of United Provinces. Believe it or not, and I was inclined not, an old woman was waiting in the entrenchment of Kanpur with a can of kerosene, threatening to burn herself alive if we approached. Allahabad and Varanasi were also pronounced dangerous. In India it is easy to whip up a crowd that becomes violent. That very day I read that a DJ on a radio station in West Bengal had been rude about the family antecedents of a local boy who had just won the TV 'Pop Idol' competition. The result was a riot leaving over fifty injured in one town alone. The police said they could no longer guarantee our safety and that left only one decision. We flew on to Kolkata the next morning.

We were left with plenty of time to hold a post-mortem – a phrase that in the circumstances seemed very appropriate. Why had all this happened? A lot may be blamed on the feverish and opportunistic state of BJP politics. It was our bad luck that our tour coincided with electioneering rallies in United Provinces: but we had played into their hands.

In my view, it was wrong for The Rifle Brigade to present their plaque without permission, and this was the start of the trouble. A little knowledge of Mutiny history tells us that it was the 1st/60th Rifles who had stood on the parade ground at Meerut that fateful morning of 9 May 1857 with their loaded guns levelled at the 'mutineers' as they were forced to strip and then were shackled. It was the 1st/60th Rifles who had fought their way back into Delhi in September 1857 with great heroism but then had taken part, as had all the victorious troops, in the barbaric sacking of the Mughal capital. This had gone beyond any forgivable act of revenge, so that the Governor General Lord Canning had written to Queen Victoria on 25 September: 'There is a rabid and indiscriminate vindictiveness abroad which is impossible to contemplate without a feeling of shame for one's fellow countrymen; a violent rancour against any Indian of every class.'

This is why Dr Amit Pathak found the presentation of the plaque 'inappropriate and objectionable'. It is difficult to find a good historical analogy, but one that comes to mind is a crack French regiment presenting a plaque to a community just outside Algiers to commemorate its losses in the Algerian War of Independence fifty years ago. Now one may say that Indian 'mutiny' history is 150 years old, and since then the British and Indian armies have fought together like brothers in arms through two world wars. One may also say that, while in India there is a great confusion between myth and history, distant events are recalled as if they happened the day before yesterday. For instance, in Kanpur it is easy to find boatmen at Satichaura Ghat who claim direct descent from those who set fire to the straw-thatched boats of the fleeing British, thus precipitating the massacre of 27 June 1857, and who still vociferously proclaim their innocence. Similarly, at Gwalior, where the Rani of Jhansi – the Queen Boadicea of the 'War of Independence' – was possibly cremated after her death in battle, the guru at the Hindu temple will tell you that he is the sixth in line of the gurus since that event, and then his disciples will haul out an old cannon (genuine) as if to prove it.

It is easy to be misled in India by the familiarity of Victorian gothic churches (not quite accurate in Meerut) to assume that we share a common history, even a special relationship. This goes to the heart of the matter. As I noted in the Introduction to this book, when the Rt Hon. John Freeman was High Commissioner in India forty years ago, in 1965–8, he wrote that Indo-British relations were characterised by 'neurosis and nostalgia'. The 'neurosis' was Indian and the 'nostalgia' was British. He wrote in his final despatch: 'We must eschew nostalgic recollections of a special relationship that over most of the field no longer exists.'The Indian Mutiny of 2007 was a reminder that in some quarters the twin moods have still not changed.

The Times of India referred to this continuing 'neurosis' in its main leader on 28 September, ruminating about the 'appalling (Indian) behaviour' during our visit.'Let's Move On' was the headline:

> What a strange country India has become. Even after sixty years of independence, it still lacks self-confidence to feel comfortable in its own skin. When a few British descendants of those who served and died in India during 1857 come to pay homage to their dead relatives, people behave as if the East India Company was back again. Will some Indians never become truly free of the foreign yoke, never be able to treat a foreigner as an equal? Do we have to be either victims or bullies?

What about the 'nostalgic recollections' on our side? I was compelled to think about these after the press office at the High Commission sent on a blog from Bangalore titled 'The Ugly Briton'. The writer was angry:

> These Britons [us], schooled as they are since childhood in the dubious theory of the 'White man's burden', simply don't get it. They are unwilling or unable to come to terms with their gruesome past and the reality that the British Empire was like any other empire in history. It was an enterprise of loot, pillage and oppression.

The writer had got hold of various quotes from members of our party including this from Sir Mark:

> I have enormous admiration for what he [Sir Henry Havelock] did and for what all the Brits who fought and lived here did. They believed that it was a good thing for Britain and even for India. Though we have retreated and gone, India survives as how a democratic system should work.

The important point about these two statements is the gulf between them. Many Indians obviously want no part of our shared history; never did. However bipartisan our commemorations at the Lucknow Residency may have been, had we flown the Indian flag (complete anathema between 1857 and 1947) and sang *Vande Mataram*, it would have made no difference. Sixty years after Independence we are strangers in a foreign land. Probably the younger generation of Brits realise this, but for those of us who remember the British Empire, even if we are not of the 'White man's burden' mentality, we must respect the point of view and sensibilities of others by keeping our 'nostalgia' to ourselves.

Despite a shared language, a shared faith, a shared sport and many other shared things, the special relationship is over. As the caretaker of St John's cemetery said, without realising the topical significance: *Woh daur kuch tha, Aaj kuch aur hai, Duniya adalti badalti rehti hai* ('Those were different times; today is a different time. The world keeps changing').

NOTES

Introduction

1. Charles Allen, 'Resuscitating the Raj', *Chowkidar* (1997).
2. Adam Clapham, *Beware Falling Coconuts* (India: Rupa & Co, 2007).
3. 'The UK and India', government press release, www.british-highcommission.gov. uk/India, 2006.
4. Michael Foss, *Out of India* (London: Michael O'Mara Books, 2001).
5. D.K. Patel, 'Indianisation: A Personal Experience', *Indo-British Review*, 15 (1989).
6. In correspondence and quoted in Trevor Royle, *The Last Days of the Raj* (London: John Murray, 1989).
7. TNA: PRO PREM 13/1574.
8. *Ibid.*
9. In conversation and in 'Britons since Independence', *Indo-British Review*, 14 (1988).

Chapter One: The Wrights of Tollygunge

1. Simon Winchester, 'The Scent behind the Smell', *Simon Winchester's Calcutta* (Melbourne: Lonely Planet Publications, 2004).
2. Quoted in *ibid*.
3. Sir Owain Jenkins, *Merchant Prince* (London: BACSA, 1987).

4. R.N. Sen, *In Clive Street* (Calcutta: Calcutta Press, 1981).

5. For this and other statistical information in this period, see Michael Lipton and John Firn, *The Erosion of a Relationship, India and Britain since 1960* (Oxford: Oxford University Press, 1975).

6. Geoffrey Moorhouse, *Calcutta* (New York: Holt, Rinehart and Winston, 1971).

7. *Ibid.*

Chapter Two: Planter Bob

1. Sir Owain Jenkins, *Merchant Prince* (London: BACSA, 1987).

2. Derek Perry, 'Tea in Assam and the Bruce Brothers', www.koi-hai.com.

3. Derek Perry, in correspondence and 'St Agnes Convent 1941–1947', www.koi-hai.com.

4. Larry Brown, in correspondence and 'My Path to Tea', www.koi-hai.com.

5. Jim Robinson, 'Childhood in Assam', www.koi-hai.com.

Chapter Three: Two Old Delhiwalas

1. Nigel Hankin, *Hanklyn-Janklin: A Stranger's Rumble-Tumble Guide to Some Words, Customs and Guidelines Indian and Indo-British* (4th edn; New Delhi: Tara Press, 2003).

2. Henry Yule and A.C. Burnell, *Hobson-Jobson: A Spice-Box of Etymological Curiosities and Colourful Expressions* (Ware: Wordsworth Reference, 1996).

3. Ashok Chakravarty, *Publicis India*; quoted in 'A Hindi–English Jumble Spoken by 350 Million', *Christian Science Monitor*, 23 November 2003.

4. Quoted by C.M. Millington, 'Whether we be many or few', *A History of the Cambridge/Delhi Brotherhood* (Bangalore: Asian Trading Company, 1999).

5. *Ibid.*, and further quotes from C.F. Andrews.

Chapter Four: Tiger Hunters

1. G.E.C. Wakefield, 'Recollections of 50 Years in the Service of India', *Civil & Military Gazette* (Lahore, 1935).

2. Jim Corbett, *My India: The Second Jim Corbett Omnibus* (New Delhi: Oxford University Press, 1991).

3. Quoted by Lieutenant-General S.K. Sinha (Retd), 'The Indian Army: Before and After Independence', *Indo-British Review*, 16 (1989).

4. *Ibid.*

5. *Ibid.*

6. Major-General D.K. Palit (Retd), 'Indianisation: A Personal Experience', *Indo-British Review*, 16 (1989).

7. K. Subrahmanyam, 'Indian Armed Forces: Its Ethos and Traditions', *Indo-British Review*, 16 (1989).

8. Lieutenant-General M.L. Chibber, 'Regimental System and Esprit-de-Corps in the Indian Army', *Indo-British Review*, 16 (1989).

9. Charles Allen, 'Resuscitating the Raj', *Chowkidar* (1997).

10. P.A. Morris *Van Ingen & Van Ingen: Artists in Taxidermy* (Ascot: M.P.M. Publishing, 2006).

Chapter Five: Kitty's Story

1. Emma Roberts, *Scenes and Characteristics of Hindostan* (2 vols; London: India Office Library, 1835).

2. *Indian Express*, 24 March 1991; repr. in *Melvyn Brown's Anglo-Indian Archive*, a desk-top publication to which I am indebted for my research.

Chapter Six: Tully-Sahib

1. Mark Tully, *India's Unending Journey* (London: Rider Books, 2007).

2. James Morris, *Places* (1972), quoted in *Simon Winchester's Calcutta* (London: Lonely Planet Publications, 2004).

3. For this and much more information about the BBC in India see the various essays in 'Broadcasting Partnerships: India and the BBC 1932–1994', *Indo-British Review*, 20/2 (1994).

4. *Simon Winchester's Calcutta.*

5. S.K. Singh, 'Imposing Sanctions', *Indo-British Review*, 20/2 (1994).

6. Quoted by Mark Tully in *India in Slow Motion* (Harmondsworth: Penguin Books, 2003).

7. Prakash Mirchandani, 'Holding the Delhi Fort', *Indo-British Review*, 20/2 (1994).

8. Mark Tully, 'Reporting India: The BBC Agenda', *Indo-British Review*, 20/2 (1994).

9. Kailash Budhwar, 'A Breath of Fresh Air', *Indo-British Review*, 20/2 (1994).

10. Mark Tully, 'National Broadcasting Systems in a Global Setting', *Indo-British Review*, 20/2 (1994).

11. Mark Tully and Zareer Masani, *From Raj to Rajiv* (London: BBC Books, 1988).

12. Tully, *India in Slow Motion*.

13. David Gilmour, *The Ruling Caste* (New York: Farrar, Strauss and Giroux, 2005).

14. Quoted in Tully and Masani, *From Raj to Rajiv*.

15. While I was visiting Mark Tully he was writing *India's Unending Journey: Finding Balance in a Time of Change* (London: Rider Books, 2007). This is a book about India and his faith.

Chapter Seven: Selling Off the Raj

1. Geoffrey Moorhouse, *India Britannica* (London: Harvill Press, 1983).

2. James Morris, *Farewell the Trumpets: An Imperial Retreat* (London: Faber & Faber, 1978).

3. Kerse Naoroja, 'Of People, Events and Happenings', *1846–1946: Royal Bombay Yacht Club Sesquicentennial Year* (Mumbai: RBYC, 1996), pp. 6–7.

4. Kerse Naoroja, 'The Founding of the Bombay Yacht', *1846–1946: Royal Bombay Yacht Club Sesquicentennial Year* (Mumbai: RBYC, 1996), p. 1.

5. For this and other incidental information from RBYC minutes I am indebted to Graham and Thelma Anthony, who made their searches, with permission, in 2003.

6. Rules of the Royal Bombay Yacht Club, 1988.

7. A. Compton, *A Bachelor's Bungalow in True Tales of British India*, compiled by M. Wise (Brighton, 1993); quoted in Amin Jaffer,

Furniture from British India and Ceylon (New Delhi: Timeless Books, 2001).

8. W.S. Blunt, *Ideas about India* (London, 1885); quoted in Jaffer, *Furniture*.

Chapter Eight: The Last Stayers-On

1. Zoe Yalland, *Traders and Nabobs: The British in Cawnpore* (Wilton: Michael Russell, 1987).
2. John Christie, *Morning Drum* (London: BACSA, 1983).
3. Eric Newby, *Slowly down the Ganges* (London: Hodder & Stoughton, 1966).
4. Sandy Lall, 'The Indian Mutiny', *Chowkidar*, 11/3 (2007).
5. Theon Wilkinson, *Two Monsoons* (London: Duckworth, 1976).
6. Sue Farrington, an interview, *Chowkidar 1977–1997* (1997).
7. James Stevens Curl, 'European Funerary Architecture in India', *Chowkidar* (1986).

INDEX